Africare

Africare

Black American Philanthropy in Africa

Penelope Campbell

Transaction Publishers
New Brunswick (U.S.A.) and London (U.K.)

Copyright © 2011 by Transaction Publishers, New Brunswick,
New Jersey.

Library of Congress Catalog Number: 2010052450
ISBN: 978-1-4128-4243-3
Printed in the United States of America

Library of Congress Cataloging-in-Publication Data
Library of Congress Cataloging-in-Publication Data
Campbell, Penelope.
    Africare : Black American philanthropy in Africa / Penelope
Campbell.
       p. cm.
· Includes bibliographical references.
    ISBN 978-1-4128-4243-3
  1. African Americans—Charities—History. 2. Africare
(Organization)—History. 3. Philanthropists—Unted States.
4. African Americans—Africa. I. Title.
   HV590.C26 2011
    361.7'7096091724—dc22
                    2010052450

Contents

Acknowledgments

As with all authors, I am indebted to many individuals for information, insight, and encouragement. Additionally, there are those to whom I owe appreciation for their work in searching for documents and for assistance in the collection of materials.

There would have been no book without the cooperation of Africare's four presidents. Each in his way was crucial to it. C. Payne Lucas first countenanced my idea to write a history of the organization and gave me valuable inside perspectives. His successor, Julius Coles, emphasized that I should write a study that presented Africare in a forthright and open manner. It was through him that William Kirker, the founder of Africare, was recognized for his role. Meeting Dr. Kirker, his wife Barbara, and several members of their Diffa team elevated my enthusiasm for the project. I regret that it has not been possible to include more about the work of the Kirkers in Niger. Finally, Darius Mans, following Julius Coles, was generous in sharing his goals as the new president.

Numerous other people, both within Africare and outside it, have been important contributors to my effort. Joseph C. Kennedy, director of international development, described the organization's methodology and aspirations. Staff members of field offices that I visited briefed me on their work and took me to see projects. Many persons allowed me to interview them. Some were Africare employees or former employees with experience working at headquarters in Washington or abroad. Others were retired USAID employees or men and women currently attached to charities, organizations, or businesses involved in humanitarian activities in Africa.

The mundane, but vital, task of locating research materials was handled capably by the Africare staff in Washington and by the librarians, under the direction of Elizabeth Bagley, at the Agnes Scott College Library in Decatur, Georgia. To both groups I am very grateful.

1

The Founding

In the 1960s, Maine-Soroa was a village of fewer than a thousand inhabitants in the Department of Diffa, one of seven administrative units of Niger, West Africa. The area, in the far southeastern end of the country at the edge of the Sahara Desert, was a vast land the size of Michigan. Vegetation was mostly scrub, water was scarce, and resources sparse. Homes had no running water or electricity, and of the few telephones in the village, the most accessible was at the post office, which opened only a few hours daily. The roads were sandy and rutted and the sole other link to the outside world was an unreliable one-line telegraph. Kanouri, also known as Munga, was the dominant language spoken, and Hausa was an important second language. Maine-Soroa itself was divided into different living and functional districts. Most people lived in the villager area of grass huts surrounded by grass walls, although a few prosperous residents had adobe houses with corrugated tin roofs and mud walls. The business area, which included the mayor's office, a grade school, and a police station, consisted of cement cinder block buildings with corrugated tin roofs. Town officials and businessmen usually lived in similar or adobe structures near this core. The hospital, with two buildings, one an outpatient center and the other an eight-room wing, was also cement block and had a corrugated tin roof. It did have a flush toilet with a ceramic basin, but that required the use of a hole in the ground and a bucket of water. There were no hotels in the village and the best accommodation available for visitors was in the school or in the mayor's house. Cows, goats, and chickens roamed about. In a desolate place that had, at most, short, scant rains, the only other livelihood was an annual crop of millet, if the season was good.

Africare began in this African village, both figuratively and literally, and the African village has remained the focus of its work. The founders were passionate visionaries whose eyes were opened to the need in Africa by service in the Peace Corps and by the desire to

perpetuate the Peace Corps' humanitarian aspirations. They began modestly in Maine-Soroa, close to the confluence of four countries, never imagining that, in a few years, their effort would evolve into the only African American development organization in the United States planning life-sustaining projects in many nations of sub-Saharan Africa. However, Africare was not just an organization. It was intended to be a movement to bring Americans of all races together in a noble cause to save Africa. Millions became involved, and together with the men and women who devoted their entire careers to Africare, they hoped that their contribution toward African development would end poverty and disease on the continent.

Six hundred miles from Niamey, the capital of Niger, the villagers of Maine-Soroa began receiving help from American Peace Corps volunteers in the mid-1960s. One of these volunteers was William O.

Kirker, a young Michigan physician who, having done his internship in Hawaii because his wife was Hawaiian, decided that the good life he could enjoy there in private practice did not match his understanding of the Hippocratic Oath. Asking himself if anyone in Hawaii would be worse off if he were not there giving medical care, and concluding "no," he joined with thousands of idealistic Americans who believed that they could be of help to people abroad. Kirker and his wife, Barbara, were assigned to Niger and Kirker became one of three Peace Corps physicians working in the Department of Diffa. Patients came not just from Niger, but from other nations, Nigeria, Chad, and Cameroon, in that crossroads near Lake Chad. Altogether, they spoke seven languages. Kirker, stationed in Maine-Soroa, found that meningitis was an annual epidemic, that malaria affected nearly everyone, and that tuberculosis was rampant. The average life expectancy was thirty-nine years and 50% of children died before they were five years old. He treated between one hundred to three hundred out-patients a day and performed sixty operations a month. Many of his most difficult cases were pregnant women with severe obstetrical complications. With limited actual medical experience and scant knowledge of African diseases, Kirker searched medical textbooks for advice on procedures and treatment. He also did a lot of praying.

Kirker became so committed to the health of Nigerien villagers during his Peace Corps term that, upon its completion, he sought an opportunity to remain in the country. The President of Niger, Diori Hamani, appointed him Departmental Director of Health for Diffa, giving him a salary of $7,700 a year and a small budget for medical supplies. In spite of the lofty title, Kirker's real job was to serve again as a physician in a region with one hundred and fifty thousand residents and many nomads. The small hospital in Maine-Soroa continued to overflow with the malnourished, the injured, the chronically ill, and victims of epidemics. The recently independent government of Niger, struggling with many development needs, could offer no additional help. This was the situation when the Kirkers left Niger in 1970 for a home leave in Hawaii. Their two years in the Peace Corps and two years' employment by the Niger Government had convinced them that they had to create an organization that would provide a modern hospital with skilled staff and support personnel. Dining in Niamey with American diplomats and Peace Corps volunteers at the home of Vincent Farley, an American Foreign Service officer, before their departure, they even announced a name for it: Africare.

Back in Hawaii, the Kirkers recruited an attorney, a bank president, and several physicians to assist them in establishing a non-profit organization that would enable them to continue their medical work under improved conditions. They had no money of their own, but received free counsel from the attorney, James Sattler, and free office services from the banker, Myra Takasaki. Consequently, Africare was recognized officially as a non-profit, charitable foundation in Honolulu on September 11, 1970, for the purpose of easing "pain and suffering by providing medical services and health care to the people of Africa beginning in the Department of Diffa in the Country of Niger." Mrs. Takasaki's First Financial Savings & Loan Association offices were listed as headquarters. The new stationery, with an outline of the African continent and the word "AFRICARE" printed across it from Senegal to Somalia, bore the inscription, "Bringing Medical Care to African Countries."

The Kirkers faced enormous obstacles as they raised public awareness of Africare, garnered financial support from the community, and planned their return to Niger. They set as a goal the creation of a volunteer group of twenty-five people to go to Diffa and they calculated that the cost for each individual for two years would be $10,000. Moreover, they wanted to be back in Diffa early in 1971. Through Barbara Kirker's uncles, photographers for local newspapers, they publicized their desire to raise funds for medical care and health services in Niger. William Kirker sought speaking engagements and gave graphic slide shows wherever he was invited. In October 1970, for example, he presented slide showings of "infectious diseases, people and customs in Niger, Africa" at the Queen's Medical Center in Honolulu to interns, residents, nurses, and technicians. He also traveled to his home state of Michigan, raising money from groups and family members.

In Honolulu, the Kirkers were particularly fortunate to have the business sense and financial support of Mrs. Takasaki. She became involved reluctantly through the persistent requests of State Senator Vincent Yano. To her, Niger was a million miles away and she believed that residents of Hawaii who needed financial help should be given first consideration. However, she admired the young Kirkers, who were willing to give up a comfortable life to help a desert nation with no major health facilities. Mrs. Takasaki provided office space, stationery, postage, and an electric typewriter that could be programmed with a form letter, but customized to individual donors. Her staff at First

Savings and Loan Association, eager to help the poor in Africa, kept the books and banked the donations. In preparing for mass mailings, the Kirkers, Mrs. Takasaki, and a small band of Africare friends stuffed and licked envelopes that went out to everyone they could think of and whose address they could find in the telephone book. They solicited as little as a dollar.

In addition to these activities, Kirker began the search for volunteers. His September 1970 notice in *The Honolulu Advertiser* produced more than two hundred applications. Selecting twenty-five people, he arranged classes for them in French, the official language of Niger, in personal health, and in the culture of the people. Getting government approval for a volunteer group to enter Niger was another challenge for the fledgling Africare organization, and it required negotiation with President Diori. Here, Kirker's personal friendship with him netted a November telegram in which Diori gave Africare permission to begin work at any time and at any place in the territory of the Niger Republic. Moreover, Diori authorized the use of his name publicly as Africare's international sponsor and offered the services of Oumarou G. Youssoufou, acting first secretary of the Niger Embassy in Washington, as Africare's administrator for the African continent.

In spite of the efforts of the Kirkers and their friends, incoming financial assistance for Africare was meager. In December 1970, only $12,000 of the projected $250,000 budget had been raised, but Africare was rescued from possible oblivion by fortuitous events going on simultaneously elsewhere. In Niamey, President Diori wanted to multiply such health programs as those proposed for Diffa and to receive American help regarding a wide range of development needs. In Washington, D.C., C. Payne Lucas, ex-Peace Corps director in Niger, now heading the returned volunteer bureau at Peace Corps headquarters, believed this was the time to realize a dream of starting his own organization to address Diori's concerns. Since his graduate school days in Washington when he dined at the family table in Yvonne Chappelle's home, met African guests, and received encouragement from her mother, he had considered the idea. Now, in daily contacts with ex-Peace Corps men and women who wanted somehow to continue their overseas service, he began to focus on them as a human pool of resources he could tap. Among his colleagues on the twelfth floor of the Peace Corps building overlooking the White House in downtown Washington, he broached the idea of a private foundation and soon offices buzzed during lunch hours and at day's end as they debated its form, structure, and practical aspects. Secretaries, such as Mary Miles and Doris Hawkins, typed out different versions of the proposal as it underwent revisions.

These three strands merged in the spring of 1971, when Diori brought Kirker and Lucas together in an agreement in which Africare would be reincorporated in Washington, D.C., and Lucas would become the executive director. Contributing significantly to this change of leadership was Kirker's early realization that his strength lay in medical care, not in administration or in fund raising. Serving the medical needs of Africans was his destiny, he believed. He came to the conclusion, as well, that Africare should be an African American organization headed by a dynamic black leader. Having a white man run it poorly fitted its desired image and appeal. Although Kirker became a charter director of the newly incorporated Africare, he withdrew from active management and concentrated on leading the Hawaiian team in Diffa.

In May 1971, the group of volunteers, sixteen in all, including the Kirkers, arrived in Diffa. Most were posted in Maine-Soroa, while a few, including staff for a mobile unit, were dispersed to two distant villages. There were mechanics, nurses, a carpenter, a handyman, a lab technician, and a secretary. Not all were from the United States; one came from Canada and two were Belgians. Some had been in the Peace Corps and one of the volunteers, Vicky Saccardi, had served in Niger previously. One man, Cosco Carlbom, Canadian by birth, but living in Hawaii where he fixed stock cars, scarcely knew the location of Niger when he heard of Kirker's plea.

The goal of Africare, as incorporated in Hawaii in 1970, was to serve the medical needs of Africans, in particular those Nigeriens living in the Department of Diffa. The cholera epidemic during Kirker's first two months back in Maine-Soroa that required the vaccination of 85,000 people illustrated the role that Africare could play. The greatest immediate concern for the future, though, was the expansion of the existing rudimentary hospital and training staff. As he treated patients for local endemic ailments and operated on patients with maladies as simple as hemorrhoids or as life-threatening as complications of childbirth, Kirker planned the construction of a hundred bed facility. In this he had the assistance of Carlbom, who was both a mechanic and a construction expert. Carlbom was the only volunteer, besides the Kirkers, who remained in Niger during the entire two years of this first Africare project. Not only did he repair vehicles and generators, but he oversaw the building of a kitchen, a well, a water tower, and the surgical block at the hospital. This was a major undertaking because building materials had to come from Niamey and be hauled the great distance across the desert to Maine-Soroa, with only rutted tracks and the occasional well or hut nearby to guide drivers.

The training of a staff to handle an enlarged hospital with more treatment facilities and more bed patients as well as a growing outpatient clientele fell to the Africare nurses, particularly Vicky Saccardi, and to both of the Kirkers. Saccardi's specialty was the operating room. With William Kirker frequently in surgery for twelve hours a day in shade-tree temperatures of 120° F, she had to find local personnel to assist both her and him. Moreover, since it was the philosophy of Africare to serve as a catalyst for change and improvement, Nigeriens had to be enlisted to be leaders and to run their own affairs. Barbara Kirker, who supervised the hospital kitchen and even grew vegetables for it, likewise trained new nurses. She also began an outreach program that taught midwives to identify risky cases, to work in sanitary conditions, and to demonstrate to mothers the proper treatment of newborns.

During the two years of this Hawaiian Africare project, the mission was beset by numerous difficulties that threatened its survival, particularly the loss of staff. Many of the volunteers, although capable and skilled, were unaccustomed to the hardships of life in Niger. Some were disenchanted by the uncertainties that accompany a new voluntary agency operating on a shoestring. They did not like it when paychecks were skipped and they had to live on credit extended by local merchants. While the Kirkers got financial assistance from the American Embassy in Niamey, from President Diori's discretionary fund, and from the United States Agency for International Development (USAID), and boxes of supplies from family and friends in the United States, the entire need was not met. The number of volunteers was reduced further by illness and medical evacuation. Even Vicky Saccardi, who had been a Peace Corps volunteer in Niger for three years, was forced to leave permanently.

In Washington, the Africare that Lucas organized was far different from that planned by Kirker. First of all, Lucas believed fundamentally in the value of village primary health care rather than in a hospital and surgical approach. He had been reluctant to assume responsibility for the Diffa project, but when a persuasive Diori asked him to take it over, he felt that he could not refuse. With Diori's encouragement,

Lucas set out to create an entirely new organization that was African American and dedicated to more objectives than health care. He thought, initially, that its work would be restricted to West Africa because of the size of the continent. The immediate task, however, was incorporating Africare in the District of Columbia and this was done early in May 1971. Taking sections of the first incorporation in Honolulu and adding his own ideas, Lucas listed the purpose of the corporation as "assist[ing] in the improvement of the health of the people of Africa, including improvement of health resulting from economic, agricultural, educational and social development in harmony with the environment." Another article stated, "no part of the activities of the corporation shall consist of carrying on of propaganda or otherwise attempting to influence legislation, nor shall the corporation participate or intervene in any political campaign of any candidate for public office." The corporation's initial office address was the home of C. Payne Lucas. Diori was made the first honorary international chairman and his representative in Washington, Oumarou G. Youssoufou, along with Kirker, Joseph C. Kennedy, who had held important Peace Corps positions in Africa and Asia, and Lucas became charter Board members. Lucas, resigning from the Peace Corps upon serving the maximum five-year term, made his home basement the operations center, and relied on the salary of his wife, Freddie, then a lobbyist for J.C. Penney, to support the family. Kennedy kept his job with the education division of the U.S. Department of Health, Education, and Welfare, but worked as an unpaid staff member in his spare time. Subsequently, in July 1971, First Secretary Youssoufou allowed Africare to make the Niger Embassy on R Street, N.W., its headquarters and Diori sent Africare a check for $10,000.

Foremost in Lucas' mind when he began to envision an African development organization was his belief that it should be led by African Americans, staffed by African Americans, and funded mostly by African Americans. He saw Africare as a way to interest African Americans from all walks of life—welfare mothers, church members, sorority sisters, businessmen—in Africa. As regional director for Africa in the Peace Corps administration, his personal philosophy had been summed up in a 1968 speech to Maryland State College students entitled, "Black Pride, Black Action," in which he challenged them to find their identity and to explore their African heritage by two years or more of Peace Corps service. He argued, "This American generation of blacks owes black Africa a hell-of-a-lot. ... [W]e must stop and give thanks to the birth of that black continent south of the Sahara which gave real impetus to the black man's struggle for dignity. ... We have come out of the bushes and on to the road of freedom because black and yellow men in other parts of the world have already *won* their freedoms and are now saying to all mankind: 'White man listen. Either we live in equality and dignity together or perish from this earth.'" He knew that very little official attention was being given in Washington to Africa's needs and that there was little recognition among African Americans of their relationship to the continent. Africare would be a vehicle for them, in a practical way, to express a renewed interest in their Motherland as opposed to simply wearing Afros and dashikis. Now, through a humanitarian movement, they could reach a helping hand to their racial brethren and, with the resulting psychological boost, reaffirm their identity.

The early 1970s was an opportune time for launching a charity appealing for support from the African American community. The momentum of an accelerating seventy-year drive for social, economic, and political equality in the United States, although frequently interrupted, had created an open and positive atmosphere. Tracing race relations back to the beginning of the twentieth century, one can see why optimism reigned. The expanding public debate among blacks about their position in the United States began both a process of politicizing them and of producing institutions that successfully challenged the status quo. A major question for them in 1900 was their response to legal affirmation of Jim Crow laws in the U.S. Supreme Court's decision in *Plessy v. Ferguson* (1896), to white opposition to their membership in the rising labor union movement, and to President William McKinley's decision during the Spanish-American War that they should share in taking up the White Man's Burden. On the one hand, Booker T. Washington, of the Tuskegee Institute in Alabama, advocated acceptance of racial segregation and advised students that most would live by the effort of their physical labor. On the other hand, W.E.B. Du Bois, professor at the University of Pennsylvania before he moved to Atlanta University, published scholarly books, including *The Souls of Black Folk* (1903), in which he rejected Washington's views of accommodation. Du Bois demanded complete racial integration, along with political and social equality. He was the convener of like-minded activists in Niagara Falls, Canada, in 1905, who founded what became known as the Niagara Movement. Four years later, it formed the nucleus of the National Association for the

Advancement of Colored People (NAACP), which used political action to lead the nation in the civil rights movement.

The NAACP was but one of many groups that came to represent large segments of the African American community and to have a profound effect on the trajectory of race relations. The National Association of Colored Women, founded even earlier in 1896 to demand racial integration and to raise the level and quality of life in home and family, achieved distinction as the oldest such organization in the United States. In 1910, the National Urban League was created by New Yorkers alarmed by the economic and social conditions under which black migrants from the South were living in their city. Helping newcomers with their employment, housing, education, and health problems, Urban League members realized that there was a nationwide need for their services, hence a rapid expansion into many cities, particularly after World War I. Carter G. Woodson, Harvard-educated as was Du Bois, provided intellectual leadership to African Americans when he founded the Association for the Study of Negro Life and History in 1915. Through his many publications, editorship of the *Journal of Negro History*, and initiation of Negro History Week in 1926, he tried to correct the image of blacks in American history and to emphasize their contributions. These four national organizations became standard-bearers of the black insistence on equality and dignity throughout the twentieth century.

In the 1920s and 1930s, there were other events within the United States that contributed to a growing confidence among African Americans. An intellectual and cultural movement known as the Harlem Renaissance gave respectability to black writers, musicians, artists, and poets who, for the first time, received recognition and appreciation as a group from white audiences. Contemporaneously, a young immigrant from Jamaica, Marcus Garvey, was in Harlem organizing the Universal Negro Improvement Association (UNIA), which was dedicated to racial pride, solidarity, and self-help. He did not just use the rhetoric of Black Nationalism, but believing that African American economic independence was essential to political freedom, started a Negro Factories Corporation and diverse businesses such as grocery stores, restaurants, hotels, laundries, and a publishing house. He also acquired a shipping company, the Black Star Line, by which he planned to carry out a great emigration scheme of helping African Americans return to Africa. That proved to be his undoing, for he was convicted of mail fraud in connection with the shipping firm, served a jail term, and was deported in 1927. While the Garvey phenomenon outwardly failed in the United States, it left a legacy of energizing thousands of black Americans, of raising the specter, if only temporarily, of a romanticized ancestral Africa, and of potential concerted social action. Back in Jamaica, Garvey entered island politics and advocated what were then radical changes, among them an eight-hour day, a minimum wage, and land reform.

The election of Franklin D. Roosevelt as president in 1932 and the subsequent twenty years of Democratic administrations in Washington brought new hope to African Americans, even as they suffered bitterly during the Great Depression and sacrificed lives during World War II. Roosevelt alternately pleased them by appointing blacks to high positions in his government and disappointed them by maintaining racial segregation in New Deal programs and in the military. When he signed an executive order in June 1941, forbidding discrimination because of race, creed, color, or national origin in the employment of workers in defense industries and in government training programs and established a committee on fair employment practice, he set a precedent of official support for racial equality. President Harry S. Truman capped the era by ordering a ban on segregation and discrimination in the military in 1948.

The decades of the 1950s and 1960s were equally significant in advancing the civil rights and political participation of African Americans. Jim Crow laws were struck down in the 1954 *Brown v. Board of Education of Topeka, Kansas*, decision in which the U.S. Supreme Court ruled that school desegregation is unconstitutional and inherently unequal. The Civil Rights Act of 1957, the first passed since Reconstruction, established a national Commission on Civil Rights and a similar body within the Justice Department. It began the legislative drive that culminated in the Voting Rights Act of 1965 by which discriminatory practices such as poll taxes, literacy tests, and other devices used by states to prevent or discourage citizens from voting were prohibited. Voter registration drives by Martin Luther King, Jr., and his supporters in the Southern Christian Leadership Conference expanded the electorate substantially in the South.

In international affairs, African Americans took particular interest in the achievement of independence by many of Europe's African colonies during the 1950s and 1960s. They could identify with freedom fighters in such countries as Ghana, Kenya, and Southern Rhodesia and felt a sense of solidarity with them. Moreover, liberation struggles

11

in sub-Saharan Africa informed their own battle in the United States. Although the Vietnam War, in which more than a million African American soldiers served, and its anti-war protests had raised fundamental questions of America's role abroad, black Americans were enthusiastic supporters of many newly independent states of Africa, notably when their leaders professed democratic values. Furthermore, as with most Americans, those in the black community had their horizons enlarged by what they learned about the work of the American Peace Corps and they admired returning volunteers who brought stories of humanitarian needs and deeds in the dozens of countries they served world-wide.

All of these political, cultural, and foreign relations aspects were important for Lucas in 1971 when he began calculating where he would raise financial and logistical support for Africare. African American leaders were being elected to important positions where they influenced American domestic and foreign policy. A analysis of the social and economic status of Negroes in the United States conducted by the Census Bureau based on the 1970 census found that there were now thirteen blacks in the U.S. House of Representatives, one in the U.S. Senate, 198 in State legislatures, eighty-one mayors, and 1,567 elected to other State or local offices. To the list of mayors were soon added Tom Bradley in Los Angeles, Coleman Young in Detroit, and Maynard Jackson in Atlanta, who became leaders of three great cities. Blacks in the U.S. House of Representatives, particularly Charles Diggs, Jr., Barbara Jordan, Charles Rangel, Shirley Chisholm, Walter Fountroy, and Louis Stokes, spoke passionately about racial inequity in American politics and economics. Most were in the House at the time of the formal establishment of the Congressional Black Caucus in 1971. Other civic leaders who brought attention to moral, social, and economic issues were Benjamin Hooks, Roy Wilkins, Dorothy Height, and Leon Sullivan. All of these individuals could be tapped for support.

Since Lucas knew that he would be dealing with American and African diplomats, he took special interest in the composition of State Department and Foreign Service staff. He noticed that, historically, leadership at State was white and that even when the man in charge of Africa policy turned out to be sympathetic with the African view point, his success was limited. A good example was G. Mennen Williams, appointed Assistant Secretary of State for Africa by President John F. Kennedy in 1961, who had little to show for his term in office after five years of preaching "Africa for the Africans." One of Williams' failures was getting President Lyndon Johnson to take an active role when Ian Smith, representing white settlers, declared a unilateral declaration of independence in Southern Rhodesia. Lucas found, too, that of the few blacks in the diplomatic corps, most were assigned to the Africa bureau, considered a backwater. A handful of African American ambassadors had been appointed by successive previous administrations, but they always were assigned to a few African and Caribbean countries in the "Negro circuit." In 1969, there were only nineteen black Foreign Service Officers, eleven Junior Foreign Service Reserve Officers, and twenty-four Foreign Service Reserve Officers, out of a total of about nine thousand on the State Department roster. Nonetheless, Lucas was optimistic about influencing the Department's policies on Africa. Looking at these factors, he believed that Africare, by appealing to the general African American community and by utilizing the growing political power of African American leaders nationwide, could generate enough financial backing to become a viable organization.

The timing may have been considered right for founding Africare, but there remained the question of how to appeal to the African American community. Lucas and his colleagues at the Peace Corps drafted documents that vowed a new approach to the needs of Africa and promised that Africa would have the opportunity to take hold of its own development. The focus of the organization was to be the health of the African people, but "health" was stretched to include improved water resources and food production, as well as any field broadly relating to health. An important component of the Africare commitment was the declaration that African governments would determine their own national priorities: "AFRICARE participates only in programs that are conceived, directed and—to the extent possible—supported by sponsoring African governments." Africare pledged its intention to assist projects in participating countries on a first-come, first-served basis, keeping in mind certain basic criteria and national population concerns.

The preeminence of the Diffa health project in the early planning of Africare programs and finances can be seen in the Africare budget for the period of January 1, 1971, to June 30, 1972. Apparently calculated in May 1971, it acknowledges that $16,000 in contributions and a $50,000 loan from Niger covered the initial expenses of Kirker's Hawaiian group, including transportation to Niger and settling-in costs. In fact, there was a surplus of nearly $15,000, in part because some expenses had been deferred. However, a sum of $15,000 was the only asset that Africare had and ahead lay the continuing monetary demands of the health project in Diffa, estimated to be more than $150,000 by mid-1972. Yet financing a single health project was quite different from foretelling the operational needs of an expanded organization. Administrative salaries, program planning (hiring a team of health and agricultural experts), fund raising, office expenses, miscellaneous costs such as telephone and postal services, and the actual beginning of projects overseas were unavoidable basic elements in any entrepreneurial venture. Altogether, the budget writers figured that Africare needed $1,000,000 by June 30, 1972. Two-thirds of the money was to go toward starting new projects. The question was: where could Africare get funding?

When Africare set up its first official headquarters at the Niger Embassy in July 1971, it had no source of income. C. Payne Lucas and Oumarou Youssoufou began visiting prospective donors in New York City. They had just enough money for train fare, but not for meals. They learned that big foundations were generally uninterested in overseas development work, and in particular, in an African American start-up with the goal of improving the health of Africans. In fairness to the foundations, however, it should be said that Africare ideas may have come across as vague, a little grandiose, and with an air of "trust me." As the year progressed and Africare founders failed to obtain funding, the financial picture became critical.

At this juncture, a benefactor made a crucial loan that kept Africare alive. She was Lorraine Ames Watriss, a San Francisco native who had served as a nurse's aide for the Red Cross during World War II. She described how she went from being a member of high society to being a nursemaid of severely injured soldiers in an autobiographical piece for the June 8, 1942, issue of *Life Magazine*; her photograph appeared on its cover. Through her best friend, Nan Tucker McEvoy, heir to the San Francisco *Chronicle* fortune and a deputy administrator at the Peace Corps under Sargent Shriver, Mrs. Watriss met Lucas. Her privileged upbringing in California had precluded contact with African Americans, but she liked "Luke," as he was called during his Peace Corps days, and thought he was ambitious. She applauded his idea of giving Africans a greater voice in how development projects were done. For her, helping Africare was in the same vein as volunteering for the Red Cross. When she saw Africare struggling in 1971, she gave a loan of $30,000, interest-free. It was, in fact, a gift. Subsequently, Mrs. Watriss hosted cocktail parties and other benefit events in Washington and in New York to introduce Lucas to influential friends. She visited Niger on several occasions, and once purchased a vehicle for the Africare staff in Niamey.

2

Building a Constituency

The goal of Africare from its inception was to be an organization financed primarily by gifts from African Americans and it immediately set up an arrangement whereby anyone could become a member through the payment of $5 annual dues. In a May 1972 piece entitled, "Blacks Helping Blacks," William Raspberry of *The Washington Post* quoted C. Payne Lucas as predicting that dues and contributions, including some from U.S. foundations, would reach $10 million in the next year. Lucas argued, "[I]t's important that we black folks carry a major share of the load. ... Admittedly we don't have as much money as whites, but even a lot of poor people can come up with $5 a year." He believed that membership gave a psychological boost to African Americans by enabling them to help racially related people in Africa and to "concretize" their concern about Africa. It offered the chance "for the brother to go one step beyond the Afro and the dashiki." Other sources of revenue were expected to be African governments, non-African nations, corporations, and private organizations. However, in two years' time, Africare enrolled sixteen hundred members and its income was less than a million dollars.

The official launch of Africare's drive to mobilize the African American community took place in Atlanta, Georgia, on June 3, 1972. C. Payne Lucas, Joseph Kennedy, and a delegation of more than twenty African ambassadors received a tremendous welcome at the airport and a police escort to Pascal's Motel in the West End. Among the prominent Atlantans greeting them were Maynard Jackson, vice-mayor of Atlanta, Jacob and Freddye Henderson of the Henderson Travel Service, and Larry Gellerstedt, Jr., president of the Atlanta Chamber of Commerce. Jimmy Carter, then governor of Georgia, did not attend the festivities, but sent a cordial letter. At a later reception, where Coretta Scott King put in a cameo appearance, seven hundred guests saw Lucas use his well-honed oratorical skills. His appeal was loaded with catchy phrases, but it carried a serious message.

He emphasized the unique character of Africare: "Africare is first an African organization. Its architect is an African president—Diori Hamani of Niger. Its agenda is an African agenda. Its personnel are predominantly Africans and Black Americans." Central to his presentation was a discussion of health in Africa and how Africare could alleviate the human suffering resulting from malnutrition, bad water, hunger, and the absence of medical assistance. He even proposed a partial solution in the creation of a corps of 110 African paramedical personnel who, like paramedics in the U.S. military, could deal with a broad range of medical needs and emergencies. (In the Raspberry article, mentioned above, Lucas is quoted as saying, "We don't intend to send a lot of white faces to Africa to do some kind of missionary thing. … We intend to use technically qualified people here and abroad to train Africans as paramedics to work among their own people.") Lucas believed that an Africare constituency in the United States, drawn to the cause because of multiple personal reasons, was there, if it could just be reached. One outcome of the Atlanta kickoff was the subsequent founding of a local Africare chapter, with the Hendersons leading it. The immediate financial return was slim, however.

As heart-rending as the stories of disease in Africa were, not one was as compelling as that of the human tragedy playing out in West Africa because of the Sahelian drought. The Sahel stretched nearly 2,600 miles and included six countries, historically among the poorest of Africa. Their ecosystems were already fragile and their combined population of twenty-five million people included sedentary villagers, farmers, and fishermen. The majority of the population, however, consisted of nomadic people whose principal livelihood came from livestock. These nations were in desperate need of food assistance and of major infrastructural improvements, including dams, wells, communication systems, and secondary roads. Decimated cattle herds had to be reconstituted and reforestation programs begun. Although the six-year drought had begun in 1968, it was not until the early 1970s that most Americans became aware of it, in large part because media celebrities and major networks began to publicize the drama through newspaper articles, television coverage, and documentaries. Graphic photographs of skeletal nomads under a blazing sun and animal carcasses strewn across the desert conveyed a picture of desperation.

Here was a gripping story that Africare could seize and use in its own anxious effort to get established and to loosen American purse strings. Hence, it set aside some of its long-term program plans to improve the health of Africans and concentrated on needs of a greater immediate urgency, saving the lives of people in the Sahel and helping them rebuild the sources of their livelihood. In early 1973, Africare began to focus on relief and restoration efforts in West Africa. Concomitant with this was a new vigor in fund raising and in publicizing the organization's goals. The Africare Famine Relief Fund was inaugurated to offer Americans a way to share in rescuing the victims of the disaster. During one weekend in July, concerned Washingtonians hosted seventy "famine parties," ranging from "grab-a-cocktail-leave-a-check" affairs to catered buffet suppers. At Africare headquarters, a number of donations were received, and although the sum donated tended to be small, the individuality of some of the donators was heartening. Among the more memorable gifts were a $20 contribution from some inmates at the Maryland Correctional Institution in Jessup and one contribution that had a note attached, "Send the receipt to God." At least ten thousand people gave and more than $300,000 was raised by 1975, about 65% from African Americans who lived mostly in the Washington, D.C., metropolitan area.

The preponderance of local support can be attributed to several factors. Two of the most influential voices raising the alarm about the Sahelian drought were Carl Rowan, at the time a journalist for *The Washington Star-News*, and J.C. Hayward, a local television personality. Rowan not only wrote poignant articles, but visited the Sahel and produced a soul-searing documentary on the effects of the drought for Washington's WTOP television station. Furthermore, most members of Africare's Board of Directors were Washingtonians prominent in business, public affairs, and religious life. At least equally as important a factor was the crusading spirit of Africare leaders, who mesmerized congregations in black churches with spellbinding stories of struggle and death in Africa. C. Payne Lucas, Joe Kennedy, Clyde Richardson, and others arranged visits through such Washington clergymen as Henry Miles, pastor of the Third Baptist Church, and John Hurst Adams, the local African Methodist Episcopal Church bishop. Their appeal to give the "widow's mite" struck a chord with parishioners who could identify with the need of a well and felt connected to the villages where their money went.

Africare's initial participation in the Sahelian relief effort was one befitting its newness to the overseas development scene, its small budget, and its lack of organizational strength. It purchased dried fish for people in Mauritania, Mali, and Chad. It provided a small motorized pump for the irrigation of an existing tomato and rice project in Senegal. In Upper Volta and Niger, it supplied several villages with oxen, harnesses, plows, and seeds. Africare often had to rely on other agencies, such as the Red Crescent and the Red Cross, to do the actual distribution of food, blankets, and medicines. Having a limited staff and limited funds, it received its first grant ($31,500) from the United States Agency for International Development (USAID) to cover transportation costs for field coordinators and relief supplies, as well as staff salaries. The Lilly Endowment of Indianapolis was the first private philanthropy to give Africare backing when, in September 1973, it proposed a $50,000 cloud-seeding project in Niger.

The accelerating participation of Africare in Sahelian relief can be seen in the financial audits for 1973 and 1974. For the fiscal year ending April 30, 1973, Africare had a total income, including grants, contributions, and membership dues, of $45,782. Expenses, counting $10,736 for the Maine-Soroa medical facility in Diffa, were $58,297. There was a deficit of $12,515, although C. Payne Lucas was not receiving any salary himself and Africare headquarters were operating with a small staff of minimally paid workers and volunteers. In one year's time, at the end of April 30, 1974, Africare's income soared to $849,028, coming from grants, contributions, and USAID. Instead of funding just one program—Maine-Soroa—Africare was now involved in Sahelian relief and restoration, health planning, water resources development, and agricultural projects. Most of its money came from such private sources as the Lilly Endowment and from USAID, setting a pattern of financial support for the decades ahead. There was a surplus of $284,282 in the Africare budget at the end of April 1974, but it included $250,000 that the Lilly Endowment had awarded Africare in late 1973 for well development in the Sahel.

The American response to the Sahelian drought brought not only life-saving measures to millions of people in West Africa, but it brought life to Africare as an organization and enabled it to grow institutionally. The appearances of Lucas and Kennedy on major network television and radio stations gave favorable national recognition to Africare's work. Increased donations enabled it to expand the permanent Africare staff. The first representatives overseas were posted in Upper Volta and Mali, where they worked closely with country officials to design and implement programs. There was an incremental growth in administrative effectiveness and sophistication as Africare went from purchasing medicines and supplies for Kirker's

hospital in Maine-Soroa, constructing a well and nutrition recuperation center for malnourished children in Upper Volta, or purchasing
meat, fish, and medicines for refugee camps throughout Mauritania
to a $250,000 multi-country water resources program in West Africa.
Nonetheless, Africare was a tiny, largely untested charity with a slim
record of accomplishment. The balance sheet at the end of the 1975
fiscal year (April 30) showed that Africare had received $157,000
from contributions and membership dues and $311,547 in grants and
contracts from private foundations and USAID. The entire budget
was a half million dollars. The see-saw nature of Africare's finances
in its early years can be seen further in the 1976 audit. Contributions
and membership dues totaled $268,941, while grants and contracts
amounted to $1,485,162. More than a million dollars of this sum lay
in Africare's bank account awaiting expenditure on large projects
already on the drawing board.

The imbalance between income from private American citizens
and from other sources, especially USAID, indicates the challenge
Africare faced in building a constituency. The Internet did not exist,
so the Africare Web site that is a very effective fund-raising tool today
was not possible. There was no money to hire professional fund rais-
ers or to publicize the organization other than by word of mouth or,
as in the case of the Sahelian drought, media attention. It was up to
Lucas, Kennedy, volunteers such as Pat Eaton and Dellaphine Rauch,
both beginning notable careers in public service, and others to visit
churches, schools, sororities, and civic groups. Within the African
diplomatic corps, some ambassadors and top embassy personnel
gave immediacy to the drive when they accompanied Africare representatives around the nation. Dr. Siteke Mwale, serving as Zambia's
ambassador to the United States, had been ambassador to all of West
Africa in the early 1970s and knew first-hand of the human misery,
not just in the Sahel, but across Africa. He was eager to sell the idea
to Americans that they could help alleviate poverty there. Oumarou
G. Youssoufou, at the Niger Embassy, continued his vital support of
the Africare cause. Some African diplomats offered their chancelleries
or personal homes for fund-raising events. For example, the ambassador of Gabon, Gaston-Robert Bouckat-Bou-Nziengui, turned over
his home in Bethesda, Maryland, one Saturday evening for a benefit
reception. Among elephant tusks, wood carvings, and Gabonese
works of art, guests enjoyed drinks and hors d'oeuvres as musicians
beat conga drums and strummed electric guitars.

Lucas and Kennedy believed strongly that the most successful approach to developing an Africare constituency was to foster the establishment of chapters in cities across the United States. One means of doing this was to encourage members of their audiences to form them. Another method was to ask people they knew in a city to start one. Examples of this tactic were the Hendersons in Atlanta and Percy Wilson in Boston. Sometimes, chapters rose almost spontaneously, as when Marion H. Jackson led a group of black women to Africare headquarters in Washington in 1972 and announced that they were organizing the very first chapter. There were eighteen chapters nationwide by 1977, nearly the high point of chapter development. While most were community-wide, two were grounded in churches. These were the Abyssinian Baptist Church in New York and the Carver Presbyterian Church in Newport News, Virginia.

The purpose of the chapters was to inform Americans about Africa, to increase membership in Africare (a percentage of dues went to Washington), and to raise donations by publicizing its programs and goals. Chapters were expected to hold special fund-raising events and pass along to national headquarters most of the proceeds. The primary target audience was the African American community in the belief that black Americans could translate an interest in their African heritage into support for an African American organization doing relief and development work in Africa.

Activities sponsored by the chapters varied. In Atlanta, there was an exhibit of contemporary Haitian art in March 1974, and in May, the world premiere of the movie *Things Fall Apart*, with the Nigerian author of the novel, Chinua Achebe, as a guest. In November 1975, Mayor Maynard Jackson proclaimed an Africare Week that featured, among several events, a city-wide church collection. The Kansas City, Missouri, chapter persuaded the mayor, Charles B. Wheeler, Jr., to declare the month of May 1976 as HELP AFRICARE HELP ... AND GIVE A CAN. The idea was to collect cans of food, sell them at half-price to Kansas City's citizens on fixed or low incomes, and donate the proceeds to the national Africare headquarters. In the early 1980s, during the Ethiopian famine, Kansas City's chapter raised $40,000 in a "Buy-a-Blanket" drive and recruited two local nurses to join an Africare medical team going to Ethiopia. At the same time, the New York City chapter, led by the Reverend Calvin Butts, provided $10,000 for the purchase of cooking pots, eating utensils, and blankets for drought victims. Under the leadership of Percy Wilson, later an Africare board member, the Boston chapter in 1976 adopted a nutrition-maternity-child care dispensary-recuperation center in Upper Volta and succeeded in getting a $10,000 donation from the southern New England Conference of the United Methodist Church. Indianapolis Africare supporters honored Charles Williams, the Lilly Endowment official who had been instrumental in selecting Africare for grants, with a thousand-person banquet in the spring of 1977. The Reverend Leon H. Sullivan, a political activist known for the Sullivan Principles that urged equitable employment practices for corporations doing business in South Africa, was the keynote speaker. Even as late as 1995, some chapters were active. Detroit Africare volunteers, for example, sponsored a ten-day trade mission to Namibia for Michigan businesses.

An outstanding example of a group of supporters who conducted an energetic educational, social, and activist program from the 1970s to the early 1990s was the Metropolitan Washington Africare Chapter. It had the advantage of being located in the nation's capital, with access to African embassies, organizations of all sorts, including Africare headquarters, and individuals knowledgeable about Africa. For some of its regular meetings, which were usually held at local libraries, it brought in guest speakers such as Walter C. Carrington, former U.S. ambassador to Senegal, and George B.N. Ayittey, a well-known African economics professor at a local think-tank. Another time, Kevin G. Lowther, Africare's Director for Southern Africa, addressed the group on the subject of "Development and Devilment in Southern Africa." On one occasion, members took a "motor safari" to five African embassies where they met the ambassadors and their staffs. They also arranged fund-raising receptions at individual embassies to learn about particular countries and their needs. A notably successful reception was held at the Embassy of the Ivory Coast near Dupont Circle in May 1991. Ambassador and Mrs. Charles P. Gomis provided an open bar, a buffet, and Ivorian music for nearly two hundred guests. The chapter turned the profits of $3,500 over to national headquarters, with the hope that they would go toward a future project in the Ivory Coast. An educational activity of a different sort was a tour of the National Museum of African Art for chapter members. They tried also to build esprit de corps by sponsoring Dutch treat dinners at African restaurants in the Washington area. The Kilimanjaro Restaurant, which specialized in East African food, and the Meskerem Restaurant, featuring Ethiopian cuisine, were popular venues for these outings. Among many overseas activities that the chapter funded was the Aghlembit vegetable garden project in the region of Tagant, Mauritania.

Its most successful long-term chapter activity was the Africare Day program that it began in 1977 and sponsored for six successive years. The mayor of Washington, Walter L. Washington or Marion Barry, Jr., annually declared a Sunday as Africare Day in the District of Columbia. For the first two years, the celebration, entitled "A Tribute to Africa," convened at the State Department auditorium and ended with a reception hosted by Ambassador Ardeshir Zahedi at the Embassy of Iran. The venue for the reception changed in 1979, and later the entire event moved to different locations. As many as a thousand guests attended in some years and as much as $18,000 was raised. In 1982, Africare headquarters assumed responsibility for Africare Day, which it occasionally made part of a larger Africare Week. Events included workshops on African development, recognition of men and women significant in promoting the cause of Africa through distinguished service awards, and fund-raising receptions at several African embassies. The last Africare Day in Washington, on June 3, 1990, was particularly celebratory, but also muted. On the one hand, Nelson Mandela, to whom the event was dedicated, had just been released from Robben Island, and Africare House, the new headquarters for Africare, had recently opened. On the other hand, Bishop John T. Walker, Episcopal Bishop of Washington, D.C., and chairman of the Africare Board, had died unexpectedly the previous September. The Bishop Walker memorial dinner, begun that fall, thereafter became Africare's main fund-raising effort both in Washington and nationally.

The effort to build an Africare constituency through the creation of chapters at the grassroots level never succeeded to the extent that Lucas and Kennedy hoped. A few—Washington, Chicago, Kansas City, and Atlanta among them—were active for years. New ones were being created well into the 1980s. Nevertheless, they did not meet their expected potential. A fundamental problem was the lack of a consensus in Washington as to what the chapters should do or be. Senior staff often felt ambivalence toward them, for while they were helpful in publicizing Africare goals and in raising money at the grassroots level, they were difficult to control. The usual absence of a chapter coordinator or advisor at headquarters who could oversee their activities and give coherent direction to leaders contributed to the problem. Several attempts by the Washington office to supply one were abandoned because the results did not justify the staff expense.

Moreover, sometimes chapters received contradictory signals of affirmation when Africare personnel confused members by seeming to promote the establishment of rival chapters. This happened twice to the Metropolitan Washington chapter. In 1987, Lucas sent Eddie Eitches, chapter president, an invitation to the inaugural meeting of "D.C. Friends of Africare." Three years later, the national staff sanctioned the founding of a "Greater Washington Chapter of Africare" and allowed organizers to hold the charter meeting at Africare House and to send invitations to members of the Metropolitan group.

The structure of the chapters was another basic flaw in their perpetuation. Most were founded in black communities of sizable American cities by men and women of some local standing. They invited their neighbors, friends, fellow parishioners, and work colleagues to come to informal meetings to discuss the plight of Africa. When the Sahelian drought or the Ethiopian famine was the main topic, there was great interest and these guests, becoming members, donated. However, after a crisis, when Africare emphasized long range programs of little immediate effect, the members felt less engagement. Another factor is that chapters were often promoted by one or two key individuals; they did not become institutionalized as organizations that would carry on if those sponsors left. Hence, the personal linkage that was often behind the establishment of chapters was sometimes the cause of their demise. There were also practical considerations that explained the failure of the chapter effort to flourish. During the 1970s and early 1980s personal computers were not widely used by the general public. Chapter leaders and members did not have modern means of keeping records or the Internet to disperse information about upcoming activities. There was no automatic mechanism for reminding members to pay their annual dues. Furthermore, there was insufficient reporting on chapter events and little accounting for the funds raised. Africare auditors, Deloitte, Haskins, & Sells, complained that "Africare exhibits limited control over chapter activities, thus exposing the organization to the possibility of unfavorable public perception ... violations of state regulations regarding the solicitation of funds, and conflicts with the Internal Revenue Service ... ."

Basing chapters in black communities and relying on contributions from black Americans also had the disadvantage of making Africare dependent on a segment of society with modest means. Moreover, this method for raising funds had the structural weakness that at its core were unpaid chapter volunteers with uneven motivation.

A 1978 evaluation done for USAID, which had given Africare an earlier $608,701 development program grant, emphasized this and added that the constituency of black Americans was not organized in a way to facilitate fund raising. It pointed out, further, that there were other regional and national organizations seeking funds from the same constituency (e.g., NAACP, CORE, SCLC, the Urban League, and others) that offered "programs with greater immediate self-interest for Black Americans than those of Africare." The evaluators warned Africare that, as admirable as it was that it had not become an exclusively black organization in its staffing or constituency appeal, its credibility as having a special relationship between Africa and America's black community was threatened by the increasing proportion of donors and donations from white constituencies. They urged Africare leaders to adopt a major new strategy of fund raising that would target black individuals, black organizations, and in particular, black churches.

Ultimately, for all these reasons, Africare put less emphasis on chapter development and worked in other ways to build a constituency. Private, secular organizations of many sorts proved to be one category of great potential. Several black sororities became strong supporters of Africare and gave sizeable donations consistently for years, right to the present. Alpha Kappa Alpha sorority adopted the African village development program in 1984 and, with its more than two hundred chapters nationwide, gave $395,000 during the next decade. The Alpha chapter at Howard University participated in that and has continued its support of Africare with an annual "Stop Hunger Fast" to build empathy with those who suffer from HIV/AIDS, homelessness, and hunger. It raised $21,000 in 2003 and set a chapter record in 2007 with $47,000. Chapters of another sorority, Delta Sigma Theta, over time gave a total of nearly $22,000, some of it for Ethiopian relief.

During the 1980s, The Links, Inc., a national black women's service organization boasting of six thousand members, contributed more than $70,000 toward famine relief, well construction, and in southern Africa, refugee assistance. The National Alliance of Postal and Federal Employees asked each of its twenty thousand members to donate $5 to planting a tree in Africa. Jack and Jill of America, Inc., a national African American family organization, supported Africare in numerous ways, including a $40,000 child survival project in Mali. In August 1988, the Shriners, holding their annual meeting in Las Vegas, added another $43,000 to the $27,000 they had already donated for beekeeping in Rwanda.

At least as significant as secular groups in contributing to Africare were black and white churches, national conferences, and related religious organizations. The administrative boards of major national denominations sent large sums. The African Methodist Episcopal Church of America, under the leadership of Bishop H. Thomas Primm, committed itself to supporting a $100,000 water resource development and well construction program in Mali. Just one church, St. Paul's A.M.E. Church in Cambridge, Massachusetts, raised half the amount during a twenty-four hour marathon that featured local dancers, choirs, inspirational speakers, and such entertainers as Babatunde Olatunji and Dick Gregory. The Presbyterian Hunger Fund donated $394,000, the Progressive National Baptist Convention contributed $264,000, and the National Baptist Convention provided $167,000.

In addition, hundreds of individual congregations took up collections and held local benefits for the purpose of building a well, buying books for school children, or trying to help the people of Africa in some other way. Beginning with the Sahelian relief campaign in the United States, Episcopalian families were encouraged by their leaders to donate at least a dollar a month to alleviate world hunger. Much of that money was funneled to Africare through the Presiding Bishop's Fund for World Relief. Typically, dioceses and individual Episcopal parishes held special weekend or Sunday events to publicize the famine. The rector of St. Cyprian's Episcopal Church in Roxbury, Massachusetts, the Reverend Richard Tolliver, utilized the religious period of Lent. He asked parishioners to take a "love box" sent by the Presiding Bishop's office and to skip one meal a week until they had deposited at least $10 in it. He gave encouragement by having the comedian Dick Gregory address a special worship service. In this way, the congregation raised $2,527 for irrigation pumps in Niger. The Presiding Bishop's Fund donated $60,000 for dike construction in Upper Volta in 1975 and more than a half million dollars for Ethiopian drought victims in the 1980s, just two of the many Africare programs that the Episcopal Church sponsored. Another denomination giving broad support to Africare was the United Methodist Church. Through its General Board of Global Ministries, the United Methodist Committee on Relief (UMCOR) and the Women's Division contributed at least $600,000 during the 1980s and 1990s. The Methodists helped Africare build dams in Mali, assist refugees in several West African nations, enable women in a Nigerien village to raise poultry, and offer AIDS education in the Central African Republic. Correspondence

27

in the Africare archives reveals a very engaged clergy and membership.

One means of getting national recognition, and hence funding, is to have celebrity sponsors. Africare, from the beginning, sought the advantage of its contacts with prominent Americans. In October 1970, Kirker parlayed his friendship with Sammy Davis, Jr., into a request that the black entertainer become the national chairman of Africare, with the primary function of raising funds. President Diori of Niger also asked Davis to accept the post. Joe Kennedy spent a fruitless night in a Las Vegas night club, expecting to meet Davis and persuade him to join the cause. Africare founders were so confident of his cooperation that they put his name on the cover of the first Africare report as the national fund raising chairman. To their regret, however, Davis never followed through with any activities that enhanced Africare recognition or coffers.

Africare came to know other celebrities through chance or circumstance, including the singer Roberta Flack, the fight promoter Don King, the boxer Muhammad Ali, and Washington Redskin cornerback Martin Mayhew. Flack served on the Board of Directors for a while after her attorney became impressed with Africare at its opening event in Atlanta. Africare's contact with Don King came through an employee, and this subsequently led to Muhammad Ali's gift of $10,000 to Africare from his fight with Chuck Wepner in Cleveland in March 1975. Ali then personally contributed $50,000 to Africare, while King gave $10,000. The money given by Ali and King went, in part, to reconstitute herds of sheep and goats, as well as to distribute highly valued donkeys to thirty-five families in the Irhazer Valley of Niger. The Africare country representative, James Toliver, described the emotional scene after the people were told that Muhammad Ali had been the donor: "The chief shouted to the group and immediately every man, woman, and child present (me included) slowly knelt to the ground, hands extended, palms upward, as the chief recited in Arabic the appropriate Koranic verses asking Allah to bestow his blessing on Muhammad Ali for what he had done ... ." Mayhew and his teammates gave $20,000 for youth agricultural training in Senegal in 1992, a country he visited as a part of a larger tour of development and relief projects in West Africa the following year.

A celebrity of a different sort who gave credibility and publicity to Africare was Lillian Carter, the eighty-year-old mother of then president, Jimmy Carter. Invited by Gambian President Sir Dawda Jawara, leader of the Sahelian nations' Interstate Committee on the Drought, to see the situation in the Sahel, "Miss Lillian" visited Senegal, Mali, and Upper Volta in the summer of 1978. Her experiences as a Peace Corps nurse in India a few years earlier and her straight-forward personality enabled her to appraise needs and programs in a realistic light. There was no pretense that miracles would follow or that she would use her influence to speed action by Africare or USAID. All she promised to do was to spread the word in the United States of Africa's need. The American delegation accompanying her, led by Lucas, saw Mrs. Carter benefit from two African customs—respect for the elderly and for mothers. Years later, Africare representatives with her remember most that she sat in a hot auditorium batting mosquitoes during a long evening cultural program and remained wide awake while other members of the delegation dozed. Photographs of Mrs. Carter in Africa and stories of her interaction with villagers, lepers, and ordinary citizens gave a boost to Africare fund raising efforts and morale.

Africare launched a comprehensive media appeal utilizing celebrities in 1979 and again in the 1990s with the airing of public service radio spots by eight well-known Americans from different walks of life. Roberta Flack, Peter Jennings, and Jayne Kennedy, among them, asked listeners to help Africare improve the livelihood, the health, and education of Africans. Three of the stars from the television series "Roots," which had run to great acclaim in the late 1970s, Georg Stanford Brown, Lynne Moody, and Louis Gossett, Jr., added their voices to the others.

In 1980, Africare's inclusion among the Combined Federal Campaign recipients marked the beginning of a significant, permanent source of program funds. The Combined Federal Campaign (CFC) had its origins in the confusion following World War II when governmental departments and agencies in Washington, D.C., ran their own on-the-job solicitations by charities. President Dwight D. Eisenhower brought some unity through a 1957 executive order that laid a few ground rules and civil service supervision. The first participating charities were primarily large and well-known: the American Red Cross, local Community Chests, CARE. Later presidents tinkered with elements of the program, and in 1971, President Richard Nixon combined all campaigns into a uniform fund raising method. Now, federal employees could contribute through payroll deduction. The really controversial issue in the 1970s was which national charities could participate. Only thirty-three were involved by the end of the decade because public policy advocacy groups, legal defense funds, and small organizations were excluded. This ended in 1980, after much litigation, and there was a great expansion of membership, including Africare, which was admitted to the general category of International Service Agencies. Although the Executive branch of the Reagan administration scored some judicial victories in the 1990s in its efforts to restrict CFC membership, Congress ultimately overrode the restrictions, resulting in a proliferation of participating charities that number in the thousands worldwide today. Africare received $362,010 from CFC during the expanded Fiscal Year 1982, which ended June 30, and that included the very first check for $2,705 issued on June 11, 1981 (through FY 1981, Africare books closed on April 30). The total received since 1981 has been more than $6 million.

Africare was not only about African assistance, but it considered its mission to educate Americans about Africa. It wanted them to see Africa beyond the images they may have received from movies as a continent of animals, jungles, and bare-breasted women. It reasoned that Americans, especially blacks, with increased knowledge of historical and cultural bonds to Africa, might become constituents. Not long after its founding, Africare began holding outreach meetings and forums for the general public. In February 1976, the first national Africare conference at the Sheraton-Park Hotel in Washington, D.C., with Senator Edward M. Kennedy as one of the honorary chairpersons, was aimed at training leaders of Africare chapters. Its theme, "Citizen Participation in African Development," was designed to inform guests about Africa and its history, about American foreign policy in Africa, about Africare and development needs in general, and about strategies for fund raising and membership growth at the chapter level. Professors, government officials, African ambassadors, politicians, chapter presidents, and Africare staff members offered an intense two-day program on such topics as "A Study of the Sahel" and "African Involvement in African Development."

One method of educational and motivational outreach was a project begun in 1984 entitled the African Development Education Program. In twenty major American cities, leaders of such community organizations as the NAACP, Operation PUSH, The Links, Inc., Alpha Kappa Alpha sorority, and the National Association of Colored Women's Clubs were asked to persuade their members to sponsor public seminars, speeches, and workshops on African development. A highlight of the 1985 activities was the speaking tour in May of eight African ambassadors to five American cities. Subsequently, eighteen of these African American membership groups continued what Africare initiated by implementing their own plans to educate fellow citizens about the needs of Africa. The Washington, D.C., affiliates of the Progressive National Baptist Convention, for example, began a pilot program entitled "One Church, One Village" that would enable congregations to establish ties with Africa.

Another educational program targeted school children. Beginning in the fall of 1981 and continuing for seven years, Africare sponsored an essay contest in District of Columbia public high schools. The general theme was the interdependence of Africa and the United States, and initially, the top prize was a summer trip to Africa to visit Africare projects. There was the added incentive of a short stopover in Paris. The first winner was a sixteen year-old junior at Woodrow Wilson High School, Stager Clay Smith, whose social studies teacher told him about the contest. Smith did not really want to enter, but pressured by his father, dean of the Howard University Law School, and hoping to get more use of the family car, he spent all his free time finding articles in the library, calling embassies for information, and requesting papers from the United Nations. He used the example of a U.N. paper to create a format and documented his essay with thirty-two footnotes. In a ceremony at the District building (City Hall) in May 1982, Mayor Marion Barry, Jr., awarded Smith first prize. His trip to West Africa that July opened the door to a larger world, and as he said, "turned on a light bulb in my head." The Tarzan image of Africa shattered when he visited village wells, reforestation projects, and food production sites. He also experienced some political realities, such as in Upper Volta, where a coup d'état had taken place. Overall, it was a maturing experience because not only did he expand his world view, but he had to obtain a passport and visa, learn what immunizations were necessary, and decide what to carry in his luggage.

Following his trip, Smith went on to college and to law school. Today, he is a lead attorney with a large international firm and is a father himself, planning to send his teenage son abroad so his "light bulb" comes on. Smith's experience in 1982 had the carry over effect of inspiring his sister, Michelle, to become interested in current events concerning Africa. She won the contest in 1984 with the essay "Divesture: Americans Revolt Against U.S. Policy in South Africa."

Africare entered into a different strategy for constituency development in 1990 when it created two new vehicles by which to reach out.

The first was the Constituency for Africa (CFA), a broad-based alliance of organizations that sought to educate Americans about Africa and affect American public policy. It sponsored various events, such as a briefing by George Moose, Assistant Secretary of State for African Affairs, and a provocative presentation at one Congressional Black Caucus annual legislative weekend. By early 1994, so many groups had joined the CFA that Africare spun it off and it became an independent organization, which it remains today, under the leadership of the man who started it at Africare, Melvin Foote.

The other initiative, called the African Diplomatic Outreach Program (ADOP), was funded by the Ford Foundation in 1991 and implemented in cooperation with the Georgetown University Institute for the Study of Diplomacy. It was aimed at African ambassadors, many of whom arrive at their embassies in Washington with little actual knowledge of the United States, its governmental operation, Washington politics, or the subtleties of their jobs. During its first year, 1992, guest speakers included Ronald Brown, chairman of the Democratic National Committee, Senator Richard Lugar of Indiana, then Health and Human Services Secretary Dr. Louis W. Sullivan, and well-known media commentator David Gergen. Among the many topics discussed were the formulation of American foreign policy, the evolution of U.S. policy toward Africa, and the role of the media, think tanks, and the business community in government decision making. Applications of space technology in Africa, uses of American pharmaceuticals and food products in Africa, and USAID programs were additional subjects of immediate practical value to the participants. Contributing to the success of these gatherings was the chance they gave African ambassadors to meet with each other and the sense of pride they felt that the venue was a newly opened Africare House with authentic art pieces and attractive facilities. The ambassadors created a sensation in 1997 when some of them participated in an "Across America" road trip to the southeastern part of the United States. They met with state and corporate officials, farmers, and housewives, but probably no contact had more impact on either party than shaking hands with a descendant of freed slaves at her house on St. Helena Island, South Carolina. On St. Helena, among the marshes east of Beaufort, one could still hear the Gullah language, find Gullah cuisine in local restaurants, and see tabby building construction.

The flagship fund raising and publicity raising event for Africare has become the Bishop John T. Walker Memorial Dinner, held in

Washington, D.C., each fall. Walker chaired the Africare Board of Directors from 1974 until his death in 1989. Born in Barnesville, Georgia, he grew up in Detroit and completed college at Wayne State University and religious studies at Virginia Theological Seminary in Alexandria, Virginia. He served as a parish priest in Michigan and New Hampshire before teaching for a year in Uganda. He came to Washington in 1966 as canon of the Washington Cathedral and in 1977, he was appointed bishop of the Episcopal Diocese of Washington.

At Africare, Walker was an icon. He brought out the best in everyone and he was an excellent fund raiser. He spoke quietly and never raised his voice. His judgment was valued. As Board chair, he was particularly adamant that Africare would not undertake any project in the Republic of South Africa as long as the apartheid government ruled. A favorite story among long-term staff and Board members is his performance in the negotiations with CARE over the use of the name "Africare." A director called it one of the funniest and most colorful episodes of Africare history. When Kirker incorporated Africare in Hawaii, he capitalized the letters. Lucas continued the practice after Africare moved to Washington. The managers of CARE in New York considered this an infringement on their own name and through their attorney, Marc Leland, threatened legal action. Lucas and Walker, along with two directors, Curtin Winsor and David Eaton, went to New York several times to discuss the issue with CARE officials. All Africare offers of compromise, such as a disclaimer, "Not associated with CARE," or dropping the capital letters except for the first, were rejected with the demand that Africare abandon its name altogether. At the final meeting in New York, when CARE persisted, Walker announced in a calm voice, "It's not going to happen." Then, still speaking softly, he warned his opponents that the wrath of God might visit them. The CARE strategy collapsed and its officials negotiated a settlement along the lines of the original Africare proposals.

Bishop Walker's death came just at a time when Africare faced new financial strains and sought to strengthen itself through the creation of an endowment. The Board of Directors and Africare management looked to Walker for leadership and believed that he would play an important role through his fund raising ability. In a way, his unexpected passing launched an event even more valuable than an endowment campaign, an annual memorial dinner. The first was held in October 1990 at the Sheraton Washington Hotel, with Roberto Goizueta, Chairman and CEO of The Coca Cola Company, serving as national honorary chair and providing the principal financial backing (E. Neville Isdell later substituted for Goizueta). Pennsylvania Representative William H. Gray III, majority whip of the U.S. House of Representatives, was the keynote speaker and honored guest. Television personalities conducted the ceremonies, greetings from the president of the United States, George H.W. Bush, were read, and prominent public figures offered their salutations. Special entertainment enlivened the atmosphere as guests met friends and recalled memories, often from their time in Africa. This became the pattern for subsequent dinners, although the venue changed to the Washington Hilton. Many prominent business people—George M. C. Fisher of Eastman Kodak, Michael L. Eskew of United Parcel Service, and Jan Leschly of SmithKline Beecham among them—helped Africare solicit support from among their colleagues by acting as national chairs. Some of the performers at the dinners were the Gateway Kids, who danced and sang from the traditional repertory of Ghana, Youssou Ndour, an internationally known Senegalese musician, and Jeff Majors, the harpist.

Beginning in 1992, Africare presented the Bishop John T. Walker Distinguished Humanitarian Service Award annually to men and women for outstanding contributions to the welfare of Africa. Archbishop Desmond Tutu of South Africa, winner of the 1984 Nobel Peace Prize, was both the first recipient and the keynote speaker. With his nation in transition from a white apartheid regime to a democratically-elected government, he pleaded, "Help us in this, the last lap of our race to the winning post of a democratic, just, non-racial South Africa. No one is truly free until all are free everywhere. We *will* be free!" The evening was capped by a special address via videotape from Nelson Mandela. Two years later, in October 1994, Mandela, on a state visit to the United States as the new President of South Africa and a Nobel Prize laureate, received the Walker Award amidst a large gathering of American and African luminaries, including Nicephore Soglo, the President of Benin, Jimmy Carter, Jesse Jackson, Coretta Scott King, Colin Powell, and Muhammad Ali. Vice-President Albert Gore, Jr., recalling Mandela's life-long dedication to the ideal of a democratic and free society, exuded, "To see him here with us tonight! What could be a more important affirmation of our capacity as human beings to transcend our past?"

The list of recipients of the Walker Award, of keynote speakers, and of other honored guests at Bishop Walker dinners for over nearly twenty years reads like pages from the *International Who's Who*.

The 1995 dinner, with a special theme, "Salute to African Democracy," honored the Reverend Leon H. Sullivan, the prominent pastor of the Zion Baptist Church in Philadelphia, whose drive for corporations to divest themselves in South Africa had earned him the friendship of Nelson Mandela and other freedom fighters and whose work for civil rights in the United States had put him in the company of Martin Luther King, Jr., and J. Philip Randolph. The audience of 2,100 included special guest President Bill Clinton, who was the recipient himself in 2006. Two men who embodied the American quest for global improvements in human rights were honored in 1996 and 1998, respectively, former President Jimmy Carter and former American Ambassador to the U.N., Andrew Young.

During 1997 and 1999, the Bishop Walker dinners saluted African American and African women. First honored was Dorothy I. Height, sometimes called "the godmother of the women's movement" for her long leadership position on the national staff of the YWCA and for her forty year tenure as the president of the National Council of Negro Women. Her civil rights involvement emerged in the late 1930s when, as a new YWCA employee in New York City, she fought for better working conditions for black domestic workers. From the 1960s and 1970s on, she participated at the highest levels of the civil rights movement in the United States. Height received the Medal of Freedom from President Bill Clinton in 1994 and subsequently, in 2004, the Congressional Gold Medal from President George W. Bush. It was a particularly festive evening at the Washington Hilton as hundreds of her colleagues in the struggle for equality joined with others in hearing First Lady Hillary Rodham Clinton praise the eighty-five year old grand dame of racial progress. In 1999, Africare paid tribute to Graca Simbine Machel, former first lady of Mozambique (as wife of the late President Samora Machel) and later first lady of the Republic of South Africa (as wife of then President Nelson Mandela). Machel is an educator and an activist on behalf of children, particularly those drawn into the vortex of war. Albert and Tipper Gore, serving as honorary patrons for the dinner, were among the large audience that heard her lament, "We have tremendous wealth in our hands, concentrated in a few people, a few corporations, a few nations. Yet the majority, billions of people not only in the developing world but also here, go hungry and without a home."

Beginning in 2000, several Bishop Walker Dinners focused on the African AIDS crisis and award recipients were recognized for their part in the battle against that disease. James D. Wolfensohn, president of the World Bank Group, proclaimed in 2000 that "the poor people of Africa are not the liability but the asset of the continent," and warned that "AIDS is not just a problem for Africa, but for all of us." Dr. Louis W. Sullivan, former U.S. secretary of health and human services and founder and president emeritus of the Morehouse School of Medicine in Atlanta, emphasized the link between health and all other human activities in his 2001 acceptance speech. Bill and Melinda Gates of the same-named foundation were honored in 2003 for their activist philanthropy in the area of global health, particularly with HIV/AIDS, and for their efforts to raise public awareness in the United States and abroad about this scourge. Unable to attend the dinner themselves, they were represented by Bill Gates, Sr., and they sent a videotaped message in which they deplored the fact that random geography determines a child's access to information, education, or a healthy life.

Not all Bishop Walker Dinners started smoothly, however. The 2002 nominee, Harry Belafonte, singer and civil rights activist, threatened to renege on his acceptance when he learned that Condoleezza Rice, the National Security Adviser, would deliver the major address. This became an embarrassment to Africare as Rice withdrew because of "scheduling conflicts" and Belafonte proclaimed on a national television talk show that his protest had been responsible. Even *The Wall Street Journal* covered the story. In a piece entitled "The Trouble With Harry, Belafonte takes on Condi Rice, and an Africa charity loses," the paper opined that Africare had countenanced Belafonte's "buffoonery" and had disinvited the wrong person. There were a few protestors with signs in the lobby of the Washington Hilton before the dinner and Africare staff apparently did interfere with journalists trying to interview guests, but the 1,800 member audience was largely unaware of scuffles. The evening's theme, "Africa and the American Private Sector: Partners for the Common Good," was emphasized by Rice's substitute, Ambassador Andrew Young, who declared, "There can be no global economy without the presence of Africa." Bono, the activist and rock musician, joined Young on the podium.

Honoring President Ellen Johnson Sirleaf of Liberia, Africa's first democratically elected woman leader, at the 2007 dinner, Africare brought First Lady Laura Bush to deliver remarks underscoring the Bush Administration's support of her. Bush called Johnson Sirleaf "an inspiration to everyone who believes in free societies" and commended her efforts to build up democratic institutions in Liberia. She spoke in particular favor of other measures being taken to improve education, especially the education of girls, and health care. Bush included Africare in the glow when she mentioned visiting during the previous June the Mututa Memorial Clinic in Zambia where patients with HIV are assisted and when she thanked Africare for its "terrific work to improve the lives of men, women and children across the continent of Africa."

In 2008, Africare awarded the Bishop Walker Distinguished Humanitarian Service Award to President George W. Bush, whose administrations unequivocally have done more than any other in American history to send assistance to sub-Saharan Africa.

For seventeen years through the selection of President Bush, Africare chose prominent world figures, politicians, leaders of governmental institutions, and philanthropists for its Bishop Walker awards. With the exception of Melinda Gates, every one was at least middle aged; most were considerably older. The audiences attracted to the dinners were largely in the same age category. Few members of the younger generation of potential supporters attended. Africare executives, becoming concerned about continuing the event's momentum and valuable fund-raising role, began exploring ways to revitalize the dinner agenda. What they learned was that, among charities also sponsoring such occasions, the trend is to bypass solemn messengers and their hard sell in favor of famous entertainers who take a soft approach. The Africare staff debated this for months before it decided, in the spring of 2009, to invite the young musician John Legend to receive the Bishop Walker award that fall. Thirty years old, he had received six Grammy Awards and been named by Time Magazine as one of the most influential people of 2009. Legend qualified as a humanitarian through the establishment of a group called "Show Me Campaign," that aimed to fight poverty through sustainable practical development programs. While attendance at the dinner was down, perhaps because the usual older ticket buyers were unfamiliar with contemporary popular culture, the ambience of the evening was lively and energetic. Not only Legend's recorded songs, but those sung in person by the Beninese Grammy Award-winning singer Angelique Kidjo filled the ballroom. Another new feature in 2009 was challenging guests to text a pledge on their mobile phones. The names of those who gave more than $250 were put in a drawing for a diamond necklace given by the DeBeers Company and Africare raised $7,200 this way.

The monetary value of the Bishop Walker Dinners is apparent in the statistics. In 1990, more than 1,325 guests attended and the net income to Africare was $198,000. Attendance quickly rose to 2,500 in 1994, in part because of the Mandela visit, and remained over 2,000 until 2002. Net income routinely exceeded a half million dollars and, occasionally, approached a million dollars. Throughout the years, attendance and net income have varied according to who was to receive the Walker Award, who was to deliver the major address, and other factors. About 1550 people came to honor President Bush in 2008 and the net income was more than $500,000. The sums raised by the dinners are particularly important to Africare because, together with individual contributions and money from the Combined Federal Campaign, as well as from churches, foundations, and corporations, they provide unrestricted funds for undertaking new programs independent of federal sponsorship. They also enable Africare to complete projects when their costs unexpectedly surpass what was appropriated for them or to assist in an overseas emergency. Africare can also meet the IRS requirements of eligibility as a private voluntary organization in which at least 20% of the group's budget in any given fiscal year is spent from private sources.

The Bishop Walker Dinner is the largest annual event for Africa in the United States and one of the largest charity events of any kind in the nation's capital. A Washingtonian, influential in African policy making and development, jokingly said, "people [i.e., charitable organizations] would kill for it." That Africare, modest in size, has the institutional capacity to manage a fund raiser with a large guest roster speaks of its operational strength. That so many distinguished guests typically come to the dinner is testimony to Africare's well-established position among African embassies, agencies of the U.S. federal government, other PVOs, foundations, corporations, private constituencies, and the academic community. Moreover, Africare itself is paid tribute by the recipients of the Bishop Walker Award and by special visitors who add their congratulations.

The heart of the Bishop Walker Dinner is not Africare, however, but Africa. Through speakers and honored guests, the audience hears first-hand about its main challenges—political, economic, social, and physical. Amidst the glitter of black tie and elaborate African national dress, men and women are sobered by a human story that demands action. Ordinary Americans, of all races and from all walks of life, American and African diplomats, and important figures in government, business, and private institutions receive the inescapable message that more must be done. It is a night for them to celebrate Africa, but it is also an occasion to renew their zeal for the aspirations of Africare founders.

3

Establishing Roots Overseas and at Home

Once Africare was reorganized in 1971, with a declared mission of engaging in more than medical assistance to one African nation, it had to decide what additional activities it would pursue and where. At least three factors pointed it geographically toward the ex-colonies of French West Africa. First, William Kirker had nearly positioned himself as the Dr. Albert Schweitzer of the Chadian Basin in southeastern Niger as a result of his years there with the American Peace Corps and then with the Government of Niger. He and his volunteers were back and operating the first Africare project. Second, C. Payne Lucas, as Peace Corps director in Niger, knew President Diori and other important government officials in the nation. He knew leaders in other countries of the region, as well. Third, the Sahelian drought gave Africare a ready-made opportunity to enter a disaster area where its small size and inexperience were not handicaps. Hence, Africare's first steps on the heels of its Diffa medical program were relief measures for the people of the Sahel. After that crisis, it was logical to focus on remedial actions that would preempt later catastrophes. Building wells in the six Sahelian countries was an obvious choice and, furthermore, Africare had funding from the Lilly Endowment.

A five-member team including a hydrologist/geologist, led by Joe Kennedy, now director of international development, left the United States for Niamey in March 1974. It stopped in Paris to study the hydrological and geological surveys that the *Bureau de Recherches Geologiques et Mineres* had collected when these nations were still French colonies. These surveys showed that the water-table in the region had been steadily declining for years and, therefore, wells tapping the water-table, except for those adjacent to lakes and rivers, had slowly dried up. Another discovery was that there were artesian aquifers throughout the Sahel; some of these had been identified coincidentally during oil and mineral exploration before independence. As an example, in the Irhazer Valley forty miles northwest of Agadez in Niger, the French carried out uranium explorations in the late 1950s. They drilled test holes and sunk pipes six inches in diameter as deep as 216 feet. While they did not find uranium, they did strike water. Each of these holes was topped with a cement plug that, over the course of time, became smothered in sand. The challenge was to locate them, uncap the pipes, and construct wells. In each country, equipment and supplies had to be brought over a nonexistent road system in borrowed or rented vehicles. There were chronic shortages of fuel and what was available came at skyrocketing prices.

In order to locate the holes in Niger, officials sent word out to the Tuaregs and other nomads that they were searching for potential well sites. What happened next in Irhazer Valley is typical. One night, Tuaregs drifted into the camp site of the Commandant and the Africare representative to tell them that they knew the location of four test holes. They all set off the next morning in a Land Rover across the desert with no roads or tracks. They zigzagged for miles, seemingly in an aimless manner, around slate fields and rocks, through scrub brush and sand until, suddenly, there were small green patches of grass. Nearby was a test hole with a cement plug. This scene was repeated until it became routine; even when the nomads pointed out a spot in the vast desert where there was no sign of vegetation, a test hole was uncovered by digging five or ten feet into the sand.

Africare selected eleven of these sites in the Irhazer Valley, based on the willingness of the Tuaregs to participate in constructing the wells and to cultivate the soil. These became part of the nomad resettlement program, a risky venture because it asked nomadic people who for generations have crisscrossed the desert with their herds to become at least partially sedentary farmers. The Africare team did have some indication that they might succeed when they learned that, at one test hole, the Tuaregs were already excavating with shovels, picks, and long crowbars. Moreover, the people had prepared nearly twenty acres of land in anticipation of a well that would irrigate their fields.

Constructing the wells, although facilitated by the pipes sunk by the French, required considerable technical skill and manual labor. Once the cement plug was located, a wide-diameter cement well casing had to be built to form the walls of the well. Then, the plug could be removed, but, even though the source of water was an artesian spring, a pump was necessary to get it to the ground surface. The last step was laying out long irrigation pipes or digging irrigation channels to relay the water from the well to the fields. Each well site was designed to accommodate fifty to a hundred families and to allow the cultivation of between fifteen and thirty acres.

In Mali, the situation with wells was quite different from that in Niger. Most of the population, whether sedentary farmers in villages and small towns or nomadic herdsmen, had some linkage to two large rivers, the Senegal and the Niger, or its tributary, the Bani. There had been mining activities that resulted in the construction of artesian wells in parts of the country, but in two regions of greatest need, outside Timbuktu and Goundam, in the heart of the Sahara desert, wells rose from water table aquifers. Some were village wells serving a semi-sedentary population; others were "village wells," but served a highly dispersed population; most typical for the area, however, were transit wells depended upon by nomadic cattle herders. The Africare water resources team found that many of the wells had dried up, collapsed inward, or produced water too salty to use. Eleven locations were selected either for construction of new wells or for deepening or repair. Africare country representative Denis Hynes, reporting in June 1975 on the village of Echelle, which was surrounded by sand dunes and had a population of approximately a thousand people, with cattle outnumbering humans by a two-to-one ratio, wrote, "[W]hat I saw on my last trip here was perhaps the poorest African village I had ever seen, whose misery was blatant, and whose very existence depended on the success of the AFRICARE well. ... Today the well is finished, functioning, and providing water to a seemingly rejuvenated population." Seventeen years later, when the Africare representative, Dan Gerber, visited Escelle, the well was still operational, as were six others of the original eleven.

The Africare water development program in Chad was centered in the relatively populous southern part of the country more than a hundred miles from N'Djamena, the capital. The people were mostly sedentary farmers and small-scale cattle herders living in highly concentrated cluster villages. Their wells, drawing from the dropping water table, were dry in many areas and needed deepening. In some cases, the villages were close enough together that the women could walk to an adjacent well that was working and, although a time-consuming, tough job in a merciless climate, they could return home with water for their households. Occasionally, however, villages were isolated and desolate. When the wells ran dry, villagers had no

43

place to go. Africare chose fifteen sites to construct new wells or to improve existing ones.

The eighteen wells built in twelve villages of the Pouni region of Upper Volta, a hundred miles southwest of the capital, Ouagadougou, were funded by a $20,000 grant from the Public Welfare Foundation and were intended to provide water for both human and animal consumption. It was an area where most people were sedentary farmers whose hand-dug wells had dried up during the drought. They needed water for the few animals they had as well as for gardening.

In the Kaedi region of Mauritania, the inhabitants had been dependent in the past on the annual flooding of the adjacent Senegal River for drinking water and for water to cultivate cereal crops and animal fodder. Needing the reconstruction and deepening of existing wells in addition to the provision of more sources of water, they were the beneficiaries, altogether, of twenty-six rehabilitated or added wells. Several years later, water resources were enhanced in Senegal by the repair of existing wells, the construction of new ones, and the addition of irrigation systems.

In each of these nations, Africare representatives worked with ministries and offices of the national and local governments. Officials from agricultural, hydrological, public works, and economic development sectors were sought for advice and for permission to embark on programs. Africare's smallness and newness to the field of charitable organizations working overseas turned out to be a big advantage. There was almost no bureaucracy at headquarters in Washington. There were no layers of administrative filtering. There were only a few very dedicated people who had been entrusted by supporters, by the Lilly Endowment, by private philanthropies, and by USAID to do something about the suffering in the Sahel. African government officials dealing with Africare found an agency that was prepared to act, to sign agreements, and to begin immediately providing water to their citizens. Africare, in its enthusiasm, charged ahead, sometimes with naïveté about the difficulties that could arise.

Related to the provision of more water to African villagers was the effort to improve their agricultural output. Here, Africare's initial foray was also limited and modest. It selected a few villages and supplied farmers with small items that could raise their productivity or aid them in enhancing their environment. In Chad, for example, Africare provided tools that villagers could use to clear farmland, repair a local dike, and maintain firebreaks. In several areas of Upper

Volta, tree nurseries were founded to enable local citizens to plant windbreaks and to prepare woodlots that, in the future, would provide cooking fuel. On a larger scale, throughout the Sahel, Africare purchased motor-driven pumps, gardening tools, and materials for village production cooperatives.

The experience gained in these small efforts soon had the cumulative effect of enabling Africare to undertake large multi-purpose and many-faceted rural projects. With a grant from USAID late in 1974, Africare began to institutionalize within its organization a capacity to plan, design, manage, and evaluate a different approach to Sahelian financial assistance: integrated rural development (IRD). Joe Kennedy pulled together a team of specialists, many of whom became long-term Africare employees, and recruited professors in relevant disciplines from three predominantly black American universities to visit Niger, Upper Volta, and Mali and write proposals that could be submitted to a range of potential donors.

The Africare Development Team made two visits to the Sahel in 1975. It spent a month each in Niger, Upper Volta, and Mali in the spring, meeting officials and technicians at both the central and regional levels of government. One purpose was to identify geographical areas in these countries that would be suitable for the IRD strategy that Africare was promoting. With the information gathered, Africare decided to concentrate on three sites: the Irhazer Valley, the village of Tara in Niger, and Seguenega Sector in Upper Volta. The other purpose, in anticipation of holding workshops to discuss development needs and explain IRD concepts, was to identify potential workshop participants and consultants.

The IRD strategy that Africare intended to introduce in Niger and Upper Volta was built on the goals of improving the quality of life of people who live in rural areas and of transforming stagnant, traditional societies into productive, dynamic economies. The "integrated" approach was based on the premise that a combination of factors was essential to achieving success. These factors were economic growth, the promotion of conditions favorable for production and distribution, value-added inputs (physical, institutional, and human), and such methods as project planning and implementation. Equally important was integrating the rural population into the development process itself. Africare emphasized that villagers must not be seen as the "target" population, but as participants who would thereby have a sense of ownership. Furthermore, Africare asserted that regional and central governments would need to provide a support system for existing rural institutions and probably have to create new ones to overcome likely obstacles.

Africare followed up its reconnaissance trips of the spring by holding workshops in November, 1975, in two of the regions where it proposed to begin integrated rural development. The first was in Agadez, Niger, to lay the ground work for the Irhazer Valley project. Before the Africare Development Team, with the professors, went to Agadez, however, it held a series of meetings in the capital, Niamey, with high officials of the central government. Representatives from the President and from the Ministries of Development, Rural Economy, Mines and Hydraulics, Human Resources, and Health offered their views on the state of development in Irhazer Valley and on various approaches to IRD. Since Africare had $100,000 for Irhazer Valley through the donations of Muhammad Ali, Don King, and the Lilly Endowment, there was discussion of its best utilization as well. Subsequently, out in Agadez, the three-day workshop brought together chief administrative officers, along with staff members from ten technical services (such as agriculture, livestock, forestry, health, and adult literacy). The conference began with a discussion of the general development needs of the region and, specifically, of Irhazer Valley. This was followed by a presentation from each technical service of the needs and priorities, as it saw them. On the second day, workshop participants visited Irhazer Valley and the eight sites that had been identified as prospects for Africare resources. The workshop concluded with a thorough examination of which sites should have priority, which technical services should be involved, what they should offer, and how all officials within the Department of Agadez would interact to achieve their goals.

Moving on to Upper Volta for a workshop at Ouahigouya in the O.R.D. of Yatenga, where the Seguenega Sector is located, the Africare Development Team and professors first discussed the development needs and the agenda with high-ranking officials of the central government in Ouagadougou. They then held five days of meetings with participants who were even more representative of the grassroots level than those who attended the workshop in Agadez. Not just top administrative officials from the regional government and technical services came, but also agriculture and extension agents, nurses, and community leaders. There were plenary sessions in which Africare objectives, funding sources, and an overview of the needs in Yatenga were discussed. Afterwards, Africare staff made short field trips locally to see *bas-fonds*, a hospital, and other potential sites for donor support. On a day-trip to the village of Seguenega, the Africare group visited a sheep-raising project, health facilities, and a reforestation project. It also looked at *bas-fonds*, with the view that these might be developed for vegetable gardening or rice production. Back in Ouahigouya, workshop participants were divided into groups that critiqued the Africare development model and designed, in theory, specific projects for Seguenega, which were then analyzed by everyone.

Gaining the approval of government officials and explaining IRD to workshop participants was just the beginning of establishing a complex program in two African nations. Other considerations, among many, were assessing the real needs in the areas where Africare proposed to work and winning the cooperation of the people. One field in which Africare excelled in its early days was in its bottoms-up approach to planning. Africare employees went out to African countries to see what their strategies were at the national, regional, district, and community level. They sought the voice of the African villager and often did not know what they would come up with. Africare proposals had no pro forma set of objectives or quantitative achievements. The Seguenega project is a good example of how Africare operated. Peter Persell, the country representative for Upper Volta, spent nearly three years experimenting with small scale projects to determine what would be a good mix for a large, integrated design. He tried dry season gardening, wet season gardening, raising goats, and well digging. He spent years residing in villages, talking to people and discussing what was needed and what would work. The knowledge he received and the experience the participants gained all went into the initial proposal for Seguenega and, later, into a multi-million dollar project.

The objectives of the first integrated rural development programs give an idea of the concept. The Irhazer Valley, almost six hundred miles north of Niamey, was an area four hundred miles long and a hundred fifty miles wide. About seven thousand people, divided into fifteen mainly nomadic tribes, lived there. Africare selected a few sites where it had already installed deep bore holes to begin. Its overall goal was to resettle nomadic cattle herders, help them reestablish their herds, and become at least part-time agriculturalists. The first step was to increase water supply for livestock production and intensive agriculture. Water would make possible the launching of a forestry program as well. Moreover, the provision of more local health services to the nomad population by the creation of village health teams would become more feasible as they circumscribed their journeys. An additional step would involve the construction of new health centers and the repair of old ones. Africare even envisioned the day when all health centers would to be supplied with ambulances that could take gravely ill patients to Agadez, forty miles away. A final feature of Africare strategy concerned adult education. As in all African countries, there was a very low literacy rate in Niger and the deficiency particularly manifested itself when citizens tried to master the technical information that accompanied new equipment, new agricultural procedures, and other innovations from the outside world. Helping villagers convert foreign instructions into language that they could understand and utilize would strengthen many other aspects of Africare programs.

Seguenega Sector, forty miles southeast of Ouahigouya, had a population of 110,000 people, mainly sedentary farmers. They lived in a hundred villages over a thirteen hundred square mile area that had one of the highest population densities in Upper Volta. Africare provided some inputs so projects could be implemented, but required villagers to contribute their own labor. Distribution of seeds, locust control measures, improvement in the production of poultry, sheep, and rabbits, and promotion of animal traction relied on Africare support. Tree nurseries, improved grain storage facilities, and farm-to-market roads depended on self-help. In addition to agriculture goals, there were health priorities: development of malnutrition recuperation centers for children, procurement of small equipment and supplies for dispensaries, increasing the capability of dispensaries to train health personnel, and securing a permanent supply of sanitary drinking water. The last goal of the Seguenega project was adult agricultural education, i.e., teaching villagers new skills in gardening, livestock management, and home economics.

The Tara IRD program was different from the programs implemented in Irhazer Valley and Seguenega in that Africare acted primarily as the coordinator of external financial assistance and provided technical consultants only for special problems beyond the experience of Nigeriens. The project itself was directed by a Nigerien and staffed by Nigeriens. Tara was a village of about five hundred families at the edge of the Niger River. The people were subsistence farmers, but much of the arable land around them was almost useless because of the uncontrolled fluctuation of the river. While Africare left the actual designing and planning to Nigerien ministries, its development team envisioned the construction of an irrigation system, with dikes and canals, to reclaim two hundred acres for intensive farming, including crop rotation and multi-cropping. It suggested to the Government of Niger the building of farm-to-market roads, the creation of cooperatives, and the establishment of health and educational facilities. Upon receiving a proposal with these features incorporated, the Lilly Endowment gave an initial $1.7 million in seed money.

Descriptions of these three integrated rural development programs illustrate their multi-faceted nature and the need of many governmental agencies to collaborate with each other and with Africare in carrying them out. Seguenega and Tara were very successful inaugural ventures, so much so that, in 1978, USAID awarded Africare a $5.7 million contract to launch a five-year program in Seguenega. A second phase of the Tara project was funded by the Lilly Endowment, several United Methodist groups, World Vision, the New York chapter of Africare, Ramapo College, and USAID. These later projects were much more complex than the earlier ones and had a degree of sophistication borne of refinement in design and an experienced technical staff. Africare efforts in the Irhazer Valley were less successful because the water drawn from the wells proved unsuitable for vegetable growing and regional officials were more interested in activities that benefited the urban population in Agadez than in those for the welfare of the nomads.

In the field of health, Africare anticipated the reorientation of its medical program to village primary health care and knew that the possible departure of William Kirker from Niger, which in fact occurred in 1974, would result in a lapse in the treatment of thousands of people who relied on his hospital, mobile units, and out-patient clinic. Receiving a contract from USAID in June 1973 to study health in Diffa Department, Africare sent a team of specialists to investigate the feasibility of a family health and child spacing program. They envisioned having well-baby clinics, rehabilitation classes, and training sessions in first aid and health education for health workers. For six months, from July to December 1973, they gathered information and conducted a household survey. The investigators found that 95% of the population was illiterate and the per capita income was less than $50 a year. Because of high child mortality, mothers were debilitated by bearing more children than either they or the food supply could reasonably support. Few people had access to primary health care and preventive health care services were scarce. Communicable diseases were endemic and nearly all water supplies were contaminated. There were very few health professionals. A single hospital and fewer than ten operational rural dispensaries served a widely dispersed population of 150,000.

With this data, the Africare team wrote a proposal that was funded by USAID in 1975. It was a three-year rural health care delivery system designed to increase availability and access to health services for people in Diffa, Niger. Primary level emergency health care as well as maternal and child health-related activities were to be established in more than a hundred villages. Health education programs, health examinations for school children, and record keeping were to be set up in many of the villages too. There was a heavy emphasis on training health workers, aides, and volunteers for these tasks. Other goals sought to provide for the communication needs of dispensaries and the collection of medical data. This activity represented Africare's new strategy in health care. Alameda Harper, a team member who later joined the Africare staff as rural health specialist and served for more than twenty-five years, recalls that when she went to Diffa in 1975 to begin the multi-million dollar project the people exclaimed excitedly, "Africare is back!" They did not differentiate between the emphasis of the Kirkers and Africare's reorientation of the medical program. They were just happy to see Africare.

After becoming established in West Africa, Africare looked at other parts of the continent to see where it could expand its three-pronged programs in water, agriculture, and health. Southern Africa looked the most promising. Of the ten nations in the region at this time, the late 1970s, only two, Zambia and Botswana, had democratic governments. Angola and Mozambique were emerging from Portuguese control and struggling to become unified as nations. An independent Zimbabwe was about to emerge from a bloody liberation struggle. Malawi was dominated by the autocratic Hastings Banda. Swaziland and Lesotho were barely viable as two former mountain kingdoms. South Africa, under the cast iron rule of a white minority, enforced an apartheid policy and punished its neighbors, the so-called Frontline States, for any assistance to liberation fighters. It controlled Namibia, too, which had been assigned as a mandate state after World War I. The big advantage that Africare had in entering southern Africa was the support and political influence of Dr. Siteke Mwale, formerly Zambia's ambassador to the United States and now her Foreign Minister in

Lusaka. He was a skillful diplomat who assisted Kenneth Kaunda in the preparation of the Lusaka Manifesto in 1969 that proposed alternative strategies for white-ruled governments of southern Africa and sought peaceful solutions to their predicaments. With Zambia being bombed by the South African air force because of the haven it gave exiled black South Africans, and as thousands of refugees entered Zambia in their flight from war in Angola, Namibia, and Zaire, Dr. Mwale realized that assistance from an organization such as Africare could help his country to ride out the present crisis.

The first Africare program in Zambia was participation in the Meheba settlement camp in the far northwestern section of the country where 10,000 refugees, mostly from Angola, had congregated. The United Nations High Commissioner for Refugees and the Lutheran World Federation had already assisted the Zambian Government in establishing a community, supplying each refugee family with five hectares of land and basic necessities, and starting primary schools. Africare contributed by building ten houses for teachers and other camp staff and by posting two agricultural assistants at schools to promote the agricultural education now mandated for all primary students by the Government of Zambia. It sent, additionally, vehicles such as tractors, farm implements, medicines, and school supplies for Meheba inhabitants. Africare's work among the refugees in Zambia was a precursor of an even more challenging situation in a new geographical region. Within two years, the UNHCR asked Africare to manage the water supply and sanitation unit for refugees in thirty-five camps and seven transit centers in Somalia. This is how Africare entered East Africa.

To become permanently established in a country, an organization like Africare or any other Private Voluntary Organization (PVO; also called NGO, non-governmental organization) has to open an office with staff. The pattern adopted by Africare was to hire country representatives, who were usually American citizens, and administrative assistants cum secretaries, also Americans. Additional expatriates were assigned to these field offices, as necessary, according to the size, complexity, and technical requirements of the projects being undertaken in the country. Local citizens were initially hired as general office workers and drivers, but as the educational and skill level within the national population rose, they were relied upon for much more sophisticated assignments, for example, as program officers heading up million dollar undertakings. Getting started in a new location demanded hard work, patience, and luck. A few examples from Africare's record will illustrate the truth of this.

Africare began to establish itself overseas permanently in Upper Volta early in 1974 when it appointed Peter Persell the country representative. Persell had spent two years in the Peace Corps in Upper Volta digging wells, a skill newly learned since his undergraduate days as a political science major at the University of Rochester. C. Payne Lucas sent him out to Ouagadougou with $10,000 to rent a house that would be both his residence and his office and to design five different types of projects in five different regions of the country. As the temporary representative for Niger and Chad also, he was to investigate opportunities for Africare there, as well. He had no money for a car, so he bought a 50cc Mobylette and a helmet. Later, with his own money, he purchased a 403 Peugeot, but it was so unreliable that, when he went out of town to inspect Africare sites, he exchanged it temporarily with a friend whose vehicle was dependable. He wrote out letters in longhand and hired a part-time secretary who came in the evenings to type them.

The experience of R.J. Benn is another example of the difficulties faced by Africare employees in setting up offices in African nations. Benn had been inspired to join the Peace Corps by the emergence in the late 1960s of what he considered a new African American people. Afrocentric hairstyles, dashikis, and such lyrics as "I'm black and I'm proud," sung by James Brown, piqued his curiosity about Africa. When he was assigned to Niger to dig wells—and he had never seen any but a wishing well—he was the only African American in his Peace Corps contingent of eighty volunteers. He spent four years there, two digging wells and two teaching English. Although Niger had received its independence in 1960, Benn perceived that white Frenchmen were still in power and he himself experienced incidents of discrimination from Nigerien officials. He saw that a lot of the foreign assistance programs were directed by whites and he asked himself, "This is Africa? Why are there no African Americans here?"

In 1974, as his Peace Corps assignment ended, Benn was sought out by C. Payne Lucas. Subsequently, after meeting Joe Kennedy and Peter Persell, he was hired as the Africare country representative in Mali with the primary task of building the Lilly Endowment wells. He was excited to be joining Africare because it was a community-based organization of African Americans who wanted to do something tangible in Africa. The salary offered was small, but he did not mind because it was still twice what he was receiving as a Peace Corps volunteer. Benn rented a house in Bamako and used a desk in his living room as an office. He had neither a separate office nor a secretary for five years. Since Africare had no money for an official vehicle, Benn rode around Bamako in shared taxis, but to visit the wells at Timbuktu and Goundam, he asked the *sous-prefets* to drive their vehicles while he paid expenses. Ultimately, the transportation issue became so critical in carrying out program objectives that Benn bought a Volkswagen and, later, a Land Rover.

Kevin Lowther inaugurated Africare's Southern Africa program when he opened an office in Zambia late in 1978. Landing in Lusaka with his wife and two daughters after a fifty-two hour flight from the United States, Lowther searched for a rental house from his hotel room. For four years, the house he found was his office and he had no telephone. He also had no assistants for four years, until he hired an administrative officer, Anatasia Mhango, who did the accounting, budget, and other office work. He talked to his supervisors at headquarters in Washington by telephone only once or twice in the five years he was in Zambia and used a public telex machine to send important communications to the United States. For Lowther, however, this seat of the pants operation, with few rules and regulations, recalled his Peace Corps days in Sierra Leone when a volunteer simply adapted to whatever happened. Furthermore, he was a journalist by profession, having left a newspaper position in New Hampshire to join Africare. He was flexible. He could type his own reports and do his own bookkeeping in those early days.

The opening of an Africare office in Somalia in 1981 was one of the most hair-raising of all Africare undertakings. Somalia, aligned with the Soviet Union soon after its independence in 1960, had recently come into the American orbit when Ethiopia, an American ally during the reign of Haile Selassie, became a Marxist state. In a diplomatic switch, the Soviet Union now backed Ethiopia and the United States began pouring foreign assistance into Somalia. When Melvin Foote arrived in Mogadishu as the Africare country representative, he found a Wild West situation. Conditions in the country were chaotic and the government fragile. As a result of wars between Somalia and Ethiopia and between Eritrea and Ethiopia, there were two million refugees. Foote headed a team of engineers, technicians, and mechanics, but none of the necessary equipment had arrived. The vehicles had not arrived either; it was nearly a year before Foote and his assistant received them. Since the telephones in the country did not work, contracts were sometimes signed at an agreed-upon location such as a lemonade stand. Foote's rented house was both home and office for two months until he insisted that he could not live in a place where staffers came and went day and night. He then rented an office and a building that could serve as a guest house for transient employees. Looking back at his experience in Somalia, Foote, an ex-Peace Corps volunteer in Ethiopia, recognizes trademarks of the Peace Corps: adaptability, improvisation, field expediency methodology, and making do with what is available.

The first decade of Africare's service in Africa was one in which basic objectives were tested and the management style created. The organization transformed itself from a charity created by one couple to treat the sick in Niger into a growing agency undertaking increasingly sophisticated and large programs in health care, water resources, and agriculture. Refugee assistance, which really launched the organization in 1973, again assumed an important role at the end of the decade because it took Africare into southern Africa and into East Africa. Another characteristic of the period was the increasing dependence of Africare on contracts and grants from the U.S. government to fund its work. The financial statement for the year ending April 30, 1980, shows that unrestricted contributions and revenue amounted to $53,000. Of the restricted funds, $171,000 came from private contributors, $209,000 from foundations, and $3 million from the U.S. Government. The Government of Niger was responsible for an additional $600,000 contract that enabled Africare to implement a rural health program, but its money originated with USAID.

In establishing the principles and practices guiding offices overseas as they were opened, Africare had to rely on the skills of its country representatives and other expatriate staff members. Many of these men and women came with a Peace Corps background. They had already been tested in the field, so culture shock was not an issue. They had friends and acquaintances in and out of governments who gave them an advantage in seeking advice, permissions, or access to important officials. Seldom, however, had they possessed experience in supervising a staff, managing a payroll, controlling and accounting for expenditures, or writing development proposals. Africare headquarters in Washington issued an employee handbook and Joe Kennedy, as director of international development, kept a careful eye on their activities, but for many of them, the duties were stupendous. There was a lot of learning by trial and error. The difficulty of carrying out their job cannot be overstated, particularly when one considers the local conditions under which they worked and their distance from Washington. Using the poor communication system available to them alone resulted in hours of frustration. Additionally, as more and more of the responsibilities of country reps involved carrying out projects funded by USAID, they had to consult with members of the U.S. Mission in the country, defend budgets or changes in design, and write elaborate reports that met USAID criteria. One long-term Africare country rep recalled, "I could do the financial report in a couple of hours for Lilly, but it would take me days to do the USAID report." In contrast, many country reps mentioned in interviews that all private foundations and groups wanted to know about their donations was "what did you do with the money?" and "who benefited?" The change in the nature of the country rep position meant that now there was a need to recruit experienced and trained overseas personnel who could manage the intricate development programs funded by USAID as well as the micro-projects favored by individual supporters, churches, and small philanthropies. They had to possess writing skills as well as a certain level of technical knowledge in order to state proposals clearly and to provide a rationale for them.

Africare, as an organization, clearly experienced a metamorphosis in character during its first fifteen years. Growing in size, it became more bureaucratic. Employees, particularly those overseas, had to seek permission from more layers of supervisors to spend money over a certain small sum, to deviate in the least from stated policy, or to take actions not specifically mentioned in the handbook. For Africare, the challenge became to retain its image as representing an African American constituency supportive of programs to alleviate suffering in Africa while, in fact, deriving most of its income from federal funding sources. Preserving its individuality as a private voluntary organization (PVO) when grouped with many other PVOs and when faced with compliance with grant procedures of USAID tested its institutional abilities. That Africare succeeded in large measure over the following years can be attributed primarily to its executive director, C. Payne Lucas, whose charisma and political savvy opened many doors. He mesmerized audiences, whether in churches, in elementary schools, or in professional gatherings. As a *Washington Post* journalist wrote in one profile, Lucas was a combination of "preacher and huckster." He may have grown up in rural North Carolina, but he could talk to presidents, diplomats, and CEOs as easily as to taxi drivers. He never forgot anyone he met and they never forgot him.

When Lucas assumed management of Africare in 1971, its headquarters were a few rooms at the Niger Embassy on R Street, N.W. Besides Lucas, the staff consisted only of Joe Kennedy, several clerical workers, and a few volunteers, including Whitney Watriss, whose mother gave Africare the critical loan. Africare's entry into Sahelian drought relief began its expansion as a charitable organization, requiring fund raising activities as well as the procurement, management, and delivery of life-saving supplies to West Africa. With Lilly and USAID funding, Africare, concentrating on the health, well construction, and agricultural objectives of its charter, needed additional professional staff to assist Kennedy in carrying them out and in planning long-term development programs. Space at the Embassy became so crammed with employees and furnishings that Africare had to look for a more permanent and functional office. Futhermore, when Oumarou Youssoufou offered C. Payne Lucas its use in 1971, both men believed that it would be only a temporary location.

In 1975, Africare moved to a building at 16th and P Street, N.W. The stay at the new headquarters was a short one, until 1977. With grants and contracts from private philanthropies and USAID totaling nearly a million and a half dollars for Fiscal Year 1976 (year ending April 30), Africare took a big leap in programming. It hired three specialists, one of whom served nearly twenty years and the other two more than twenty-five years: Robert Wilson, agriculture; Alameda Harper, rural health; Alan Alemian, public health. All came with a Peace Corps background. Wilson had served as the Peace Corps director in Togo and Zaire and Harper as the associate Peace Corps director in Liberia. Alemian was a volunteer in Uganda. The addition of these staffers meant an increase of support personnel and the preparation of more proposals to circulate among prospective donors, large and small. There was great enthusiasm and energy at Africare about what could be done in Africa. The results were the detailed design of large IRD projects at Seguenega and Irhazer Valley and the implementation of a rural health care delivery system in Niger. Africare also gave reinforcement to the Government of Niger and its ministries in their design and completion of the Tara program.

By the summer of 1977, the offices on 16th Street overflowing with employees and equipment, Africare had to move again. Now, Lucas rented the entire sixth floor of a building on Connecticut Avenue at the northeast corner of Q Street (1601 Connecticut Avenue, N.W.), one block from Dupont Circle. The staff was told that, while the facility would be spacious at first, it should expect to have to double up later as the organization grew. Africare was not planning another move. Some of the individual offices needed painting, but anyone who wanted a make-over would have to do it himself, with Africare paying for supplies. Lucas asked staffers to watch the newspapers for office furniture sales.

Africare's growth in the next ten years can be illustrated by looking at the budgets, the programming, and the number of African nations served at the beginning of the period and at the end. For the fiscal year ending April 30, 1978, total public support and revenue, which included grants, private contributions, membership dues, and USAID money, was $2,240,609. Africare's main operations were in six Sahelian countries whose immediate needs were relief from drought and recovery assistance. While it had provided an irrigation pump for four hundred families in the Wabe Shebelle valley of the Ogaden region in Ethiopia in 1976 and had joined with the Government of The Gambia in 1975 in an agricultural demonstration project where improved varieties of vegetables and rice were introduced, these were random projects. Their chief benefit to Africare was in giving it later entry to broader channels of participation in Ethiopian drought relief and Gambian agricultural development.

The situation in 1987, when Africare moved into the Africare House, was drastically different. Total support and revenue, from the same sources as before, was $13,333,466. It now worked in seventeen nations. Projects in the Sahelian countries of West Africa remained the major focus, but several English-speaking countries there, Nigeria and Sierra Leone among them, were added. There was expansion of programming to southern Africa: Zambia, Mozambique, Malawi, and Zimbabwe. Major relief activities in Ethiopia and Somalia addressed problems of drought and regional wars. Rwanda and Kenya benefited from several small projects. Although Africare's main emphasis overseas continued to be water, agriculture, and health, the diversity of its efforts showed a willingness to tackle many needs identified by villagers. School repairs, women's clothing production, refugee orphanages, credit unions, and provision of school books were tangential to the big three objectives, but considered complementary to their success.

The search for a permanent home began in late 1980 when the seventh floor of the building at Connecticut and Q Street, N.W., became vacant. The Africare office on the sixth floor bulged with employees and space was becoming tighter as computers, printers, and copy machines replaced outdated equipment. With the 1981 budget at $6,000,000, a small sum in the world of charities, Africare management sought opportunities to expand geographically and programmatically. Staff members became excited at the prospect that Africare might rent another floor, but several, particularly Cassandra Moore and Gladys Tackie who kept the books, knew that Africare could not afford the additional cost. Instead of promoting this opportunity, they used their lunch hours to walk the streets in the neighborhood east of Connecticut Avenue, looking for reasonably priced small office buildings or houses. They could not locate any, but, during the months that followed, someone mentioned to Michael Miller, Africare's Director of Finance, that the District of Columbia government regularly auctioned local schools that it deemed surplus and private properties that it had acquired. Miller began receiving the monthly list and, during 1981, he and Moore looked at eight private properties and twelve District schools. The big issue was whether anything east of 16th Street N.W., was worth having. The gentrification of downtown Washington, which revitalized large areas of the inner-city in recent years, and the opening of the entire Metro system were still far off.

In December 1981, the Morse Elementary School building on R Street, N.W., between 4th and 5th Streets was offered at auction. With authorization from the Africare Board to bid up to $150,000, Miller and Joe Kennedy, acting in his capacity as Secretary of the Board, attended. Their only serious competition was another PVO whose representative apparently had similar instructions from his employers. When the bidding got to $150,000, Miller and Kennedy were in a quandary. Convincing themselves that they were within the range of Board approval, they kept raising their hands until their opponent dropped out and theirs was the final bid at $159,000.

Africare employees were jubilant when Miller and Kennedy returned from the auction with news that they had bought the Morse school. Piling into cars and dashing the dozen or so blocks from Connecticut Avenue east to 440 R Street, N.W., their enthusiasm was dampened by what they saw. Houses were dilapidated and trash, especially liquor bottles, lay about. The only people on the street were winos and the homeless sitting on doorsteps. There was no sense that the neighborhood was inhabitable. The school building was an early 1900s brick structure that had been boarded up for years with numerous bird's nests and holes in its roof. It took imagination to believe that Africare could transform the property into a handsome headquarters, but with a pioneering spirit, the staff set out to do just that.

Altogether, the conversion of the Morse school into Africare's international headquarters took nearly six years. A zoning variance had to be obtained from the District of Columbia government to change the function of the property. Engineers were hired to study the soundness of the structure. The architectural firm of Joseph Handwerger, of Washington, was engaged to conceptualize the transformation of school rooms into spaces for offices, meetings, and general use. The Africare staff spent hours in collaboration about its wishes for a building that would provide three times the working area of the Connecticut Avenue facility. In 1983, using Handwerger's preliminary drawings, a Bethesda, Maryland, firm, Scharf-Godfrey, Inc., gave Lucas a pro bono estimate of $959,000 for the renovation. Related expenses were not included. Allocating $200,000 of its unrestricted funds, Africare launched a capital fundraising campaign for the Africare House that June. Raising money for a new headquarters from the private donor community in the mid-1980s, however, was seriously hampered by the return of drought to the Sahel and by a drought in Ethiopia that superseded in misery anything seen earlier in West Africa. Africare had the dilemma of asking the same benefactors to join in two causes and many of them were not affluent enough or willing to give to more than one.

Fundraising took many forms. Brochures were printed and mailed to Africare members and friends. Africare chapters were urged to raise money for a volunteer chapter room in the new building. The metropolitan Washington chapter contributed $20,000 from its Africare Day receipts to this purpose. The honorary chairman of the Africare Board, President Kenneth Kaunda of Zambia, visited ambassadors from African nations at their Washington offices to ask for gifts. Board chairman Bishop John Walker used his connections to the religious community to appeal on Africare's behalf. No one at Africare headquarters, however, was as successful in fundraising as C. Payne Lucas. He knew hundreds of political, business, diplomatic, philanthropic, and government figures. He soon had Vice President George H.W. Bush addressing a luncheon of corporate leaders from Abbott Laboratories, Pepsi, U.S. Steel, IBM, and similar business giants. Mayor Marion Barry, Jr., was persuaded to co-host, along with C&P Telephone Company, a Washington fundraiser in April 1984 at the unconverted Africare House site. In July 1984, Lucas secured a $250,000 challenge grant from the Kresge Foundation. The main condition required Africare to raise its entire goal of $1,294,000 by March 15, 1985. He was responsible, also, for gifts of $275,000 from the Royal Kingdom of Saudi Arabia, $63,000 from General Motors, and $24,000 from the Pharmaceutical Manufacturers Association. Other donors that received the special Lucas approach had supported Africare projects overseas and some participated in the capital campaign. Among them were the African Methodist Episcopal Church, Alpha Kappa Alpha sorority, the Besser Foundation, The Links, Inc., and the Presiding Bishop's Fund for World Relief.

Africare employed many arguments in its appeal to prospective donors. In financial terms, it pointed out that it was paying $84,940 a year to rent 4,655 square feet of office space at its Connecticut Avenue headquarters. The Morse school would provide 15,900 square feet. Using a formula to account for operational and maintenance costs and to factor in 6% per annum inflation over a twenty-five year planning horizon, Africare calculated that the new building would be enormously more cost efficient than the present location. Additionally, ownership would strengthen Africare by providing a margin of safety. It was a good investment.

The practical arguments were really surpassed by a philosophical, emotional rationale for building an Africare House, or as the promotional literature called it, the "House of Africa." The Africare staff emphasized the purpose of the Africare House beyond its function as office space for executing the business of the organization. In one brochure they wrote, "In Washington, D.C., the capital city of the United States, Africa has no single, all-encompassing, outward and visible symbol. Africare House will be that symbol." It would be a focal point for African Americans and for Africans visiting the United States as the Pan American Union building represented Latin America. They expected that it would be the site for important events. African heads of state and other high-ranking Africans could hold press conferences, official briefings, and receptions. African embassies in Washington could utilize facilities and resources for public outreach programs. Community groups, church congregations, students, businessmen, and others could attend Africa-related presentations. Africare staffers also mentioned features whose expansion in the new building would make them much more accessible to the general public than they were on Connecticut Avenue. There was the Resource Information

Center that school groups and community organizations would have easy access to and the language laboratory for local students whose public school foreign language facilities were inadequate.

In its fundraising campaign, Africare put great emphasis on the positive benefit it could have in connecting to an African American neighborhood. The Morse school was at the edge of a historic district, named Shaw for a Civil War commander, just north of the U.S. Capitol and of the federal government's offices downtown. After the Civil War, its rural character changed slowly to urban and it attracted a mix of German, Irish, Italian, and other immigrants in addition to African Americans, who became the majority population by 1920. It was the home of Carter G. Woodson, the "Father of Black History," and the birthplace of Duke Ellington. Many other famous African Americans—Langston Hughes, A. Philip Randolph, Malcolm X, Dorothy Height, and "Sweet Daddy" Grace—are linked to the area. World War II and the post-war era had the effect of diminishing its quality through crowding, subdivision of privately owned homes into rental properties, and the cheapening of businesses. Shaw's fortunes were further affected in the 1960s when national residential housing restrictions and patterns changed and citizens, black and white, moved to the suburbs. Their flight accelerated after many businesses were destroyed by fire in the 1968 riots following the assassination of Martin Luther King, Jr. The people who remained began to rebuild their surroundings by the early 1980s, in part because the Washington Metro system, then under construction, planned a station nearby. Africare, an African American organization, would be sharing with them in revitalizing the community. Furthermore, the Africare House, with flags of African nations flying above its lawn, would become a local landmark that symbolized ancestral pride for Shaw's black population.

Actual conversion of the Morse school into the Africare House began on September 30, 1985, and was completed enough for the Africare staff to move into it in March 1987. The estimate of $959,000 given by Scharf-Godfrey in 1983 had risen to $1,176,000 a year later and that did not include such auxiliary costs as furnishings and equipment or moving fees. They were another $118,000, bringing the entire estimate to $1,294,000. In January 1985, Africare signed a construction management agreement with the firm of Blunt-3D/International of Washington, D.C., and Houston, Texas. Blunt-3D/I performed its own updated project cost based on the final architectural drawings of

Joseph Handwerger, AIA. The new estimate came in at $1,803,321. It had ballooned in part because of construction cost increases over the life of the fundraising campaign. Negotiations between the Africare Board of Directors and Blunt-3D/I in March and April resulted in a list of project cuts that would save nearly $350,000. This is when the Board made the decision, later rued, to eliminate the elevator from the plans.

Throughout the spring of 1985, Blunt/3-D/I put the Africare House project out for bids from prospective sub-contractors. The first round was a failure, due to overly strict completion deadlines, disinclination of subs to bid, or pricy submissions. The second round, after Africare's budget-reducing cuts, produced four bids, but all were significantly over Africare's revised budget. The lowest bid for the line item called "construction," by Cardiff Construction Company, was $1,060,000, although it was listed as $834,115 in the budget. In addition, there was the $90,000 cost of a skylight being manufactured separately and a $50,000 sum required for general condition items such as building permits. When all the financial figures for the Africare House were compiled in June 1985, the Board faced a total cost of $1,340,000. That was $325,885 over the revised April budget and $485,525 more than funds on hand. Africare contracted with Cardiff to begin the renovation, nonetheless, and continued its fundraising efforts. By the time it celebrated the opening of the Africare House on October 8, 1987, it had spent nearly $1.6 million on the project. It still needed $300,000 to pay off the building. The total cost came to more than two million dollars.

The Africare House, as designed by Joseph Handwerger, stands as a good example of creativity and imagination. The old rectangular red brick school house is now a light gray structure of painted brick and glass surrounded by simple landscaping and a decorative fence. The glass walls of the narrow entrance lead to a lobby with a soaring atrium running vertically three floors through the heart of the building and ending in a tower above the original roof line. A wide staircase with open risers gives more light to the interior. Private offices, large regional offices shared by employees, conference rooms, and equipment areas surround the central core. There is a sense of openness and spaciousness. The ground floor, the least public section, has a large conference room and an employee lunch room/kitchen, but otherwise accommodates such functional responsibilities as accounting, computer management, and housekeeping.

In a review of the Africare House for *The Washington Post* on March 5, 1988, architectural and urban design critic Benjamin Forgey applauded Joseph Handwerger's renovation of the Morse school. He noted that it both met Africare's "familial" style of operation and presented an airy, open, welcoming face to the community. He praised the entryway, the gabled top, the glass walls, and certain interior characteristics. Forgey called it a "handsome, indeed a striking, new presence on R Street." Declaring that the Morse school was a plain Jane with little architectural merit, he concluded that "Handwerger's changes fundamentally improve the building. His architectural approach deftly combines minimalism and a respect for the existing structure."

The aspirations of Africare leadership in building the Africare House have been fulfilled in large measure. First, it has been valuable because it gives the organization a tangible, unique identity. It is a handsome physical structure decorated with art from the entire continent of Africa. It is a permanent site that conveys the message that Africare has a long-term commitment to African development. It gives Africare credibility with donors, with African dignitaries, with African Americans, and with many types of visitors. Secondly, Africare House has been the site for important events, just as envisioned. Receptions for heads of state, such as Nelson Mandela of South Africa and Ellen Johnson Sirleaf of Liberia, have been held there. Ambassadors of African nations hold briefings, news conferences, and monthly meetings. The spacious conference rooms are perfect for other gatherings, such as those of the African Diplomatic Outreach Program and the Shaw Advisory Neighborhood Commission, a community forum. Literally hundreds of meetings of all kinds have been held there. Thirdly, Africare House has served an important educational function. Groups of students representing all levels, from primary to university, have learned about Africa by touring the building and hearing staff presentations about the work of Africare overseas. University interns now regularly spend a term imbedded in the intricacies of managing a development project and watch their mentors guide employees in the field.

Africare's renovation of the Morse school was one of the first community initiatives in the long process of revitalizing the Shaw neighborhood. As a landmark and an anchor, the Africare House had little company in the struggle for urban renewal for nearly a decade. Fortunately for the Africare pioneers, they drew gradual support from a number of external factors. The Washington Metro system connected Shaw to the rest of the city by building the green and the yellow lines and opening the Shaw station in 1991 (later called Shaw-Howard University). Suburbanites, tired of long commutes as metropolitan Washington, swelling with population in the 1990s and thereafter, sprawled toward Fredericksburg, Manassas, Annapolis, and Baltimore, reconsidered city living. The District of Columbia government itself studied ways to halt the deterioration of its inner core. The construction in the 1990s of what is known today as the Verizon Center, which led to the gentrification of the Chinatown/Gallery Place neighborhood, had a beneficial effect on the adjacent Shaw, as did the opening of the even closer Walter E. Washington Convention Center in 2004. These circumstances and others led to a slow show of interest by developers and individual "urban guerillas" that were attracted by the location and the potential profit. A motivation of a different type inspired churches to build new sanctuaries and low-cost housing for the poor or elderly. The consequence has been that, in the twenty years since Africare moved to its new international headquarters several blocks from the Metro station, many houses have been renovated, new businesses have opened, small condo projects are under construction, and the streets, while not litter free, look presentable.

4

Health Care

William Kirker, beginning the first Africare project, held a conventional view that delivering medical care in a centralized hospital system was the greatest contribution Africare could make in southeastern Niger. Treating patients in wards, performing surgeries, and controlling epidemics were his main objectives, although he considered mobile health units, health education, and outreach activities important adjuncts. He did not address other economic or social needs in the region and, given the limited scope of his resources at the time, it was a realistic approach. In contrast, C. Payne Lucas, upon becoming executive director of Africare in 1971, brought with him a belief that while the improved health of villagers was a vital first step to helping them, it was but one part in achieving other essential development goals. Consequently, as the organization expanded geographically and programmatically, he linked health components to Africare proposals in water, agriculture, resource development, and other types of projects whenever possible.

In 1976, primary health care at the village level replaced Kirker's emphasis on a hospital-centric approach. Over the next thirty years, this focus continued, but Africare soon widened its base by tailoring funding proposals to accommodate what ministries of health in African nations and public funding sources, as well as private sources, saw as priorities. Accordingly, when improved child survival rates and better maternal health became their primary goals in the early 1980s, Africare quickly moved to meet them. When ministries of health in The Gambia, Sierra Leone, Nigeria, and other nations acknowledged both an inability to purchase pharmaceuticals for their citizens and a deficiency of trained staff and infrastructure to manage them, Africare, situated in Washington, D.C., where it had access to representatives of American pharmaceutical companies, could deal with those problems as well. Africare was also pro-active in offering African governments solutions to pressing health problems that could be alleviated by the transfer of western technology and medical advances. Programs to deliver packaged hospital units to rural communities and to assault river blindness and malaria in many nations were eagerly undertaken. Since all African nations had a shortage of dispensaries and health clinics, Africare often constructed them as adjuncts wherever it was already active. The rise of the HIV/AIDS epidemic in the late 1980s offered funding for programs as diverse as training health workers or supplying school books for children of AIDS victims. The imperative for clean water in African communities has always been a primary focus of Africare work. The consequences of these increased health initiatives were, often, the challenge of recruiting field staff with relevant skills and expanding to parts of Africa beyond Africare's initial regional roots. Reaching outside the Sahel, where it was centered during its first eight years, Africare undertook additional health projects in Anglophone West Africa and, later, in nations spread around the continent.

Succeeding the Kirkers' work in Maine-Soroa was the Niger Basic Health Services Delivery Project in Diffa, begun in 1976 and continued until 1981. As described earlier, it aimed to train health aides, workers, and volunteers; to offer basic and emergency medical care; to build new or to improve rural dispensaries; and to incorporate school children into a health surveillance system. Once this project was completed, the public health doctor and other personnel moved on to work with the technical assistance team of a new rural health improvement project, co-sponsored by the Government of Niger and USAID. Africare continued to provide logistical and administrative advice.

Contemporaneously with the health project in Diffa, Africare initiated the primary health care component of the five-year integrated rural development plan at Seguenega Sector, Upper Volta. Organizationally, it was structured as a pyramid. Beginning with a base of thirty villages (out of a hundred and forty-four), each had a health team comprising of a non-salaried health aide and a midwife trained and equipped to handle basic health problems. Aside from offering diagnostic, curative, and midwifery services, it was expected to collect basic health and demographic information. It was to involve villagers in health education, applied nutrition, personal hygiene skills, immunization programs, and environmental sanitation. Some villages were to have a salaried *animatrice* (community development leader) who would supervise the teams. Above the village level were to be four rural health posts, each with a dispensary staffed by nurses and midwives and providing improved maternal and child health care. Overseeing them in the Seguenega village was to be a health post center, with a pharmacy, dispensary, and expanded professional staff. At the pinnacle of this superstructure would be the departmental hospital at Ouahigouya, forty miles away. Since some of the rural dispensaries and many of the villages needed new or deepened wells, Africare linked the provision of water resources with the solution of health issues too.

During the life of the Seguenega IRD, in which funding was extended and it became a ten-year project, professional evaluations of the health component pointed out the difficulties for such organizations as Africare in working with people and bureaucracies at the village and regional levels in the countryside, far from cities. Whereas the objective had been to bring thirty villages into a medical framework, Africare staff could not get that number to participate. The fundamental problem can be traced to Africare's effort to introduce more democratic rule in the villages by the creation of Village Development Committees. These were to be composed of elected leaders who represented everyone in airing grievances and common problems and in planning ameliorating activities, rather than traditional figures who, in the past, had made political and economic decisions unilaterally. The villagers did not understand the procedure, the purpose of the new groups, or that the newly-elected had responsibilities to carry out. Africare, for its part, failed to realize the effort necessary to win acceptance of what were revolutionary ideas and practices in communities where, heretofore, the opinions of only a few people mattered. Putting the mechanism in working order required much more organization and guidance from experienced field staff than was originally envisioned. Since the Village Development Committees were at the core of the Seguenega program, every aspect of its success depended on their effectiveness.

Implementing the Seguenega health component was a challenge for Africare in other ways. In the villages, the quality of service was jeopardized by a lack of supervision, whether over the health workers, the dispensary pharmacy, or in record-keeping. The aides and mid-wives, receiving no salary, had little incentive to maintain regular schedules, keep data, or offer health promotion activities. A major deficiency at the four health posts was the provision of a clean water supply. In addition, there were serious problems in personnel matters, in work performance, and in the creation of procedures for the use and control of equipment, materials, and supplies. The Central Medical Center at Seguenega had a similar need for procedures and it likewise suffered from management and monitoring deficiencies. Furthermore, the effectiveness of its pharmacy was constrained by a situation in which the pharmaceuticals were all labeled in English, but the pharmacist did not read English. There was no refrigeration for certain drugs, either, a limitation at the health post pharmacies as well. These challenges were not unique to Seguenega, but proved to be common as Africare attempted to improve health care in numerous African venues.

Africare embarked on another health strategy in the mid-1980s that stressed the survival of children under five and maternal health care. There were many parts to the program: childhood immunization, oral rehydration therapy, child spacing advice, nutritional counseling, training medical personnel, and supplying key equipment to rural clinics. Childhood immunization vaccines for measles, whooping cough, tetanus, tuberculosis, polio, and diphtheria, available in the West, were scarce in Africa. Dehydration, a major killer of infants, stemmed from severe diarrhea and was often caused by foul water, but could be cured by a simple formula of sugar, salt, and clean water. Elementary sanitation, better nutrition, and growth monitoring did not require sophisticated technology, but called for increased knowledge among mothers about the importance of washing their hands, breast feeding, weaning practices, and using locally grown food. Although Africare had already utilized certain aspects of the health initiative in such nations as Chad and Upper Volta, it combined them in Nigeria, Sierra Leone, Central Africa Republic, Ethiopia, and other nations.

Nigeria became the site of one of Africare's largest, most comprehensive, and longest lived health care efforts. In 1985, working with the Nigerian state and federal ministers of health and funded by USAID, Africare surveyed more than a hundred rural clinics in ten states to assess their need for basic equipment and technical services. With that information, it sent the states large quantities of non-pharmaceutical supplies and medical equipment and drew up a broad plan for immunization, oral hydration, and family planning services. The following year, Africare evaluated rural clinics in the rest of Nigeria's nineteen states and sent more equipment. It trained hundreds of medical practitioners, from physicians to midwives, in improved health habits, better clinical procedures, and measures by which to encourage mothers to think ahead about their family's future. Disease prevention took the form of supplying 144,000 doses of measles vaccine to the Ministry of Health in Imo State. In 1988, when the Nigeria Federal Ministry of Health began a nationwide Family Health Services Project, Africare was selected to procure and supply family planning equipment to eligible public clinics and hospitals. It subsequently inspected nearly three hundred clinics and provided equipment to more than a hundred of them. It found a Nigerian manufacturer of high-quality obstetrical and gynecological equipment, thus supporting the local economy while avoiding the higher cost of imported goods. Later, recognizing that improved women's health was directly linked to their literacy, it started a "Literacy-for-Health" program in Kaduna State. It first developed the educational materials and then trained local teachers to maintain the program. Literacy projects for women were spread to more Nigerian states after the initial success in Kaduna. Africare sustained its Nigerian projects in child survival and maternal health care throughout the 1990s and on into the twenty-first century. Comparable efforts were pursued elsewhere on the continent as well.

One segment of child survival and maternal health programs in all of the nations where Africare had them was an effort to treat people with malaria and to help with the distribution of malaria prevention materials. Medical experts estimate that 90% of Africans are infected with malaria, the foremost killer of people in Africa. It is also an underlying cause of poverty because it affects its victims both physically and mentally, making it impossible for them to be economically productive.

Two recent examples of Africare work come from East Africa. In 1999, with assistance from USAID and in support of the Ugandan Ministry of Health's overall strategy to improve child health, Africare undertook a large project entitled "Ntungamo District Community-based Integrated Management of Childhood Illness." A second phase of the project ran from 2003 to 2008. Ntungamo District, in the far southwestern area of Uganda close to Rwanda, has 450,000 residents, engaged mainly in small-scale farming and in pastoral activities. The five main intervention areas of Africare's program were malaria, nutrition, diarrhea control, immunization, and assistance to those affected in some way by HIV/AIDS. Many goals were educational in nature, but a major obstacle to the implementation of some objectives was a population widely scattered among hills in small, remote villages reached by dirt trails miles off the few paved roads. Most people, especially women, did not have radios and even if they did, they were too occupied with survival to listen very often. Public service announcements such as Americans hear reminding them to have their children vaccinated before school begins would be a largely wasted effort. A further constraint to the program's effectiveness was that educational outreach activities needed to be supported by the local availability of vaccines, antiretroviral treatment for patients with AIDS, and other medical remedies. Africare, having no control over this, was dependent upon the Ministry of Health and other service providers that often could not provide help. However, Africare could put its message into action by emphasizing improved nutrition. It did this by sending field workers to villages where they introduced such new vegetables as carrots and spinach. Soon, thousands of householders were growing them in backyard gardens. Field workers also helped communities establish fish ponds and they promoted rabbit production. (People in this area of Uganda do not eat rabbits because they consider them children's food.)

In Ntungamo, where almost half the population suffers from malaria, small children and pregnant women were the primary targets in its reduction and the methods used to reach them varied. Some methods were educational, as with sending trained drummer and drama groups out, equipped with loud speakers, to sensitize communities, particularly to the value of using insecticide-treated bed nets. They were very popular. Another tactic was to distribute mosquito nets in villages. Although people were often too poor to buy them, Africare did not just give them away. Rather, it encouraged villagers to form clubs and contribute to a central pool each month until, slowly, every family could be the recipient of a net. A factor that has emerged in Uganda and elsewhere in Africa recently has been the question of using DDT for spraying mosquito habitats. It could be an important asset to Africare and to other development organizations in their struggle against malaria, but a major concern fueling the debate is whether agricultural exports will be rejected on the international market because of its use.

Tanzania is another African nation where Africare has become a participant in a national program to treat malaria patients and to prevent malaria infection. Here, under the auspices of the Global Fund—an organization founded in 2002 to fight HIV/AIDS, tuberculosis, and malaria, and funded by governments worldwide, international institutions (such as the United Nations), and private sector sponsors—Africare personnel have taken the leadership role in building a network of a hundred and fifty NGOs. Their task is to pull these NGOs together as a team to find donors, plan programs, hold forums where health issues are discussed, and prepare a broad assault on the disease. The first step, Africare staff believes, is to work with rural communities to help them see that malaria is their problem and that they can contribute to lightening its toll. Since every development organization enters a country with its own strategy, its own way of doing things, and its own mission, it is a great challenge to get each one to think about acting jointly with others and to adjust to local circumstances. Africare's job in Tanzania is to synchronize the activities of network members in order to reach all regions of the country and to avoid redundancy of effort.

Many African nations, within two decades of independence, realized that a major constraint in their health plans was the absence of medicines and their inability to manage the purchase, storage, control, and distribution of pharmaceuticals. Africare became a major participant in the solution of this deficiency, beginning in 1981, when it received a grant of $15,500 from four drug companies—Merck, Sharp & Dohme, Schering-Plough, Smith-Kline, and Sterling Drug—to help the Ministry of Health in The Gambia decide which drugs were most needed in the nation, determine the most cost-effective means of procuring them, and figure out how to deliver them to villages over poor transportation and communication networks. Subsequently, ten drug companies, under the aegis of the Pharmaceutical Manufacturers Association of the United States (PMA), gave cash and in-kind support of about $200,000 that enabled Africare to assign three pharmacists on a short-term basis to advise members of the Gambian Medical and Health Department on how to strengthen systems and practices of record-keeping, inventory control, and distribution. Africare also provided specialized filing and record-keeping equipment and $50,000 in basic pharmaceuticals, which enabled the government to transfer an equal amount of its funds to the cost of staff training. Africare's success in this work later led to its selection by the Gambia Family Planning Association to improve storage, record-keeping, and inventory control of family-planning commodities.

Africare's work with pharmaceutical management and distribution needs in The Gambia was soon replicated in Sierra Leone, Ghana, and Ethiopia, again with some financial support from members of the Pharmaceutical Manufacturers Association. In the mid-1980s, Africare advised the Government of Sierra Leone on drug ordering, inventorying, and distribution procedures. After a study of national pharmaceutical needs, the Sierra Leonean Ministry of Health designed a pilot program that began with the construction of a model central warehouse for medical stores in Freetown, the capital, and established procedures for how medical stores would be handled as they were distributed to district-level hospitals and on to rural health facilities. Funding from the PMA enabled the government to build the warehouse and to implement the pilot in three districts. Later, the program was extended to the rest of the country and UNICEF asked Africare to offer staff training and provide technical support.

A very different type of medical intervention was Africare's decision in 1978 to participate in the conveyance of packaged hospital units to African nations. During the Cold War of the 1950s and 1960s, when Americans feared nuclear attacks from the Soviet Union, part of the national civil defense plan was to organize self-contained hospitals and to locate them in communities where they would be available in an emergency. Each contained the equipment and supplies for a two-hundred bed facility. It had four operating rooms, surgical instruments, a clinical laboratory, X-ray equipment, and sterilization vats. Bed sheets, toilet paper, and other amenities considered essential in an American setting were also included. All that was needed was a structure with four walls and a roof. Many state and local governments in the United States decided, by the 1970s, that these units were no longer necessary or functional and gladly passed legislation that donated them to charitable organizations that could use them overseas. At least thirty-five were deeded to Africare. Receiving them, however, was just the beginning of the challenge. Africare had to get funding for their trans-oceanic and inland transport, oversee the substitution of updated medicines for those outdated, refurbish some equipment, provide technical training for the repair and maintenance of the equipment, and locate suitable sites in African nations for their placement.

Funding for the multiple tasks associated with getting hospital units from American communities to African villages was soon accomplished by donations from many sources. The first was a two-year grant of $153,000 from the William H. Donner Foundation, accepted by Africare with the condition that the hospital units be integrated into existing rural health care programs. Other supporters were the Public Welfare Foundation, Tea Importers, Inc., Ethiopian Airlines, Ford Motor Company, Mobile Oil, Lykes Brothers Shipping Company, and Smith-Kline. USAID and the Embassy of Rwanda were two government sponsors.

This health support program was the first of Africare's continent-wide projects. By the mid-1980s, at its conclusion, thirteen nations, from Guinea to Somalia and from Egypt to Zambia, had received one or more hospitals. None went in its entirety to a single community, but each was broken into components that were distributed widely to remote clinics. Africare hired an American biomedical equipment technician to oversee the installation of hospital equipment and to train African technicians in its maintenance and repair.

The strengths and weaknesses of this program can be gauged by looking at its implementation in Senegal, which received three units. The equipment and supplies were carefully assigned to small clinics over much of the country, even to Casamance, a region almost cut off from the rest of the nation by its neighbor, The Gambia, a spear-shaped political entity physically little more than the two banks of the Gambia River. The clinics had scant equipment, sometimes not even a pair of scissors, and their shelves were bare. The arrival of medical paraphernalia and supplies must have seemed like a miracle to the lone nurse who received little material or moral support from elsewhere. Yet, frequently, she took steps to share or to maximize Africare goods. It was not uncommon for her to divide her shipment and to send on to the next village clinic an extra pair of scissors or sterilization equipment. Or, she split the bed sheets, much too large for African beds, and proudly showed visitors how, like Jesus and the loaves of bread, she had multiplied them. Hence, in terms of helping to overcome the profound shortage of furnishings critically necessary for a medical facility, the Africare hospital units were a success. They were also beneficial to the Senegalese Ministry of Health because it was able to reassign funds allocated for similar purposes to strengthening its primary health system.

Looked at in a different manner, however, one must make a more cautious assessment. The main focus of the civil defense emergency units was surgery. They contained operating tables, overhead surgical lights, forceps, and catheters. Among the greatest health needs of the Senegalese were malaria prophylactics, vaccines for childhood diseases, and maternal care education. None of these was addressed by packaged hospital units. Another limitation to the effectiveness of this health program was the failure of the Government of Senegal to keep its promise to Africare that it would make whatever improvements necessary in communities for the use of the equipment, if Africare donated it. The best example of this regards the power supply. Many of the clinics were in villages that had no electricity, but such items as surgical lights and X-ray machines were useless without it. The absence of power also meant that there was no refrigeration for medicines and that the sterilization equipment was not operational. Even if the government had followed through on electrification, there would have been another obstacle to the use of some equipment: the availability of physicians with the skills to utilize it. So few Senegalese doctors were willing to serve in rural areas that the government had to draft them into the military and assign them there. Considering that there were gaps between their deployments, that they took annual holidays, and that they attended professional conferences and other events, most military doctors spent negligible time in the countryside.

Onchocerciasis, or "river blindness," is the world's second leading infectious source of blindness, after trachoma. Its cause is a parasitic worm carried by small black flies that breed on the banks of rapidly flowing rivers and lakes. It is found in thirty-five countries, twenty-eight of them in Africa, mainly in the western and central regions. Ninety-nine percent of the thirty-seven million people affected worldwide live in Africa and many millions more are threatened by this disease. As terrible a condition as blindness is, more victims experience skin lesions and rashes, severe itching, and disfigurement than visual impairment. The consequences in rural Africa, aside from the obvious debilitation of its victims, are depopulation of fertile river valleys, decreased agricultural production, increased poverty, and, sometimes, even famine. People with pronounced symptoms may suffer social ostracism. In Africa, the first attacks on river blindness used aircraft to spray chemical and biological insecticides on river valleys with the object of destroying black flies. That strategy was superseded in the 1980s when the pharmaceutical company, Merck, discovered that the drug Mectizan (Invermectin) successfully treats and prevents onchocerciasis by killing the larvae of the parasitic worm. Just one pill taken annually is required. In 1987, Merck established the Mectizan Donation Program that, in partnership with the World Bank, UN agencies, Ministries of Health, and many other organizations, not only gives away the drug, but contributes to the costs of worldwide distribution.

Africare began its work with onchocerciasis in 1989 when it collaborated with the International Eye Foundation to study the feasibility of a blindness prevention program in Kwara, a state of Nigeria, a nation whose citizens are among the most vulnerable. With a grant from the Public Welfare Foundation, Africare distributed thousands of doses of Mectizan to health clinics in 1990 and it accelerated its efforts in succeeding years by expanding to four more states. It added six provinces of southern Chad in 1992. Africare estimated that it reached about three million Nigerians and Chadians in these projects.

All of the preceding health programs were carried out by the availability of large grants and contracts from foundations, private donors, and federal or international sources. While they supported Africare's work overseas, they did not enhance Africare's image as a PVO sustained in large measure by the gifts of ordinary Americans, particularly African Americans. That dilemma was addressed in part by Africare's success over the years in persuading churches, sororities, and other organizations to participate in the construction of at least a hundred health facilities in African countries. A few examples will illustrate the breadth of participation by private Americans acting together and the continent-wide reach of their donations. In Burkina Faso (formerly called Upper Volta) and Mali, Alpha Kappa Alpha sorority, the Presiding Bishop's Fund for World Relief, and the United Church Board for World Ministries built dispensaries. Jack and Jill of America underwrote the cost of a maternity clinic in Mali and the National Association of Colored Women's Clubs paid for a health center in Senegal. The Amherst African Response Coalition funded a health clinic in Somalia and Howard University Medical Center co-sponsored with Africare the reconstruction of three health centers in Rwanda. The Bwanunkha village health center in Zambia owes its existence to a contribution from the United Methodist Committee on Relief (UMCOR).

Other dispensaries and clinics received funding through the generosity of corporations and foreign governments. Village dispensaries in Zambia were built by IBM, NCR Corporation, and Burroughs. The Government of Germany gave a maternity facility to the town of Divinhe in Mozambique and a health clinic to the village of Revue. The Embassy of Canada donated a health clinic to Brava village in Somalia and the then British Overseas Development Administration (now called the Department for International Development) contributed a health clinic to a village in Mozambique. The American diplomatic

75

corps also helped when the U.S. Embassy Self-Help Fund paid for the construction of two village health centers in Zambia.

As admirable as it was to construct a rural dispensary or clinic, having the physical building was not the entire solution to community health needs. In many cases, ministries of health, which assumed management responsibilities once the structure was built, were unable to spare funds for medicines or trained personnel. Sometimes, they could not persuade health workers to relocate to remote rural areas because there was no school for their children or adequate local housing. The facility then just stood vacant. Or, if supplies, medicines, and health workers were present, there frequently were other constraints that limited effectiveness, for example, the obstacles that arose on a wind-swept savanna near the small village of Kongwa, Tanzania, where Africare built a dispensary. The head health worker had basic supplies and pharmaceuticals, but possessed no gas refrigerator for the storage of vaccines and medicines. She had no transportation, not even a bicycle, which would still be difficult to maneuver through roads of deep sand. Sometimes, in the middle of the night, she would be fetched for a childbirth or medical emergency and, by the time she reached the home in question, the baby had been born or the patient had suffered a serious setback. The nurse often had to search for interpreters to help her talk to patients, for few people in that area of central Tanzania spoke Swahili, the national language, but instead spoke many different languages. Finally, the dispensary building was not large enough for her to keep critically ill patients overnight. Those were the circumstances that confronted a dedicated nurse who had a modern building, plenty of clean water from adjacent wells, and a facility relatively well-stocked with necessities.

Since the late 1980s, activities associated with the HIV/AIDS epidemic in Africa have had a prominent role in Africare work throughout sub-Saharan Africa. In 1988, Africare advised the Rwandan Government about plans to coordinate disease treatment and prevention measures among its population. The same year, the Nigerian Ministry of Health, already concerned about the threat of HIV/AIDS even though it knew of few cases within the country, asked Africare to conduct a national workshop on the subject and, the next year, to offer a regional workshop on AIDS prevention for forty participants who, in turn, would train more health workers in their home states. Africare undertook larger programs in Nigeria in subsequent years to inform everyone who had any role in health care about the disease.

It soon expanded its AIDS awareness campaign to the Central African Republic, which established an AIDS Education and Training Center in Bangui, the capital. As Africare became more professional in its development of AIDS training and public information materials, the World Health Organization, the World AIDS Foundation, USAID, and other sponsors entrusted it with increasing responsibility in the fight against AIDS in Africa. For example, in the early 1990s, Africare was chosen to prepare educational resources in Portuguese for the Lusophone nations of Guinea-Bissau, Angola, and Mozambique.

Africare's continent-wide work with AIDS awareness, prevention, treatment, and assistance to those, especially children, affected by loss has become a signature cause. In the past twenty years, it has helped more than twenty-five African nations in this struggle. Realizing the magnitude of coordinating many types of programs, and of working with ministries of health and health professionals in nations with different national languages, different political systems, and diverse populations, Africare hired a seasoned health veteran, Clarence Hall, in 2000 to develop a comprehensive strategy. He had first been associated with Africare in The Gambia when he assisted in the procurement, storage, and distribution of pharmaceuticals. He established principles to guide overseas operations, such as maintaining Africare's community-based approach of raising AIDS awareness and of utilizing local volunteers in educational efforts. HIV/AIDS activities were now to be integrated into all Africare development programs, much as health concerns were earlier incorporated into as many Africare proposals as possible.

Africare's decision in 2000 to put more of its resources and efforts than ever before into the struggle against HIV/AIDS coincided with increasing concern within Washington about the spreading worldwide menace. In his State of the Union address in January 2003, President George W. Bush announced the creation of The United States President's Emergency Plan for AIDS Relief, or PEPFAR (it is also called the President's Initiative or the Emergency Plan). He committed the United States to a five-year, $15 billion assault on the disease that would be managed through the Department of State rather than through USAID. Fifteen nations, twelve of them in sub-Saharan Africa, were the focus. Together, they had half of the world's thirty-nine million people infected by HIV. PEPFAR designed a managerial structure whereby host countries were to have one national plan, one national coordinating authority, and one national monitoring and evaluation system. There was a three-pronged strategy: treatment, prevention, and care for people living with and affected by HIV/AIDS. A major therapy measure was the use of antiretroviral drugs, which are effective in treating the disease itself and for certain other purposes but require laboratories and trained health workers in order for the proper dosage to be determined and for patients to be monitored. Prevention necessitates behavior change and such measures as the administration of antiretroviral drugs to HIV-positive pregnant women who may transmit HIV to their babies. The PEPFAR-funded projects adopted many approaches to behavior change, particularly one encompassed by the acronym ABC (Abstain, Be faithful, and consistent use of Condoms). PEPFAR's goal to care for people living with and affected by HIV/AIDS aimed at children who have become orphans, elderly people who must assume responsibility for bereaved grandchildren, widows, patients on ARV drugs who suffer common unpleasant side effects from the medicine, and people bedridden from other maladies. PEPFAR was renewed by the U.S. Congress in 2008, with an even larger budget than before.

An important feature of PEPFAR's strategy has been the use of local organizations as partners. In Fiscal Year 2006, 83% of all participants in PEPFAR operations were indigenous. A good example of how this works is Africare's affiliation in Zanzibar, Tanzania, with at least a half dozen diverse groups that share in recruiting volunteers for home care, for providing school support, and for raising seed money for income-generating activities. They include the Zanzibar AIDS Association for Support of Orphans, Zanzibar Association of Farmers and Fishermen, Zanzibar Moslem Women's AIDS Support, and the Zanzibar NGO Cluster for HIV/AIDS Prevention.

Africare's first response to the President's Initiative was to hire a Health/HIV/AIDS director, Charles DeBose, to carry out its strategy of incorporating HIV/AIDS projects into as many Africare development programs as possible. Under him, many activities carried out in African nations to help improve their health systems were unified in a broad approach that recognized the futility of all other efforts—child survival, maternal health, reproductive health, nutrition, malaria, acute respiratory infections, diarrhea, and immunization—unless the disease is conquered. A few illustrations of Africare operations in some African nations will show the holistic tactics that DeBose, Hall, and their staff adopted. They will also demonstrate the effect of HIV/AIDS on communities, the logistical problems of trying to reach people already infected or most vulnerable, and the strategies adopted to encourage behavior change.

Through PEPFAR, Africare, in 2003, received funding for a program it called COPE, standing for Community-based Orphan Care, Protection, and Empowerment. It organized a consortium in four nations, Mozambique, Tanzania, Uganda, and Rwanda, all in PEPFAR's group of fifteen focus nations. These were countries in which Africare had already been working for years. Africare set up a Project Manager Unit (PMU) in Dar es Salaam, Tanzania, to synchronize activities and hired individual project coordinators for each country. Together, they developed five strategic objectives for COPE: build institutional capacity within communities, train volunteers, and ensure supervision; form school clubs in which students and teachers participate and where information about HIV/AIDS is disseminated; distribute material benefits to schools such as uniforms, lab equipment, or desks, often to offset tuition costs for orphans; improve health and nutrition through messages about mosquito nets, proper food, and sanitation; help care takers with skill enhancement, record keeping, group dynamics, and income-generating opportunities.

The Ntungamo District in southwestern Uganda is a good example of how the COPE model has worked in one locale. The densely populated area, a transportation crossroads between Kampala and Lake Victoria and central Africa, was even more affected by the HIV/AIDS crisis than the rest of the nation. Project manager Gad Sam, a graduate of Makerere University in Kampala, began by winning the approval of district leaders to reach influential people in the governmental structure below the district level. These were political figures, religious leaders, and opinion-makers in the counties, sub-counties, parishes, and villages. He then held large meetings to explain the project, the beneficiaries, and the strategy to these individuals and he sought people who would assume responsibility for the many tasks involved. It was an effort to institutionalize the structure of COPE. Before long, service corps volunteers who visit villages, orphan care committees, caregiver support groups, and school clubs were being organized within the district.

The implementation of COPE strategy in Ntungamo reveals a number of useful points and the presence of challenges that can be extrapolated to other COPE projects. In holding meetings, whether large inclusive gatherings or village discussions, Africare staff found that women were far more interested in the success of the program than men because they are the caregivers. It was typical for as many as 80% of the group to be women. Furthermore, men tended to be target seekers. They came to obtain a mosquito net or some other material benefit. Women stayed at meetings to learn about nutrition, malaria prevention, and sanitation. Because of HIV/AIDS, women, many of them widows, are learning to be self-sufficient and, whereas in the past they did not have much voice in family decisions, they now are making them on their own. Women are also getting leadership positions in the neighborhood, receiving training, and learning about team work. Gender issues receive more attention than before.

With regard to the design of COPE, the Africare staff found that there is occasionally a gap between its application and practical consequences. Part of the program is to encourage the creation of support groups for orphans who are school drop-outs (usually because they lack tuition or face other obstacles stemming from HIV/AIDS in their family). Volunteers teach them life skills, creative thinking, self esteem, and non-violent conflict resolution, but they do not give them any means of earning a living. There is only a very limited vocational skills portion in the instruction manuals and with the severe shortage of technical schools in Uganda, most teenagers never have a chance for additional education. In one group of 190 boys and girls, only two were chosen for vocational training and even if many more had been selected, there would not have been the teachers or facilities to handle them. While this deficiency is not the fault of the COPE design per se, it does point out how reality can interfere with goals.

Another practical consideration that Africare COPE staff in Ntungamo faces as it works in the district is the absence of legal protection for orphans and widows. Orphans, in particular, need help in holding on to the property they inherit, for it is not unusual for an uncle or other relative to want to sell it, either for the child's benefit—school tuition, for example—or for his own. Africare is joining other charitable organizations in submitting a proposal to the Ugandan Ministry of Gender, Labour and Social Development for laws and policies to protect orphans.

The Government of Uganda is also caught in a dilemma between how the Ministry of Health has been implementing HIV/AIDS programs and the personal beliefs of its political leaders. The backbone of the prevention message publicized on billboards, in the media, at schools, in the COPE program, and through other health providers has been ABC: abstinence, being faithful, and condom use. The State

House, specifically the First Wife (Janet Musaweni), disapproves of the use of condoms and wants the acronym to be ABY (abstinence, being faithful, emphasis on youth) or ABC (abstinence, being faithful, changing behavior). This insistence that condoms not be a part of the prescription has skewed the type of organization that receives funding and is allowed to work in Uganda.

One facet of the COPE program is helping caregivers earn money to underwrite their living costs. Africare has sponsored a number of income-generating activities that have been very successful or are promising. One of them is drying fruit for export. In this area of Uganda, such fruit as apple bananas (good for drying), pineapples, and mangoes are plentiful and the caregivers could bring them either from their own gardens or from the local market. The project manager, Gad Sam, identified a company in Jinja called Fruits of the Nile, which exports to Europe, as willing to assist four groups of caregivers. The company sent its carpenters and extended credit for construction labor costs to the communities. It built solar driers and trained the people how to dry fruit. Africare provided the materials. Each group has its own bank account and every member must contribute a small amount each week. Already, the venture is proving to be profitable. A more risky, but potentially worthwhile, income-generating activity is the growing of an anti-malarial plant, *Artemisia*, which a private company, East African Botanicals Ltd., in Kabale contracts with caregivers to raise. They get the plants from the company, cultivate them, dry their leaves, and then sell the leaves back to the corporation, which processes them for their beneficial properties. When successfully executed, the process can be very lucrative to the caregivers.

The COPE strategy in Tanzania in the vicinity of Dodoma, several hundred miles inland from Dar es Salaam, also yields examples of how the program works and its challenges. About ten miles south of the paved, but narrow, Dar es Salaam-to-Dodoma highway, past cactus, occasional palm trees, and scrub brush, is the village of Kongwa with five thousand inhabitants. Near there, the secondary school has ninety-five students and four teachers. On the backboard in one classroom where the students are studying Africa's pre-written history is the weekend assignment. They are to learn answers to the following questions: What was the Iron Age? What was the difference between the Middle Stone Age and the Iron Age? What were four uses of iron? (All instruction in Tanzanian schools from the primary level up is in English.) The school lacked desks, chairs, teachers' materials, and

81

general supplies before Africare awarded it a block grant in which AIDS orphans and vulnerable children were admitted tuition-free in exchange for the commodities. Students still must share desks and chairs, but they no longer sit on the floor.

East of Dodoma and eight miles of washboard dirt roads north of the paved highway through a vast area of scant vegetation there is an oasis of three thousand people along a tree-lined river bed. Its primary school has 669 students and eight teachers. The greatest need here is for faculty housing. In response to that need, Africare has built a house for a teacher and his family. The energetic principal has established a small tree nursery and is planting trees around the school grounds, but he is frustrated by another shortage—equipment and teaching materials.

In a Dodoma suburb, a village committee of thirteen members—men, women, and children—has canvassed its dense neighborhood searching for the most vulnerable children in the community. It has ascertained that 136 need assistance, usually several in the same household. Economic reasons are the foremost explanation for their difficulty and behind the financial distress often is early pregnancy or a single parent. With the encouragement of Africare, the committee has set up a bank account with the money it has collected and has laid out an action plan. Africare enabled the committee to bring eighty-two of the children into the program by supplying mosquito nets, exercise books, pencils, soap, and water treatment kits. Committee members hold meetings for the children at school or in the village office where they counsel them, offer recreation, and supervise income-generating activities. While HIV/AIDS education and prevention are not explicit goals, they are implicit and, furthermore, this is an example of a community organization taking responsibility for local problems.

Zimbabwe—where at least a quarter of the adult population is infected with HIV/AIDS and where life expectancy at birth has plummeted to little more than forty years—is also important in Africare HIV/AIDS prevention and care programs. However, there are unique aspects to Africare's operations in that country. Being very sensitive to the activities of foreign organizations, the Government of Zimbabwe requires Africare and other NGOs to register and to receive permission from local and provincial authorities to work in specific districts. Staff members have to get police clearance to hold community meetings or to bring visitors into the community. Since only routine, repetitive activities already established are exempted, the working environment is shaped by government surveillance. Another distinctive feature of Africare's Zimbabwe HIV/AIDS activities is the urban orientation of many of them, a stretch beyond the rural commitment of Africare's past. The explanation lies in the accelerating economic and political turmoil following Zimbabwean independence in 1980 that drove many villagers from their ancestral lands to towns and cities in search of employment and government services. Concomitant with a mobile population congregating in new shanty towns adjacent to urban areas was the spread of HIV/AIDS across the African continent. Subsequently, Zimbabwean health officials realized that reaching the ill and the susceptible required a concentration of their limited resources on certain groups of citizens, wherever they resided, and Africare adjusted to the new situation.

A key target of government programs became adolescents and young adults, individuals at a malleable and vulnerable stage of life. Africare, receiving support from the Bill and Melinda Gates Foundation, soon began participating in the national effort through a regional southern Africa adolescent reproduction health project. One of its main features in Zimbabwe was the sponsorship of AIDS Action Groups, similar to COPE school clubs elsewhere. These were launched in primary and secondary schools to disseminate information and literature on HIV/AIDS and reproductive health. Through the assistance of teachers and patrons, usually parents, and the use of films, drama productions, and sympathetic discussions, the students are encouraged to consider the perils of casual sex and to be more thoughtful about their own conduct. They learn the medical aspects of sexually transmitted diseases and they are urged to take a caring, understanding attitude toward those afflicted. A practical feature of the AIDS Action Groups is the establishment in each of an income-generating activity through which the participants are trained in such business principles as organizational structure, finances, and bookkeeping.

There have been many restraints and challenges to the implementation and success of the AIDS Action Group strategy in Zimbabwe. Most of them are equally applicable to similar programs elsewhere in Africa, whether managed by Africare or by other PVOs. Students often have home chores that limit the time they can devote to club activities. Furthermore, especially in rural areas, the lack of transportation is an impediment both to their participation and to collective action. In creating an income-generating project, students have no access to funding sources with which to begin, whether it is raising rabbits or chickens or cultivating medicinally useful herbs. Naturally, there is no financial cushion to protect them when disaster befalls their venture. The program objectives of disseminating information and literature, making condoms available, and affecting student behavior in a positive manner are also thwarted by practical circumstances. Sometimes there is not enough material on HIV/AIDS and reproductive health to meet the demand. In regard to condoms, in some cases parents threaten Africare if it makes this contraceptive available to their children. Elsewhere, there may be a shortage of condoms due to a poor distribution network. Two societal characteristics also enter into the picture. First, very few boys participate in the AIDS Action Groups as compared to girls and, second, by the time students reach secondary school, most are already sexually active. Through necessity, the girls become the focus of efforts to help them avoid pregnancy and sexually transmitted infections.

An example from eastern Zimbabwe illustrates how AIDS Action Groups operate. Out in the Mutare District on the slopes of the Eastern Highlands that divide Zimbabwe and Mozambique is Hauna valley, well-known for large English tea and coffee estates. Fifty students at the secondary school in Mandeya, a community of a thousand inhabitants scattered over the hillsides, demonstrate a typical meeting. A sixteen year old girl in her blue school uniform reads several stories from the manual furnished by Africare about a woman infected with AIDS and a child who is also sick. Of her classmates she asks what their response should be to the situation and the general discussion elicits empathy and compassion for the ill. The children then take visitors to see their herb garden and although the rain turns from a drizzle to a downpour, they pick chilies, basil, and other herbs. They explain the medicinal value of each—this for malaria, that for toothache, another for backache. Finally, they show off the rabbits they are raising. They have learned how long it takes rabbits to mature (three months) and that cross-breeding is necessary to prevent deterioration of the stock. The group has a distribution program similar to that of the Heifer Project in which a person receiving a rabbit gives away the first litter to others. There is no cultural bias against eating rabbit in Hauna valley, as in Ntungamo, Uganda, although some apostolic sects forbid it.

Peer education became another Africare strategy to reach adolescents and young adults, and in reality, it may reach as wide an audience through its methodology as the action groups. In multiple wards of eastern Zimbabwe, for example, headmasters, nurses, teachers, priests, traditional leaders, and local health workers were selected to receive training about HIV/AIDS and to promote activities within their communities to ameliorate its effects or to halt its advance. These peer educators held awareness days and organized informal discussion sessions and counseling workshops. They sponsored public lectures and drama performances. One particular category of youth that they targeted for peer education has been that of school dropouts. As elsewhere in Africa, many left school because they are orphans who cannot pay tuition or buy school uniforms, or they must care for a family member ill with AIDS, or because of other unfortunate family circumstances. The groups commonly meet at youth centers in small towns where they see videos about reproductive health and about sexually transmitted diseases, including HIV/AIDS. Peer educators and patrons lead discussions designed to discourage high risk behavior and to provide a supportive environment for those already affected in some way by AIDS. For these young people, however, the future looks bleak and even if given encouragement by community-backed programs, they feel a need for a vocational component that will help them earn a living.

One of the challenges Africare faces in managing its HIV/AIDS prevention and care activities in Zimbabwe has been the cultural context in which the people grow up. Women have traditionally provided most of the labor in the fields, done household chores, and looked after children, old people, and the ill. The fact that 60% of adult cases are women compounds the impact of the national HIV/AIDS epidemic and, consequently, quickly makes apparent that men have to accept more responsibility for fighting the disease. This recognition that Zimbabwean men must be enlisted to help their families and communities coincided with a transformation of thinking internationally about the role of men in economic and social development programs, including HIV/AIDS prevention. Social scientists and researchers investigated ways to broaden beliefs about gender roles, masculinity, and cultural norms that would make male involvement in orphan care, community health, and improved treatment of women socially acceptable.

To test the latest theories, Africare launched the Male Empowerment Project in 2002 in the Mutasa District of eastern Zimbabwe. Its purposes were to increase care and support to families and individuals affected by HIV/AIDS, particularly to women who are the primary caregivers, and to reduce the stigma attached to the disease while increasing information about it. Men were to learn new skills, adopt behavior changes that benefit the community, and assume more responsibility for the safety of their families. It was an effort to redefine masculinity as including caring and supportive behavior. The first step in the project was recruiting a group of eighty voluntary caregivers. Project staff members trained them in basic home care features: patient exam and history, hygiene and nutrition, wound and skin care, pain control, and general nursing duties. They led discussions about stigma and discrimination, about condom use, and cultural practices that promote HIV transmission. Finally, the men were given home-based care supplies and condoms. The names of home-based clients, all men, came from a number of sources. They were referred by hospitals or clinics, by community health workers, by pastors, and by village chiefs, but the largest number came from the voluntary caregiver's own family.

In assessing the Male Empowerment Project in Mutasa District, Africare found that male caregivers were uncomfortable performing tasks, such as bathing or feeding, that traditionally belonged to women, but willingly provided counseling, spiritual support, and exercise for the patient. In terms of assisting the primary caregiver with gathering firewood, gardening, or fetching water, there was a dissonance between the expressed willingness of the male caregiver and his reported performance. Important lessons emerged from testing the hypothesis about male empowerment in eastern Zimbabwe. Since home-based care is an extremely intimate undertaking and deals with a disease laden with the baggage of stigma and fear, caregivers needed continual in-service training and consistent monitoring. They and their clients required observation periodically by field officers. Another lesson was the difficulty that male caregivers had in discussing "safe sex," aspects of HIV prevention, or providing counseling on preparation for death and bereavement. Cultural taboos on these topics caused them, at most, to inquire generally about the health of the household or to discuss community news. Furthermore, the absence of testing services for HIV in the district made it possible for clients, even those with obvious symptoms, to deny the cause of their illness, instead blaming other diseases, curses, or witchcraft.

One of Africare's contributions to the assault on the HIV/AIDS epidemic in Africa has been in strengthening the institutional capacity of national ministries of health in their struggle to prevent the spread of HIV, to manage sexually transmitted infections, and to make wise policy decisions. A major USAID-funded Africare project in Benin, a small nation on the west coast of Africa with a population of seven million and high fertility and population growth rates, is a case study. Although the prevalence rate of HIV in Benin is only 2%, infant mortality is high, public health services are scant, and there is very little usage of condoms. For four years, beginning in 2002, Africare administered the Benin HIV/AIDS Prevention Program (BHAPP) as a part of the *Programme National de Lutte contre le SIDA* [National Program in the struggle against AIDS]. The goal, at the national level, was to assist the Ministry of Health in program planning; establishing norms and standards for HIV, AIDS, and STI prevention; drafting a national HIV/AIDS law; and policy development. An important function of Africare BHAPP technical experts was to transmit their knowledge to the Ministry of Health's SIDA staff. Regionally, BHAPP aimed to organize the outreach activities of more than twenty-five indigenous NGOs, to strengthen the capacity of personnel in health zones within five of the country's twelve departments to diagnose and treat STIs, and to promote what it called "condom social marketing." The population groups that the Ministry of Health expressly tried to reach were sex workers, truck and taxi drivers, market women along the national thoroughfares, and out-of-school youth.

There were solid achievements during the four years. Technical documents that spelled out norms, standards, and procedures at the national level for every aspect of the fight against AIDS and sexually transmitted diseases were written. The ability of the government to discuss, formulate, implement, and disseminate health policies was improved, thus strengthening the institutional capacity of the Ministry of Health. A major accomplishment of BHAPP was shepherding a national HIV/AIDS law through the National Assembly in 2005 and having the new president of Benin sign it in May 2006. It was the first piece of legislation of its kind in the West African region. At the regional and community level, where twenty-three clinics or health facilities were selected in health zones, many health workers were trained in the diagnosis and treatment of AIDS and other STIs. The percentage of health workers who were capable of correctly explaining prevention standards and caring for STI/HIV cases rose from 15% in 2003 to 47% in 2004. Health supervisors learned the value of close staff surveillance in delivering comprehensive, high quality services. In these zones, knowledge about the causes and prevention of HIV increased considerably within the targeted population too. For example, among truck drivers, the percentage capable of listing at least two risk reduction methods for the sexual transmission of HIV rose from 7% in 2002 to 40% in 2005. Sadly, however, among the truck drivers during the same period there was a slight increase in their encounters with occasional sexual partners, although this figure is offset by a significant increase in the use of condoms. The main purpose of the indigenous NGOs was to communicate information locally about behavior changes needed in the fight against HIV transmission. NGOs selected peer educators from among hair dressers, truck drivers, bicycle taxi drivers, and employees at travel hotels who received training in presenting the message to their respective groups and in identifying individuals with symptoms. As on Zanzibar, the structure of local institutions was enhanced by the involvement of thousands of newly active citizens. One facet of the BHAPP project in Benin that was less successful than the others was the objective of facilitating condom distribution by community health workers and peer educators. Although the peer educators, after their training, were sent back to their locales with supplies of condoms that they were to sell within the target groups with which they worked and to create a revolving fund to refill their diminished stock, they were stymied in knowing how to find social marketing outlets or how to establish a revolving fund. Consequently, the number of condom sales was far below what BHAPP had projected.

The lessons learned from the BHAPP project in Benin are illustrative of the delicacy and complexity inherent when an outside actor (Africare) enters a nation in order to help it with a health program, especially when the host already has personnel and an organizational structure in place. From the beginning, the two staffs in Cotonou, Benin's largest city, lacked agreement on the definition and scope of such operational terms as "capacity building" and "technical assistance," with the Benin professionals objecting to assumptions by BHAPP employees. There were other problems in the relationship between the two staffs that involved communication and coordination of activities. Out in the field, the choice of just twenty-three clinics and health facilities in the health zones of five departments created jealousy and resentment among those not selected. Evaluators recommended that the number of health zones be reduced so that all medical centers within these fewer confines could be included. The indigenous nongovernmental organizations, whose existence relied almost entirely on external donor assistance, were shown to be of value in reaching local communities, but they viewed the BHAPP project as another source of financial support, their capacities and skills varied, and they needed to teach outreach workers to customize their messages to individual cultures. Furthermore, the role that traditional chiefs, elected officials, and traditional healers could play became more apparent in light of the complicated functioning of local NGOs. The lesson learned in regard to the social marketing of condoms was the need for more training of peer educators, more orientation to how the system works, and improved linkages between NGO outreach workers and vendors. Finally, a general recommendation that the evaluators of the BHAPP project made for further USAID-funded activities was the application of "vigorous concentration" in similar projects to the issue of gender imbalance. As they traveled through Benin, the evaluators had found that no women had management positions of any importance in the NGOs, none of the leadership of the health facilities they visited was female, and women were in a distinct minority among peer educators. If this situation were to be changed, they wrote, the gender imbalance had to be addressed with firmness and specificity.

A health issue that has escalated as a concern at Africare in the past two decades is the provision of clean water under sanitary conditions for human consumption and the related hygienic disposal of waste. When Africare drilled its first wells in the Sahel in the mid-1970s, its primary interest was in supplying a life-dependent need to nomads and their animals. Then, it set the goal of persuading them to become at least semi-settled and agriculturalists, which involved irrigation. The early approach was all technical: the delivery of water to remote areas. Annual reports until the late 1980s enumerated the number of wells built in different countries and thanked many donors, but the focus was on how they enhanced agricultural production, reduced women's labor in seeking water, and ameliorated drought conditions. In fact, however, a significant program component was evolving because Africare employees had soon realized that they could improve the health of recipients if they collaterally emphasized sanitation and personal hygiene. Among their first successes in inculcating these values in West African communities that received wells was the decision by local women to fine anyone who stepped on the concrete lip in her sandals.

One step toward a broader appreciation of how Africare could use water resources in development came in the mid-1980s when it began cooperating with various African nations in child survival programs. Dehydration and diarrhea were the foremost causes of childhood illness and death, but, as mentioned earlier, it could be prevented or cured by the use of clean water and a simple sugar solution. Africare gained more insight into the value of hygienic water systems when it assisted Sudanese refugees in southwestern Ethiopia in 1989 and 1990. It was 1993 when Africare first apprised supporters in strong terms of the correlation between disease and access to clean water, sanitation facilities, and knowledge about personal behavior. It published broad, undocumented general statistics, such as the fact that 61% of rural Africans have no clean water, that 85% of rural Africans have poor sanitation facilities or none at all, and that as much as 80% of all illness in Africa is thought to stem from the quality of the water supply. Africare's new thrust in water resource enhancement was to be in southern Africa, where a severe drought threatened the lives of millions of people. Camps filled with refugees from several civil wars had inadequate amenities, and primitive toilets or open defecation were still standard in many communities.

More than a decade later, improved sustainable access to safe drinking water and basic sanitation has become a United Nations Millennium Development Goal. While it is impossible to compare the 1993 Africare figures with those from WHO and UNESCO that undergird their objectives, a similar picture emerges about the imperative to help African nations with their water systems. The percentage of people, rural and urban, in sub-Saharan Africa who had access to "improved" drinking water in 2006 was estimated at 58%. The percentage of the rural population from all of Africa using improved sanitation—that is, private facilities that flushed or pour-flushed into a piped sewer system, a septic tank, pit latrine, a sanitary pit latrine, or a composting toilet—was 28%. More disturbing than this was the finding that 36% of the rural population practices open defecation. These macro statistics from United Nations entities become more vivid when the situation in an individual African country such as Rwanda is analyzed. It is densely populated, with abundant water resources, yet only 41% of its rural citizens have access to clean water. That means that three and a half million people are without it. Although 80% of rural Rwandans possess latrines, only 8% of these are sanitary, putting more than six million rural residents in danger of an unhygienic environment. Many sub-Saharan African nations report similar circumstances, but one factor that sets some apart from Rwanda is the absence of plentiful groundwater.

Africare's major programs in water resources during the early 1990s in southern Africa were unique in that they represented a regional approach targeting multiple nations. Malawi, Zimbabwe, and Zambia were always included in projects, but at times, Mozambique or Namibia was added. A commitment to the U.S. Office of Foreign Disaster Assistance (OFDA) and to USAID to provide emergency water supplies for about 260,000 residents in selected provinces of Malawi, Zimbabwe, and Zambia was one such regional undertaking. It is also an example of obstacles that Africare sometimes encountered in dealing with USAID Missions in the respective host countries. American officials in Zimbabwe and Zambia, whose approval and cooperation were essential, were directing so much of their attention to food relief that they were unenthusiastic about water projects. Moreover, in Malawi, USAID's drought coordinator, pointing to a number of valid technical questions about Africare's proposal, expressed his belief that Africare, along with other NGOs that approached the agency, had "no experience [in water relief] behind them." He and others at the Mission were convinced that non-U.S. NGOs had a competitive advantage in water extraction. Nonetheless, Africare received the contract because the coordinator decided that, "we'll only know if the NGO can do the work by letting them [sic] do it."

In all three nations, Africare, through its drought coordinators, cooperated with national ministries, district and local governments, and special water task forces to identify existing wells, boreholes, and water points. It searched sites for the construction of new water sources. By the end of the project, more than nine hundred wells and boreholes had been rehabilitated. However, one reservation about the project's success concerned the standards of the finished product in some locations. Professional evaluators hired by OFDA complained that the program did not address in any substantive way the general issue of water quality. They pointed out that, even in an emergency, the water provided must be potable and that not only may health be threatened, but in extreme cases it might be worsened if the water is not. Among factors accounting for unsatisfactory well protection were the haste to provide water, inadequate staffing and equipment levels, and inexperienced or untrained supervisors. A specific deficiency affecting the outcome of the entire project was the dearth of seasoned water engineers.

Running simultaneously with the effort to provide immediate water to people in drought-stricken Malawi, Zimbabwe, and Zambia was a longer-term project that focused on improving health through community mobilization and the construction of latrines and wells. Spread across four years, from 1993 to 1996, and funded by private, international, and American governmental donors, including the Besser Foundation, Coca Cola, the Canada Fund, UNICEF, and USAID, it employed a new methodology in the implementation of its objectives. Africare staff, administering earlier programs elsewhere in Africa, particularly those in health care and child survival, had assumed that, if mothers and others received information about how behavioral changes would benefit their families, they would adopt new practices. In fact, however, final evaluations often found that target audiences were more influenced by community norms than by their own awareness and that the best route to success was in increasing the knowledge and in changing the attitudes of influential individuals in the community. The inference to be drawn was that there should be more emphasis on active, participatory learning and adult education for village chiefs, men, old women, and other respected local figures. Accepting the growing evidence that their project designs would be more effective if reoriented, Africare employees now utilized the WASH approach in this multi-national undertaking.

WASH, an acronym for water sanitation and hygiene, emphasized the role of individuals and groups of citizens in assuming responsibility for the outcome of water projects, in sharing the duties required for their implementation, and in adopting habits that would reduce the incidence of water and fecal-borne diseases. It was an effort to get rural people to "buy in" to a new mode of living. What Africare was also seeking to benefit from were the hard lessons it had learned in earlier construction programs in which, expecting the government to build and maintain wells, boreholes, dams, and other water facilities, villagers typically were unwilling to expend much labor or to maintain water points that had been given them free of charge.

The methodology of WASH began with introducing the project to the community and in gathering baseline information about the number of wells and latrines, the incidence of water-related illnesses such as diarrhea, and how much time women spent fetching water. Next, a water and health committee was established with the duty of promoting hygiene and sanitation. On a self-help basis, individuals undertook the construction of latrines, using Africare-supplied material and training. The water and health committee stressed their use and maintenance through local education. The community then selected a water source to be protected and, on a self-help basis, with Africare training builders and villagers, it completed a clean well or spring. Water source caretakers were trained in its maintenance and the entire population was reinforced in its knowledge of hygiene, proper use of protected water sources, and the handling of water at the household level.

At the end of the fourth year, Africare reported that it had completed about 250 wells and more than 10,000 latrines in Malawi, Zimbabwe, and Zambia. It estimated that 115,000 people, the larger number of them women, since women are a distinct majority in most rural areas of southern Africa, had benefitted. Africare staff believed that their work had sparked a strong local interest in developing the indigenous capability to improve water availability and sanitation. Nonetheless, there were obstacles in the implementation of the program. In Malawi, during the one-party regime of President Hastings Banda, development initiatives were associated with the regime and citizens cooperated only reluctantly. In the early 1990s, as opposition leaders arose and subsequently replaced him in power, many of them encouraged voters to resist self-help projects because these were linked with Banda. Africare had to enlist the help of community leaders and government officials to persuade villagers to participate. The area where Africare drilled for wells in Zambia suffered from a declining water table and the presence of underground rock formations. It had to shift sites. The problem to overcome in Zimbabwe was a cultural one. It was taboo in many communities for both sexes to use a single latrine and gradual acceptance of the idea that one unit per family was adequate came through the urging of project committees. There were also unintended consequences of this program. Training builders in the construction of latrines gave them skills to construct simple houses or to work on such public enterprises as bridges. While this was of overall value to the community, it offered the men the opportunity to find more remunerative employment elsewhere. Specifically in Zambia, the success of Africare's efforts and the prolonged drought in central Zambia drew migrants into areas where there was improved water access, causing greater demand for wells and latrines. The issue of whether women benefitted or not from the closer proximity of water sources and to what degree drew mixed conclusions from project managers. Women in Malawi were depicted as saving enormous amounts of time by having safe and adequate water within a reasonable distance of home, but those in Zimbabwe were characterized as having expanded labor because more water is required for hand washing after latrine use.

The WASH approach was viewed skeptically by donors, by African governments, and by other PVOs when Africare proposed its use in Malawi, Zimbabwe, and Zambia. For them, direct action seemed imperative without the time-consuming search for community input and support. In the last decade, however, enthusiasm has grown so much that WASH is being implemented throughout Africa and even outside the continent. For example, in Uganda, where good sanitation and hygiene have actually decreased since the 1960s because of political turmoil and civil unrest, only 33% of the country's thirty million people have improved sanitation coverage. In 2003, the Ugandan government united six ministries into a National Sanitation Working Group to coordinate and promote hygiene and sanitation, using WASH activities. It made Janet Museveni, First Wife, its chief promoter and advocate. Another sign of growing WASH acceptance was the UN General Assembly declaration of October 15, 2008, as the first Global Hand washing Day (GHD). It was celebrated in thirty-five sub-Saharan African nations and in about forty other countries.

Another validation of WASH has come to Africare from its selection as the recipient of funds collected annually by Bono's U2 fans on his birthday, May 10. Knowing of his earlier activism on behalf of African causes, they aim to provide access to clean water to everyone in Africa. Hence, they established the African Well Fund in 2002 on the belief that water is not merely a basic human need, but a Basic Human Right. Every year, they emphasize a slogan in their fund-raising campaign. In 2006, it was "Walk 10 Miles in Her Shoes," in reference to the distance some women must walk, roundtrip, to the nearest water source. They asked volunteers to raise at least 84,480 pennies ($844.80), which, if all lined up, would equal one of the ten miles women in Africa typically walk for water. The group has raised more than a half million dollars in less than a decade for clean water and sanitation projects in Uganda, Angola, and Zimbabwe.

The need for clean water in a hygienic environment continues to dominate African communities. The United Nations' designation of 2008 as the International Year of Sanitation gave attention to the programs of Africare and other PVOs, as well as a prod to international and national agencies to allocate more funds to water resource activities. Private foundations and corporations also took interest in the long-term health implications of the existing situation. Africare's most recent commitment to improved water supply, in 2009, came in partnership with Water for All, an American non-profit organization founded in 2004 to provide clean drinking water to schools and communities in Africa, but active so far only in eastern and southern African nations. Together they pledged to take clean drinking water and hygiene education to three hundred locales in Zambia, Uganda, and Malawi. The mechanism for accomplishing the technical goal is a South African invention called the "Play Pump Water System." Although devised by an anonymous engineer and professional bore-hole-driller to entertain lonely children on South African farms, it was adapted by an advertising executive, Trevor Field, to do social good. The play pump is a merry-go-round attached to a pump. As children spin it, they draw water up and into a large sealed storage tank that rests on a tall stand. The tank can be used also for posting public service messages.

The non-profit company that grew from Field's ingenuity has been incorporated in the United States under the name PlayPumps International and it received a $10 million contract from USAID in 2006 to provide 650 water pumps across several African countries. In addition to play pumps, the firm makes solar pumps that will be installed in some places. Africare is cooperating with Water for All by identifying promising sites for pumps, helping in the selection of the type of pump suitable for the location, providing hygiene and sanitation education, and giving agricultural guidance to communities. It is also responsible for monitoring and evaluating the program. Malawi, where Africare has significant experience, will receive a hundred pumps for primary schools, just part of the $1.6 million total cost expected in its collaboration with Water for All.

5

Agriculture and Food Security

The effort to alleviate suffering from malnutrition and starvation has always been central to Africare's work and it dates to involvement in Sahelian relief during the early 1970s. That experience jump-started its agricultural focus by illustrating that residents of the six stricken West African nations, once they survived the drought, had to rebuild in its entirety the economic base of their livelihoods. Nomads had to reconstitute herds, find grazing routes across the desert where water was available, and in some cases become partially sedentary farmers. Villagers, confronted with diminished soils, environmental degradation, and depleted resources, literally had to begin life over. Africare's integrated rural development projects in Niger and Upper Volta (Burkina Faso), already described, were designed to meet the multiplicity of needs. They were built on smaller agricultural activities, many of a trial and error nature that preceded them.

The perusal of Africare annual reports from the late 1970s to the present reveals progression in the sophistication and tenor of its agricultural endeavors. The use of new financial means to expand its range is also evident. During the 1980s, large sections described "agriculture and small scale irrigation" and "integrated rural development." More than half of Africare's annual program budget went to these categories. Dip tanks for cattle, fish farming, irrigated vegetable gardens, poultry production, and rice cultivation were featured prominently. Water resource development received less specific attention, perhaps because its cost was often submerged within a larger expense framework or the stand-alone outlay was slight in comparison to the overall financial picture. In fact, the relatively small gift necessary to sponsor construction of one or several village wells was a major factor in attracting churches, civic groups, sororities, and many other American organizations as Africare supporters.

Annual reports during most of the 1990s referred to the variety of agricultural activities as "Food, Water and the Environment." With one exception, greater than half the budget each year was spent on activities within these categories. Now, Africare informed its donors not just of many more projects than before, but of new themes as well. There was assistance to a local Zimbabwe solar lighting enterprise, Solarlite, which provided financially affordable and environmentally friendly illumination to rural areas. Groups in Zambia, Zimbabwe, and Mozambique, primarily of women, were introduced to low-cost, manually operated presses with which they could extract edible oil from sunflower and sesame seeds. Farmers used milling machines in Senegal, Chad, Zambia, Zimbabwe, and Ethiopia to generate extra income through grinding corn and peanuts for oil or dried tomatoes for powder. Africare even helped to privatize garbage collection in Conakry and Kigali, capital cities of Guinea and Rwanda, respectively, thus improving sanitation. Africare's attention to environmental challenges became a major topic of its publications in the 1990s. Whereas, previously, agro forestry, village-level tree nurseries, sand dune stabilization, water collection and storage, and irrigation had been discussed as discreet projects in individual nations, Africare now presented a larger, holistic picture of what they meant collectively. "Environmental management" and "natural resource management" became watchwords. Perhaps the biggest innovative leap was participation in Title II of the P.L. 480 program ("Food for Peace"), established by the U.S. Congress in 1954, which allowed PVOs to obtain surplus agricultural commodities, which they monetized overseas in support of their efforts.

However, Africare supporters still found plenty of familiar programs in the 1990s. Animal traction—the use of oxen or mules instead of humans to pull plows through fields—was as important to new Africare initiatives in Mozambique as it had been earlier in Niger. Clearing land, draining it, and extending the cultivation of vegetables, rice, cotton, sunflowers, and many products either edible or income-producing remained typical activities. Well-digging and construction of water systems continued to be significant. Agribusiness education and credit support for farmers, fishermen, women's cooperatives, and agricultural enterprises in many countries aimed to give local people more control over their economic future and to encourage private commerce. Agricultural extension work was enhanced in Zimbabwe by partnering with the Canada-based Farm Radio Network to develop programming aimed at eastern and southern Africa in crop production, animal husbandry, agribusiness management, and land-use management.

Since 2000, Africare has used its annual reports to emphasize the linkage of agriculture, environment, and water in providing food security; the Food for Development program, based on P.L. 480, plays an increasing role in the narrative. They now reflect more intentionally than before solidarity with the objectives of international organizations and attention to African nations facing domestic political crises. An essay in 2000 quotes the definition of food security enunciated by the 1996 World Food Summit in Rome and elaborates on it. More recently, annual reports repeat information from the 1996 World Food Summit and use illustrations, with statistics, from the World Bank and UNICEF. The overall impression is of Africare as a partner in a world-wide, international effort to help Africa. It is magnified by coverage given concurrently to Africare's concern with major global health issues, particularly the HIV/AIDS crisis.

Agriculture is the basis of livelihood in Africa and most Africans are small farmers scattered in villages over the continent. While the Sahelian drought sadly illustrated the immediate effects of an environmental disaster on one region of Africa, it overshadowed for a time a fundamental truth about all of Africa, that is, that almost everywhere the soil is poor, only primitive tools are available, seeds and plants are genetically inferior, and water scarcity is a daily fact of life. Furthermore, farmers lack knowledge of modern agricultural practices, cannot afford to purchase fertilizer, and have no access to credit. Beginning with helping the people of Niger and Upper Volta overcome these obstacles, Africare slowly undertook a multiplicity of projects geographically encompassing half of Africa.

Mindful that the variety and types of food available to African households were important determinants of healthy diets, Africare, from the early 1980s, began encouraging a diversity of food-raising activities in African nations. First, it promoted vegetable gardens. Women, at the heart of farming in Africa, were organized into cooperatives and with the technical help of Africare staff and critical inputs of seeds, fertilizer, and pesticides, learned to cultivate vegetables for their own home use and for sale at local markets. In Niger, women in the villages of Ramsa and Goubre grew tomatoes and eggplants that were actually flown to France. Since vegetable growing was a dry season occupation, other crops, such as sorghum, were planted during the rainy season. The obstacles to overcome were many and project designs attempted to incorporate all components of successful farming. Every aspect required back-breaking labor. Wells, essential for an irrigation system, had to be dug. Fences and windbreaks had to be erected to protect gardens. The construction of passable roads was often necessary, since markets for the produce might be a considerable distance away. A typical project in the village of Badje Koaro in Niger illustrates the interlocking factors needed for success. Africare helped 248 women vegetable growers through the construction of two wells and the provision of donkeys to draw water. It donated fencing, materials, seeds, and fertilizer, and established a revolving credit fund to create a sustainable endeavor. The large first harvest of onions, tomatoes, and okra was the beginning of change in that community.

At about the same time—the early 1980s—Africare engaged in teaching youth in several African nations about growing vegetables. They were the future and attracting them to farming had the multiple promises of offering food security and stemming the tendency to migrate from rural areas to urban. In the small town of Quallam, Niger, fifty miles north of Niamey, it trained forty-five students, ages thirteen to eighteen, at the area's secondary school in agricultural principles by establishing a garden plot and supplying everything from seeds to tools. The students shared farming tasks and their successful cultivation of many crops, including lettuce, carrots, hot peppers, and potatoes, was so remarkable that the Nigerien government decided to initiate similar programs at fifty more secondary schools nationwide. Meanwhile, the Government of Zambia decreed that every primary school would teach agriculture to its students and have demonstration gardens. Africare participated at the Meheba Refugee Settlement in northwestern Zambia by constructing teacher housing, supporting agricultural agents, supplying tools and other needs, and providing farm equipment. Concurrently, Africare helped train a group of selected teenagers at the Isenge Youth Training and Settlement Center near Ndola, Zambia, in the Copperbelt. For various reasons, they had not finished school and were unemployed, but they showed an aptitude for farming. The Burroughs Corporation enabled Africare to provide a classroom setting for learning the principles of agriculture and supplies for small crops of corn, soybeans, sunflowers, and vegetables. Subsequently, vegetable production was increased by drilling a deep well and laying irrigation pipes.

Several more illustrations can further establish the positive impact of Africare's focus on vegetable growing. One thousand people in the Senegalese village of Keur Assane N'Diaye, just east of Dakar, were constrained in growing vegetables by a very dry climate and inadequate water. Africare helped them construct wells, including one fitted with a wind-powered pump, and water storage basins. Three hundred and fifty women in two villages of the Nigerien district of Boboye, with assistance from Africare, modestly began the intensive cultivation of thirty acres. Over time, they slowly dug more wells, improved their irrigation system, and cleared additional land. Their harvests of squash, potatoes, okra, and onions were impressive enough that in March 1984, the president of Niger, Senyi Kountche, visited them and praised their contribution to the country's food supply. Year after year, these women continued to excel in their garden.

Farmers everywhere across Africa faced similar hurdles, from the nature of the climate to the paucity of resources. Africare recognized that, with a modicum of input and oversight, it could have a valuable impact among rural populations, so the encouragement of vegetable production became one of its key programs, continent-wide. The examples cited here were replicated in hundreds of locations over the next thirty years and vegetables became important in enhancing the diet of African families.

Helping farmers upgrade the quality and increase the quantity of rice, a major staple in the diets of many Africans, was another contribution to their better health. Africare's exceptional success with rice production in its Tara-integrated rural development project in Niger provided easily transferable knowledge to other African nations. It sought to improve crop yields by extending the infrastructure in rural communities, teaching better agricultural techniques, enlarging the number of growers engaged in rice production, and expanding the amount of land under rice cultivation. As with vegetable gardening, extension agents worked closely with farmers. Farm-to-market roads were up-graded or newly built. Demonstration plots tested which varieties of rice grew best and the steps necessary to nurture rice from the seed to the dinner table. The construction of rat-resistant granaries that advanced the safe storage of rice and prevented half its loss provided knowledge that had important applications elsewhere in villages. The provision of a reliable water supply by way of new or rebuilt wells, irrigation, and electric pumps was necessary, too, in most locations. One example is the village of Richard Toll, north of Dakar,

Senegal, where families cleared more than two hundred acres of land along the banks of the Senegal River for new rice production. Africare, with support from Alpha Kappa Alpha sorority and USAID, built a large electric pump to raise water from the river to the fields. Local men did the preliminary preparation of digging channels through sand and rock for the placement of pipes and equipment.

The job in Richard Toll relied on cooperation of Africare employees and villagers. A larger, multifaceted five-year project (1981-86) to increase rice production and small farmer income in northeastern Zambia, however, illustrates challenges that arose when government ministries and Africare tackled a much more intricate challenge together. In this case, agricultural extension activities among farmers in Chama District were basic to the program and the Government of Zambia's Ministry of Agriculture and Water Development had agreed to provide extension personnel. It was never able to hire the full complement of workers and those assigned to Chama were deficient in training and motivation. The road construction promised by the government never occurred, due to erroneous cost estimates and lack of leadership. Its accounting skills were sorely lacking too. Africare officials realized, with hindsight, that the unsatisfactory performance of Zambia's participating ministry in Chama District was not due to indifference or disagreement, but rather to a shortage of administrative capacity and resources. Acknowledging the impossibility of determining the degree of success at the end of the project because of these problems and—equally as important—the incomplete and inaccurate baseline data used, evaluators for USAID concluded, nonetheless, that the project had increased rice production and had raised net income (primarily by introducing mechanized cultivation and intensive farming techniques). One notable achievement, they wrote, was the formation of farm management groups that were doing an excellent job of maintaining the tractors and other equipment supplied. They recommended greater coordination between the two sponsors and the elicitation of more input from farmers as well as more self-help aspects.

Recognizing that meat has often been a staple of village life, providing valuable protein, Africare encouraged projects across the continent that increased the production of cattle, pigs, sheep, and poultry. Its actual beginning in animal husbandry was in helping the people of the Sahel replenish their livestock after the Sahelian drought. When Africare entered southern Africa, it found that cattle in Zambia and

Zimbabwe, nations with a large stake in this economic activity, were susceptible to fatal tick-borne diseases. Africare constructed large tanks in various locations that could be filled with pesticide. These dip-tanks, which Africare also placed in other cattle producing nations, enabled communities to preserve both an important source of income and a basic part of their diets. Somalia was another nation in the 1980s whose economy was heavily reliant on cattle production. Two-thirds of the population was engaged in this activity and 70% of the country's foreign exchange came from it. The biggest problems were frequent droughts and land degradation. Calculated to reverse the long-term consequences of these environmental blows, Africare's plan was to persuade communities in a northeastern region to harvest rainwater and to construct reservoirs where livestock could be watered and ground cover grown. This initiative in rangeland management laid the foundation for later programs in Tanzania. Africare also assisted Somalia's National Range Agency in its pilot effort to pinpoint species of grass best suited to dry-season planting nationwide by establishing a twenty-five acre fodder production nursery.

All over Africa south of the Sahara are examples of Africare efforts to increase the output of poultry, pigs, and sheep. In the Casamance region of Senegal, the southern department separated from the rest of the nation by The Gambia, Africare encouraged growers of all three species of livestock, with the help of the Heifer Project International and the United Methodist Committee on Relief (UMCOR). Pig farming was especially welcome in such nations of southern Africa as Zimbabwe. Four of many nations where poultry breeders gained from Africare attention were Burkina Faso, Niger, Somalia, and Mozambique. Southwest of Ouagadougou and close to the northern border of Ghana, residents in Leo, Burkina Faso, for example, raised hens and roosters at a poultry center established by Africare. Breeding activities, egg production, and increased meat availability locally subsequently inspired students at a number of young farmer schools, using their own money, to build chicken coops and learn the skill. Extension staff from the center visited these schools and other poultry producers to give vaccinations and medical advice. A particularly heartening aspect of this Africare project was the likelihood of long-term growth and the prospects for sustainability of its effort. Another remarkable story occurred in four villages of Niger in the mid-1980s. Two hundred and forty women joined in cooperatives received start-up stocks of hens, training in the management of chickens, and assistance in the construction of chicken coops. In one year's time, they raised 2,800 hens that produced 200,000 eggs. Not all such ventures were successful. Sometimes, wind storms destroyed hen houses or chickens died of disease; not infrequently participants lacked capital to begin anew.

The milk, cheese, and meat produced by sheep had the advantage of benefitting individual household meals and income in three ways. Moreover, milk and cheese were renewable resources. An early Africare endeavor in sheep-raising occurred with one hundred and forty families in the Tangenhamo Cooperative, a part of its large integrated rural development program in the Gaerezi Settlement Area of eastern Zimbabwe. This was 1983, just after Zimbabwe achieved independence and began to move black farmers from the poor, overworked, and overcrowded tribal trust lands allotted them by Rhodesian white governments to more productive agricultural areas. In successive years, Africare helped the Gaerezi people build wells, cattle dip tanks, a health clinic, and other elements of infrastructure. The personal side of the project included adult literacy and cooperative management training. To its dismay, however, Africare found that the Gaerezi, who had a special pre-independence relationship with Robert Mugabe, were not disposed to working together for capitalist aims. The reconstitution of sheep herds in West Africa, a continuation of Africare tradition in the Sahel after the drought, was more successful. The women of Farak, Niger, provide another positive example from the late 1980s.

In many of the illustrations of crop cultivation and animal husbandry just mentioned, improving water access was *sine qua non*. Indeed, Africare employees, over the years, found few villages that did not put water at or near the top of their list of development priorities. The climatic and environmental conditions of most African nations, together with the technological inability for deep drilling or efficient water distribution, would seem to explain and support that conclusion. After Africare built wells with Lilly Endowment funding, donors entrusted the organization with so many well-digging operations in West Africa that it became acknowledged as the leading PVO in that enterprise. Its reputation brought invitations from governmental agencies and private foundations to spearhead water resource efforts across Africa. The construction of wells and boreholes was just one of many water resource activities in which Africare engaged. In many locales, it built earthen dams and reservoirs. In other places, it built large-scale irrigation systems. A specific use of water to which Africare applied its knowledge of hydrology was that of fish culture.

Fish is food of high protein value that Africare program planners, from the early 1980s, promoted in discussions with villagers and government ministries. With Africa's many estuaries, rivers, and lakes, fish was already appreciated as a food, but in many places there had been over-fishing or fishermen lacked seaworthy boats and effective nets. Africare saw aquaculture as one answer to the food shortage in some nations and as contributing nutrients to local diets elsewhere. Close to the Malian village of San, just inland from the Bani River, a major tributary of the Niger, Africare completed a fish breeding station in 1983. The ten ponds, four holding tanks, canals and drainage, water pumps, and laboratory had the goal of countering overfishing in the region. Africare imported more than a thousand fingerlings from the Ivory Coast and, in six months time, the number had doubled, proving the feasibility of the Mali location. Africare and Malian extension agents helped local farmers improve their own fish breeding operations and encouraged others to raise fish. Several years later, when the effects of drought threatened the viability of the project, Africare helped fishermen run pipe from the Bani to the ponds and install a pump to move water.

Enabling fishermen to engage in profitable fishing by giving them access to credit was another solution to the challenge of food insufficiency. The Kafue River Basin covers around 20% of the total land area of Zambia and, though relatively small, accounts for half of the nation's population and a great concentration of mining, industrial, and agricultural activities. One section, the Kafue Flats, an extensive region of wetlands and floodplains along the Kafue River west of Lusaka, has so little slope that it may take two months for water to pass through, hence the name "flats." The local people, the Lozi, have followed the ebb and flow of water forever, moving villages toward the river and away from the river according to the season, as they engaged in cattle grazing, agriculture, and traditional fisheries. In the 1980s, fishermen were hampered in getting good catches because of their poor boats and meager equipment. Africare saw the opportunity to make a difference by offering self-sustaining revolving credit funds. With a Lilly Endowment grant and the cooperation of several Zambian sponsors, including Barclays Bank, more than $20,000 was lent to participants chosen by the fishermen themselves through their own oversight committees. As fate would have it, a drought curtailed fishing partially during the project span, but the fishermen turned to vegetable gardening and repaid the loans.

Lake Madarounfa, Niger—a small, shallow body of water near the border with Nigeria—and its large city of Katsina offered year-round fishing, but local fishermen lacked training, adequate equipment, credit, and extension services. Africare assisted seventy-five of them by constructing a research station, hiring extension agents, and establishing a revolving credit fund that enabled them to buy boats and nets. An additional feature of the plan was the teaching of basic literacy and elements of credit management. The fishermen were successful to the point of having surplus fish to sell retail and to donate to the nutrition program at the Madarounfa Maternal and Child Health Clinic. After three years, a larger group of fishermen reorganized its cooperative into subgroups representing villages so there would be better coordination of fishing activities and expansion to nearby ponds. The result was a substantial increase in the catch, going from two and a half tons of fish in the first half of 1988 to eight and a half tons in the corresponding period of 1989.

As Africare gained more working experience with basic agriculture, it began to expand its range of activities. Its efforts in African nations had helped farmers in many communities increase the productivity of their crops, but, in some respects, that success was bittersweet because of the additional labor it conferred on them. Where the harvest was sunflower seeds, sesame seeds, soybeans, or corn, women (it was usually women) had to pound it to extract cooking oil, an arduous and inefficient task with the primitive equipment they had. Late in the 1980s, Africare introduced newly-invented mechanical presses into a few villages of southern Africa and, thereafter, facilitated their spread to thousands of communities. The transfer of other new technology, such as improved milling equipment and systems for converting soy beans into various nutritious food products, likewise added value to crops while reducing the onerous labor required.

The story behind the creation of the oil presses is interesting in itself. Appropriate Technology International (ATI), a small, non-profit organization in Washington, D.C., recognized in the mid-1980s that rural populations in sub-Saharan Africa, not having access to locally processed oil, were forced to pay high prices for either imported oil or oil produced by urban processors. It set out to invent a machine appropriate for village-level use and developed one, called a ram press, that had a long handle that two men pulled down to squeeze oilseeds through a metal cage. Later, ATI improved the design to a size where one woman could operate it. The advantages of this new technology were advertised as low cost and simplicity, faster processing time of raw materials, and a much higher yield compared to the amount produced using traditional methods. There were many potential benefits to the community too. Farmers would have a greater incentive to increase productivity. Local consumers could purchase much cheaper cooking oil than before. There would be more money in the community, especially in the hands of women. In addition, the availability of fodder in the form of oilseed cake, the roughage left over after pressing, would contribute to animal husbandry, particularly of cattle, in the area. An entrepreneurial spirit would be fostered as participants, from farmers to traders, learned principles of business management.

This new technology spread rapidly to many African nations because oil presses could be made by small manufacturing companies wherever there were materials. One oilseed processing project in Zambia provides a good test case of how theories about their value corresponded to the reality of their usage. During the late 1980s, Zambia's annual production of edible oil consistently failed to fill the gap in domestic demand caused by the suspension of crude oil vegetable imports from the United States under the P.L. 480 program, the limitations of commercial producers, and by the government's structural adjustment policies. The Ministry of Agriculture, Food and Fisheries (MAFF) decided to collaborate with Africare and some other groups to promote locally-made oil presses that would be adopted at the village level. Hence, in the early 1990s, Africare contracted with four different engineering firms to make the Yenga Oilseed Press for farmers in the southern province of the country, in particular for those growing sunflowers. Altogether, 424 machines were sold between 1992 and 1998, 56% through Africare employees and 44% by various marketing agents. The total cost of acquisition, accessories, and a training component for a household was less than US $200, but out of the reach of many prospective buyers. One solution, adopted mainly by women, was to form clubs that purchased the equipment.

An important first lesson for Africare in Zambia was the value of encouraging the adoption of oil presses by giving demonstrations in rural areas to show how they work and their advantages. Another vital need was to train new owners in the operation, maintenance, and repair of the machines. A third essential mission was to make available to farmers improved sunflower seeds that yielded large crops and were easy to crush for oil. All of these tasks required a large roster of extension workers to visit villages in order to mentor farmers and distribute seeds. In looking at Africare's performance in these three aspects, it is clear that its awareness campaigns were cost effective; 47% of Yenga oil press owners had heard about them during demonstrations, more than through any other source. However, within several years, only 47% of total Yenga press owners were active, most of them hardly crushing a fifty kilogram bag of sunflower seeds a day (the value of its oil would be from US $6.76 to US $9). The critical factor for some of them was not the efficiency of the machinery, but the availability of harvest. For other owners, it was a matter of broken equipment left unrepaired because of the owners' unfamiliarity with the technology or a shortage of spare parts. There was a scarcity of local artisans with the capacity to fabricate parts and of neighborhood dealers from whom to purchase replacements. The problem was compounded by a lack of standardization among the manufacturing companies and the incompatibility of components for older machines.

Although Africare distributed more than twenty-two metric tons of seeds in the southern province of Zambia in the 1990s, sunflower production declined while that of corn, cotton, and peanuts increased significantly. The reasons were two: an inability of farmers to buy improved seeds locally at the time of planting and the non-affordability of the seeds. Farmers simply reduced the area under cultivation and/or switched to other crops. Another factor in their reducing sunflower cultivation was the decrease in the demand for local oil and a consequent fall in prices for their oil precipitated by national government liberalization policies that allowed for cheap imported oil to be dumped in Zambia.

In spite of these deficiencies and difficulties in southern Zambia, the introduction of Yenga oil presses demonstrated that with greater crop production, expansion of the market outside the local towns, and increasing the economies of scale among the farmers, crushing sunflower could be a profitable business. The cooking oil extracted through the Yenga press enjoyed popularity in the area because its natural properties and high viscosity made it desirable for frying fritters, a dietary specialty. Requiring only manual labor, it was a relatively inexpensive way for households to enhance their food and nutrition security. A field survey found that most farmers who purchased presses experienced a rise in household income, an improvement in their life style, and a greater ability to meet family financial needs. They were pleased to see their social status elevated too. At the community level, the oilseed processing technology added value to crops, encouraged farmers to try new, improved strains of sunflowers, increased business for tradespeople and artisans, and where there was no livestock, provided sunflower cake that could be used as manure in vegetable gardens. A professional evaluation of the oilseed processing project by the Food and Agriculture Organization (FAO) in January 2002 agreed that the introduction of the Yenga oil press to Zambia had contributed to the enhanced income and improved nutrition of owners while offering affordable sources of cooking oil for local consumers at the household level. It also praised the technology for other benefits. Nevertheless, this Africare project is a good example of partial success and partial failure if measured by the numbers at its formal conclusion. Were sustainability of its program counted, Africare would score well in that a group of citizens formed the Sunflower and Yenga Press Association of Zambia in the late 1990s to take over and continue the business operations Africare had organized. Contemporaneously with its work in southern Zambia, Africare accelerated the distribution of presses to women's cooperatives and farmer groups in Mozambique, Zimbabwe, and other African nations.

Processing such crops as tomatoes and peanuts was also arduous and inefficient, given the methods used in most African communities. The first step, however, was to improve the yield and the profit in farming. There is a good example from Chad that illustrates how positive change can be brought about through the efforts of knowledgeable agricultural agents and the entry of simple new machinery. Ouaddai Prefecture begins almost three hundred miles east of N'Djamena, Chad's capital, and ends at the border with Sudan. While it is deep in the Sahel and suffers often from drought, its farmers, using irrigation, raise large quantities of vegetables, mainly onions, tomatoes, and garlic. Africare representatives found that producers, not having access to regional and national market prices because of their isolation, were unable to negotiate on an even footing with buyers for the going rate of vegetables. Some did walk up to three days to reach the large daily market in Abéché, the prefectural capital, because their local markets were held just once weekly. Among other deficiencies that limited the success of farmers in Ouaddai were inadequate storage facilities.

Farmers could not maximize their profits by holding vegetables past the prime of the harvest season. Both of these problems were tackled by a large Africare project in the early 1990s in which staff members gathered statistics and devised solutions to improve knowledge of fair market prices and to lengthen the shelf life of onions and garlic.

The next step was upgrading the processing of tomatoes and peanuts. Traditionally, farmers sliced their ripe tomatoes in half and spread them on the ground in the sun to dry, which took fifteen days. The dried tomatoes were then bagged and taken to mills in N'Djamena. They were pulverized into powder, repackaged, and distributed over the country, including back to Ouaddai Prefecture. Africare field-tested a platform made of local materials on which tomatoes dried in nine days, retained their natural red color, and were free of dirt and other contaminants. There was good acceptance of the innovation and farmers learned that consumers would pay more for the better quality dry tomato. The stage after this was to give farmers the ability to capture the value added to tomatoes by milling them locally into powder. Here, Africare ran into resistance. In villages where Africare representatives were working, almost all tomato growers preferred to sell dried tomatoes rather than powder and, furthermore, not one of the male cooperatives was willing to operate an Africare-supplied mill. There were several explanations, but one may have been that the men, already overworked, did not want to take time from their ordinary chores to travel to Abéché, where, for logistical reasons, the mill was located. Africare overcame this problem by recruiting a women's group, a sensible choice because more than 90% of tomato marketing and milling is done by women. The results were enhanced profits for tomato growers and traders and better prices for consumers. In one aspect alone there was considerable saving. That saving occurred in transportation costs, since dried tomatoes no longer had to be taken to N'Djamena and tomato powder could be distributed from Abéché. There were setbacks, as when motors had to be replaced because they burned out after a relatively short service life. This new technology, however, was transformational for a remote people eking out a living in a severe climate. After several years, Africare sold the mill to the women's cooperative, which paid for it through a five-year loan, continued to operate it, and expanded business.

Peanuts made up more than a third of the rain-fed crops grown in Ouaddai Prefecture, but peanut oil, preferred by cooks, was always in short supply because only a negligible amount of the peanut harvest went into its production. The reason was the tedious traditional extraction process that most women used. In the only large town, Abéché, dehulling was done by a hand-operated tool and a peanut paste was made by using a cereal-grinding mill. Women in villages, however, where most lived, dehulled peanuts by hand and ground them by pestle and mortar. In either case, the paste was then boiled and squeezed to extract the oil. Africare selected six villages in Ouaddai and distributed, on a cost basis, twenty-four improved hand mills (originally designed for corn grinding) among six women's groups. Finding that the size of the groups limited access of members to the mills, Africare set up a revolving credit fund so they could purchase more of them, ideally making one available to each household. Data collected during the first year and a half showed that, whereas a woman using traditional methods had an output of three liters a day, she produced ten liters if she used an improved hand mill. The net result was that, during that time, women increased their income from peanut oil processing by 57%.

Another example of how the introduction of simple new technology can have a significant impact in communities comes from the invention of the VitaGoat food processing system by Brian Harrigan, founder of the Canadian organization Malnutrition Matters, in 2002. It was designed initially for use with soy beans, which have the advantages of being cheaper to produce, having a higher yield per acre, and being less labor intensive than other crops such as corn. In some African nations such as Zimbabwe, however, the precursor to implementing the VitaGoat program was persuading farmers to begin cultivating soy beans in addition to the cotton and corn that they traditionally grew. The VitaGoat consists of four main components: a steam boiler that burns wood, other hard fuels, or liquid gas; a bicycle grinder with adjustable speed pulleys; a stainless steel cooker; and a stainless steel press. The process begins by grinding soy beans into a coarse meal that is then cooked and, finally, passed through the press to make milk. From it, tofu and yogurt can be derived. In actual usage, the VitaGoat has many more applications than these. Certain parts of the equipment can be used to prepare fruit and vegetable sauces, purees, and juices. The bicycle grinder is handy for pulverizing many grains into flours and meals or for making peanut butter. Malnutrition Matters calculated that, with a base price of $2800, the VitaGoat would pay for itself in one year if it were operated three or four hours a day. Subsequently, the VitaCow (also called SoyCow), which requires electricity and will process only soy beans, was developed by engineers at Malnutrition Matters.

Africare began installing VitaGoats in African nations in 2004, with the selection of Guinea, Chad, and Mozambique for pilot projects. In Dinguiraye, Guinea, where Africare was deeply involved in monetizing commodities for increased food security, a women's group, Diarou Folly, undertook the operation of a VitaGoat as a micro-enterprise. Soymilk became a popular drink, but the women were limited in their success by a shortage of soy beans to process and by equipment breakage. Since replacement parts had to come from Canada, there was sometimes an interruption of months in production. The women later decided to process shea nuts into shea butter. This was so successful that two other women's groups also purchased VitaGoats. The twenty people in Chad who each contributed $50 to getting a VitaGoat and formed a group to run the business were fairly successful financially, but abandoned the effort within several years. They had insufficient access to raw materials (soy beans), lacked refrigeration to preserve the output of the VitaGoat, and keenly missed the support of Africare staff members who had left the area.

The Mozambique pilot program is a particularly illuminating case study of one individual's effort to improve her financial position while benefitting a whole community. Rita Lazaro was a widow in the Manica Province of Mozambique who had participated in Africare's large food security project in the late 1990s by demonstrating good nutrition and hygiene practices to local women. During this time, she had also acquired an oil press to supplement her income and employed three workers to crush sesame and sunflower seeds. Because of her energy and skill, Africare picked her to receive the first VitaGoat to come to Mozambique; it arrived at the port of Maputo in March 2004. After two days undergoing customs clearance, the equipment was transported to her large compound in the Sussendenga district and a technician spent another two days assembling it. Lazaro used the VitaGoat only to handle soy beans and was immediately successful in producing a large quantity of milk every day. Soon thereafter, though, problems arose. The provincial health authorities closed her operation because of their concern about sanitation and hygiene. A lack of raw materials made it impossible for her to utilize the machinery to its capacity and she found that she needed better packaging to extend the life of the milk beyond twenty-four hours. Finally, she learned from its functioning that, because of fumes and sparks, the boiler should be in a building separate from the rest of the mechanism. That required more capital expenditure. The fundamental difficulty for Lazaro was finding a consistent market for her products, particularly with their short shelf-life. Nevertheless, she has persevered to the point that she now owns a house with indoor toilet and a corral of livestock.

After the installation of VitaGoats in Guinea, Chad, and Mozambique in 2004, Africare decided to introduce VitaCows to seven African countries, including Nigeria, Benin, Uganda, and Zimbabwe. A women's farming group in Zimbabwe that was participating in a soybean production program initially had great success with the VitaCow, but later ceased operation because of technical problems. In Uganda, the cost and inconsistent supply of electricity and competition from locally produced cow's milk resulted in mediocre success. Various difficulties in other countries likewise made VitaCows a poor choice for most Africare projects because they were too complicated and expensive to function well under existing circumstances. Subsequently, Africare went back to VitaGoats, which it incorporated in food security programs in Namibia, Burkina Faso, and Rwanda. In particular, soy milk became important in the HIV/AIDS fight because its high nutritional value was beneficial to patients receiving anti-retroviral therapy (ARV). Another advantageous feature of the machinery was the opportunity to use HIV/AIDS volunteers in its operation.

An environmental catastrophe gave Africare its first real entry into African development. After assisting nations, international agencies, and other charities in relief assistance, Africare considered the best strategies for mitigating future natural disasters. Consequently, it began promoting programs in reforestation, establishment of wood lots, windbreaks, erosion control, local tree nurseries, and forestry extension services. An early effort incorporated a goal to plant 330 acres of trees in selected villages into the integrated rural development (IRD) project at Seguenega, Upper Volta. By the time of the mid-project evaluation, almost half of the acreage had been planted, but there was a low survival rate (40 to 60%) and there were other difficulties. The first problem was an insufficient supply of water for the transplants to become established. Trampling or grazing by livestock, lack of safe pesticides, and the use of extremely marginal land for the trees also undermined their viability. These were physical limitations. At the human level, villagers could not agree on whose land the trees would be planted or who owned the trees once they reached maturity. All of this was compounded by a delay in the distribution of seedlings and by the lack of qualified technical personnel who could guide participants. The heart of the issue, wrote the evaluators, was the failure of Africare to convey to the community the purpose of reforestation, which was soil conservation. An additional problem became the unwillingness of the villagers to take an interest in an activity whose benefits were years away. This sector of the overall IRD project proved to be one of the least successful in reaching its objectives.

The inclusion, where appropriate, of different types of environmental enhancement became standard in the designs of most large multifaceted, million dollar Africare projects thereafter, but often more limited plans were carried out separately through the donations of small philanthropies, churches, citizen groups, and individuals. One example is the $2,820 that the Albert Kunstadter Family Foundation gave in 1978 for the creation of a five acre demonstration woodlot in Senegal, where population increase and drought had put severe pressures on the availability of wood. Building materials, stakes, and fencing were scarce. Women and children found every day's search for firewood more difficult than the day before and they often reduced live trees to skeletons with just one branch as other sources vanished. A subsequent private grant to Africare from the al Dir'iyyah Institute paid for the cost of a forty-four acre lot. After their success, other private donors, USAID, and the Senegalese government supported the spread of woodlots and regional nurseries and the training of farmers in their management. USAID, for example, funded a five-village reforestation project in which 475 acres of communal forests were established in the regions of Kaolack and Thies. More than 90% of the trees survived. Through Africare efforts at that time, thirty-five thousand Senegalese benefitted from its attention to agro forestry.

There were similar endeavors elsewhere in Africa during the 1980s, most notably in Somalia and Burkina Faso, but Africare did not draw any comprehensive picture of all the ways it tackled environmental challenges until a major emphasis occurred in the 1990s. Beginning in 1991, Africare began to stress the balance between nature and human activities, the need to conserve natural resources, and the importance of including environmental management in its programs. The following passage from the annual report that year referred specifically to West Africa, but the crisis existed over the entire continent:

> Most of West African nations fall within the Sahelian zone. Many include parts of the Sahara itself. As such, they have some of the

harshest, driest environments on earth. Yet, for centuries, millions of West Africans have survived and made their living on these lands. In so doing, however, as populations have increased and national economies have changed, the fragile balance between nature and humankind has been lost. Farmers must produce more food, so they over-cultivate their fields, leading to soil erosion and infertility. Herders over-graze their livestock. Householders, pressed for wood for fuel and construction, denude the countryside of trees, shrubs and other ground cover. All these actions, never intended to be environmentally destructive, have, nevertheless, become exactly that.

These trends Africare set out to reverse with renewed energy.

Rwanda was among the numerous African nations where Africare attempted to interconnect environmental improvements. It began working there in 1983 following the influx of 45,000 refugees from Uganda. After distributing 180 tons of clothing, Africare designed a refugee resettlement project around Lake Nasho, which is at the southern tip of Kagera National Park just inside the border with Tanzania. The area was relatively unpopulated and fertile, but infested with tsetse flies, which cause sleeping sickness, and deficient in potable water. The original idea was to overcome these problems and provide a permanent refuge for 2,500 Ugandan cattle herders. However, they returned home and Rwandan farmers migrated in. What was to be refugee resettlement assistance metamorphosed into a multifaceted development agenda that continued through the decade and on into the 1990s, encompassing more and more elements of environmental supervision. One of the first undertakings was to replace the destructive pattern of wood collection by supporting reforestation efforts. Agricultural groups in six villages and surrounding provinces received thousands of fast growing seedlings that, as they matured into trees, were selectively harvested for fuel and for construction materials. Africare also introduced fuel-efficient stoves into two hundred households. This good progress was sadly interrupted early in 1994 when civil war erupted following the assassination of the Rwandan president. Africare supplied humanitarian relief for the thousands of Rwandans who crossed the nearby border to Tanzania. Within the year, an uneasy peace settled over Rwanda and, thereafter, Africare shifted to postwar reconstruction around Lake Nasho. It picked up where it had left off in its earlier efforts to preserve the habitat by helping to rebuild the infrastructure and by establishing new villages for returning refugees.

Concurrently, Africare spread its broad approach to environmental improvement elsewhere in Rwanda through training farmers to use terracing to control soil erosion on hillsides.

At the same time that Africare encountered difficulties in establishing a long-term environmental management plan in Rwanda—the early 1990s—it began similar, but even more inclusive undertakings in Senegal and in Tanzania. The Kaolack Agricultural Enterprise Development Program (KAED), an $8,000,000 USAID-sponsored project, ran for six years in the Kaolack region of Senegal, about a hundred miles southeast of Dakar. The goal was to increase agricultural productivity and farm income through sustainable use of natural resources. Demographic pressures and changes in climate had caused degradation of the environment for a population relying on traditional methods of cultivation. Africare's job was to train farmers in the restoration and preservation of soil fertility and to demonstrate new agricultural techniques. It also wanted to provide infrastructure and needed equipment, offer literacy and management training, organize a rural credit system, and ensure the participation of women.

Utilizing an already established Senegalese approach to community development, Africare organized groups that it called Agricultural-Based Enterprises (ABEs) in fifty-six villages. These had institutional and legal status under national law. A large, specialized staff worked at the field level to familiarize local citizens with the strategy and to solicit their input about desired objectives. Central to the program was the creation of a ten-acre demonstration field within walking distance of each village. Obtaining the title to such a piece became a great challenge because 80% of ABE membership consisted of women and, as typical in Africa, few women had outright control of land. In Kaolack, for example, 41% of female members of ABEs borrowed fields that they farmed and only 32% of women had inherited land. [By the end of the KAED project in 1998, most demonstration fields had been granted conditional titles by Rural Councils, which gave women a more secure access to land than previously held and recognized the equal right of women in legally recognized groups to be granted land titles.]

Once the demonstration plots were identified, Africare field agents introduced a wide range of new agricultural and environmental techniques and practices. While the ABEs were free to grow what crops they wished, they had to rotate the types, so most planted half of the area in peanuts and the other half in millet or in millet and something else. Every field required live fencing around it to keep out livestock and retard soil erosion. Furthermore, windbreaks of trees that preserved the top soil and reduced water loss by evaporation were planted within it. When mature, they could provide fuel, construction material, livestock forage, and ingredients for traditional medicines. One particularly valuable innovation was the introduction of the idea of composting crop residues. In the past, whether peanuts, millet, or other crops, the stems, leaves, stalks, and roots were sold, fed to animals, or burned at the end of the harvest. Very little organic residue was incorporated into the soil. Years of following traditional practices had produced an agricultural region that was in a state of advanced soil degradation.

Two more contributions of the KAED program in Senegal were introduction of improved cooking stoves and help with setting up village tree nurseries. The traditional African stove consists of three stones in a triangle on which a pot is perched. As a result of an open flame, much of the heat produced by the firewood underneath is dispersed into the atmosphere. The improved stove, developed in East Africa, begins with the three stones, but embeds them into a low convex circular wall made of a fermented mixture of clay, millet chaff, cow manure, and water. One hole is left for insertion of firewood and, when the dried combination of materials is heated, the stove becomes as hard as ceramic. Africare found in Kaolack that the improved stoves required no more than a third as much fuel as the old ones, that they were transportable, and that they were even being given as wedding gifts or being sold as an income-generating activity by ABEs. The rate of adoption in the area was high, 43% among women members and 37% of ABE households.

Unlike O-lan, the thrifty wife in Pearl Buck's *The Good Earth* who buries the peach pit on her wedding day and lives to see it become symbolic of her own fruitfulness, most Africans were not so lucky with direct seeding of trees. Harsh environmental conditions jeopardized the success of this method and only careful nurturing in a monitored situation would work. However, ABE members in Kaolack had neither tools nor primary inputs until Africare provided watering cans, wheelbarrows, plastic planting bags, seeds, and pesticides. They had no nursery knowledge or skill until Africare field agents trained them. Ultimately, the ABEs established sixty-five village tree nurseries that produced a million tree seedlings for demonstration fields, village woodlots, and individual planting.

These and many other aspects of the KAED program in Kaolack left a permanent legacy of benefits to the local population, whether members of ABEs or not. Almost all residents of the fifty-six ABE villages acquired knowledge about the management of natural resources and a large percentage of them adopted at least one new technique. Demonstration fields illustrated improved agricultural practices to communities and soon non-participatory villages were emulating them. Classes in functional literacy and numeracy gave students, most of them women, more facility in running business enterprises and in handling their private affairs. Men and women with reading skills were better able to understand technical information that was being introduced to them too. As befitting the name, "agricultural business enterprises," these groups aimed to increase farm output, whether of an animal, cereal, or vegetable nature, so they could sell surpluses at the market or could trade in other commodities, such as homemade soap. They needed credit to get started, however. Africare, in conjunction with *Caisse Nationale du Credit Agricole du Senegal* (National Agricultural Credit Fund of Senegal), established a credit program and, subsequently, twenty-six ABEs organized their own revolving credit funds. Most of the borrowers were women and the repayment rate was nearly 100%.

The goal of increasing food security in the Kaolack region was at the heart of the KAED project and it succeeded. Whereas 80% of all households in ABE villages claimed an average annual shortage of cereals during approximately four months of the year in 1997, by the end of 1998, through village-level measures of credit and stockpiling, that time had been reduced by a month and a half. There was still great need in the area, but the local people now possessed more technical knowledge, new management skills, an enhanced infrastructure, and a greater institutional apparatus to continue the impressive progress they had made in the previous six years.

On the other side of the continent, Africare sponsored a resource-saving project aimed at increasing food security of quite a different character. From colonial times, Tanzania has been recognized for its outstanding wildlife populations, especially of elephants and lions. Both pre-independence and post-independence governments, which ultimately set aside a quarter of the country's land area for national parks, game reserves, and forest reserves, capitalized on tourism and big game hunting for a significant percentage of their revenue. In the 1970s and 1980s, however, in spite of the passage of the first wildlife conservation act in 1974, Tanzania's wildlife was nearly decimated by poachers seeking elephant tusks and black rhino horns and by villagers, suffering from the government's socialist policies, killing animals for subsistence. The crisis led to a government review of its wildlife management policies and organizational structure as well as to reaching out to international donors for help. Consequently, in 1998, the Government of Tanzania issued a new wildlife policy that envisioned village-based Wildlife Management Areas (WMAs) that "would allow rural communities and private land holders to manage wildlife on their land for their own benefit." Through this mechanism, villages would zone a portion of their land as a wildlife conservation area and, in return for not cultivating the section or inhabiting it, they would receive a quota of animals that they could either hunt themselves or sell to a hunting concession. The broader plan behind WMAs was to promote community conservation knowledge and action through the improved economic incentives. This is where Africare entered the picture.

The Ugalla ecosystem in central Tanzania southwest of Tabora is an area approximately the size of South Carolina with a million and a half people. Livestock grazing, agriculture, fishing, hunting, beekeeping, and harvesting of forest products provide the main sources of income, but they are jeopardized by a population growth of 3.6% per year and a small annual influx of refugees from Burundi. In the late 1990s, the central government sanctioned the formation of two wildlife management areas in Ugalla to complement the two game reserves and twenty-six forest reserves it had already established. Theoretically, they were to be under local control, while the central government was responsible for deciding national policy and providing technical assistance. Africare consequently received two and a half million dollars from USAID/Tanzania Mission for a five-year program involving one game reserve, Ugalla, and two proposed WMAs, Uyumbu and Ipole. It was called the Ugalla Community Conservation Project.

Africare analysis found numerous conservation problems in the Ugalla ecosystem. There was over-fishing and indiscriminate cutting of trees for fish smoking, construction of canoes, and charcoal making. Trees were killed by debarking them to make beehives. There was also excessive and uncontrolled timber harvesting. Deforestation was further accelerated by agricultural patterns and population pressure. Instead of leaving part of their lands fallow to be incorporated into the Wildlife Management Areas, villages were encroaching on the soon-to-be designated zones for the expansion of tobacco cultivation and for settlement. With tobacco, land was cleared for new crops and forests were cut to provide fuel wood for curing tobacco and building drying barns for tobacco leaves. Another environmental problem was the poaching of animals, easily done because of a paucity of game scouts to patrol the vast area.

Among Africare's many tasks was to change attitudes among the population about conservation and the responsible use of natural resources. It also had to convince villages to allocate part of their area so that the boundaries of the WMAs could be demarcated. Then, the promotion of appropriate technology and economic activities that utilized basic materials became important. A fundamental goal was assisting communities, government technical agencies, and district officials in strengthening institutional structures to control natural resources. For example, the Tanzanian Government required that all villages participating in the WMAs join in forming and registering a representative community-based organization that had management authority. Together, the communities then created a strategic plan, individual village land use plans, and a general zoning plan for approval by various government agencies.

Although five years is a short time to inculcate different ways of thinking about the environment and to persuade people to incorporate new practices into daily life, many of Africare's original objectives at Ugalla were largely achieved by 2004. Conservation officers and staff had been hired and, working with individual communities, had delineated the tentative boundaries of the WMAs. They had completed a base-line socio-economic study of the area and held consultations with local groups. Adoption of new ram presses for extracting oil from sunflower seeds, better beehives, and improved stoves represented valuable technical advances, although there was not wholehearted acceptance of the latter. Honey and beeswax production had increased. The training of 151 Village Natural Resources Scouts had reduced poaching and illegal acquisition of forest products significantly in the WMAs. Game Scouts were trained specifically for the Ugalla Game Reserve and, later, received radio communication equipment to improve law enforcement. As a result of the communities' collaboration in putting nearly a million acres of land under their control into a protected status, there was already a noticeable increase of fauna and flora within the ecosystem. It had become common to see elephants, reedbucks, warthogs, and other wildlife. Women were entering the mainstream of economic life by engaging in such previously male-exclusive activities as beekeeping and fishing, the latter being particularly significant environmentally because now both men and women were switching to fish farming. Women were also benefitting from the introduction of new cash crops such as sunflower, palm oil trees, and Moringa trees, all used for oil.

In spite of these achievements, it was apparent that enormous efforts would have to continue to sensitize people to the value of conservation so that they utilized environmentally-friendly practices and, through their communities, implemented resource management plans. The first phase of the Ugalla Community Conservation Project fell short, for example, in certain critical respects. Only nine of forty-two villages had been persuaded to initiate participatory land use management planning. Consequently, Africare staff succeeded in reaching just 74% of its modest goal of putting 442,000 acres under sustainable land use plans. The underlying problem was the ambiguity of the land tenure system. Another deficiency in the project was the absence of reliable baseline data on natural resources and the institutional/organizational makeup of the Ugalla locality. Africare depended on anecdotal evidence to evaluate the situation in the region when it began and measured accomplishments against estimates.

Overall, Africare received high marks in evaluations for developing awareness among the people in Ugalla about the environment and how they can contribute to their own welfare by cooperating in the management of their natural resources. Moreover, some project deficiencies were understandable in light of certain circumstances. For example, the failure of village governance to be fully participatory or of village committees to be more autonomous than they were was explainable by the history of traditional leadership and legitimacy in Tanzanian society and by past State dominance over decision-making. Finally, some issues, such as land titles, were beyond the control of Africare because it was up to the central government to promulgate the necessary legal instruments.

On the basis of the foundation that Africare laid during this first effort at instilling principles of environmental management among the residents of the Ugalla ecosystem, USAID awarded Africare contracts in 2005 for a second phase, called the Ugalla Community Landscape Conservation Project. The goals, in many respects, were a continuation of the original objectives: involve local residents in the management of natural resources, encourage them to adopt practices and new technologies that enhance the environment, help them create income-generating activities that are both profitable and environmentally sustainable, and assist them in organizing their game reserve and WMAs into beneficial enterprises. Some new objectives broadly concerned the provision of credit opportunities for farmers, digital mapping of natural resources in the Ugalla area, illustrating conservation farming techniques, and HIV/AIDS education. Africare specifically wants to stimulate beekeeping (organic honey is under consideration) and encourage beekeepers to establish savings and credit associations as well as cooperatives. It intends to expand fish farming and it recognizes that communities, especially if they plant the highly regenerative Miombo tree species, could find the timber industry as profitable as wildlife. What Africare is attempting in Ugalla is long-term and highly complex. Its ultimate success depends on many factors: Africare's own performance, the perseverance of the Tanzanian people, the cooperation of the Tanzanian Government, and the continued generosity of foreign donors. An official evaluation at the end of five or ten years cannot truly gauge the effect of any project, although donors, for understandable reasons, want immediate measurable results.

6

Monetization's Role in Food Security

By the late 1980s, after nearly two decades of service, Africare matured as an African American development organization. The geographical spread of its programs extended to every region of Africa. Funding sources stabilized to a pattern in which large undertakings—national health drives, refugee relief, dam construction, and integrated rural development—were underwritten by USAID, foundations, corporations, and similar benefactors. Churches, civic organizations, Africare chapters, clubs, and individual donors usually sponsored the more modest, but equally lifesaving efforts involving wells, vegetable gardens, dispensary repair, reforestation, and child nutrition. In 1987, however, Africare began considering an entirely different source of financing and another approach to its rural development projects in sub-Saharan Africa. After careful scrutiny of the U.S. Congress' Food for Peace Program, it set up its own Food for Development unit at headquarters in Washington. It then witnessed the slow evolution of a complex program that moved it into intricate dealings and regulatory requirements with such American government entities as USAID, the United States Department of Agriculture, and the United States Congress; with foreign governments; with shipping companies in the United States and abroad; with sales agents in African countries; and with African consumers. The new era was marked by the use of food from the U.S. Government and its monetization in African commercial channels to finance program costs.

President Dwight D. Eisenhower signed the Agricultural Trade Development and Assistance Act that established the P.L. 480 Program ("Food for Peace") in 1954. Among motives behind this Congressional initiative were recognition that American economic prosperity was interdependent with that of other nations and the awareness of American farmers that their incomes improved with overseas sales.

The disposal of agricultural surpluses was a particular goal and, in theory, it would stimulate international trade. There was also willingness in the Congress to continue such aid efforts as those of the Marshall Plan because they demonstrated American leadership in international affairs. A third motive had to do with the complicated subject of world-wide foreign exchange flow. At the end of World War II, most nations had what were called nonconvertible currencies, meaning that their money was useless outside their own national borders, and they had very low quantities of hard currency, or foreign exchange, such as the US dollar and the British pound. One part of the P.L. 480 Program (Title I) initially allowed commodities to be paid for with the local currency of the recipient countries. In this way, the United States stockpiled funds in these nations that it could use for humanitarian purposes locally and recipient countries conserved their foreign exchange, which they could spend in hard currency nations such as the United States. Sometimes recipient governments received food shipments on long-term credit and were able to use their national treasuries for internal development needs.

In the first years of the P.L. 480 Program, the bulk of transactions, in fact 70% were sales of commodities for local currencies or on credit (Title I) and the United States Department of Agriculture administered it. Title II of P.L. 480 provided for transfers of U.S. agricultural commodities to meet humanitarian food needs, whether emergency or non-emergency, in foreign countries. It was managed by USAID. At first, most of the food went overseas on a nonemergency government-to-government basis. Recipient governments sold it on the open market and disbursed the proceeds to their ministries. PVOs and such intergovernmental organizations as the United Nations' World Food Programme (WFP) and the International Red Cross also received nonemergency food, which they used for family feeding programs, reforestation, food-for-work, and similar projects. CARE and Catholic Relief Services were the two PVOs receiving the most grants. During P.L. 480's fifty year history, many adjustments were made in emphasis and detail, according to different presidential administrations and Congresses. Humanitarian aims, foreign policy objectives, human rights concerns, and just plain economic self-interest all figured in the formulation of P.L. 480 strategies at one time or another.

A change in Title II methodology came in the late 1980s as USAID became concerned about more frequently-occurring famines in

Africa. It decided to utilize additional PVOs in the delivery of its food aid programs and it suggested to C. Payne Lucas and Joseph Kennedy, Africare's top officials, that Africare consider becoming a cooperating sponsor, as participants are called. Their initial reaction was skepticism, on the basis of their belief that direct food distribution created dependency and, furthermore, did not fit Africare's philosophy that every activity must foster national development. Nonetheless, they were willing to investigate how Food for Peace operated and the experience and perspective of other PVOs with Title II involvement.

With a six-month pre-enhancement grant from USAID, an Africare team began a feasibility study in June 1987. The big question for Africare was whether food can be used to promote developmental activity within Africare's *modus operandi*. The staff study found that, in Africa, most PVOs began participation in Title II food distribution programs as spin-offs of their emergency relief operations after natural and man-made disasters. Establishing sound practices and precedents or enlisting local involvement received little attention, for it was a matter of getting food to desperate people any way it could be gotten to them. Africare decided, though, that food resources could have a far greater impact if their use was properly programmed, monitored, and integrated into a well-designed project. In fact, they could be more versatile and appropriate than other types of contributions. This was the main conclusion: "food is just one input in the design of a project."

As a result of its investigation, Africare formulated policy guidelines and strategy with which to enter a new era in its institutional history. It rejected the use of the terms "food aid" and "food assistance," opting instead for "food resource" because the latter better fit its intention to use food as an integrally programmed component in development projects. It insisted that external expenses accompanying the administration of food resources programs, such as moving commodities inland from coastal ports and hiring additional field staff, would have to be funded by non-Africare sources, and by that it meant primarily USAID. Africare proposed that food management costs be paid for through monetization itself, local currencies available from USAID missions in overseas posts, contributions from local communities in the recipient countries, and OutReach grants (from the State Department).

Monetization, most simply defined, is the sale of Title II agricultural commodities to one or more buyers in a foreign market. When cooperating sponsors were first allowed to use it in 1986, they could sell up to 30% of the commodities they received through Title II to cover warehousing and transport costs, but they could not apply any money toward financing the project itself. Africare recommended that USAID regulations be altered with respect to the quantity of commodities that could be monetized for these purposes. Further, it argued that cooperating sponsors should be allowed to employ proceeds in carrying out the programs. Africare subsequently had a major role in USAID's 1988 policy changes that embodied the suggestions. It also joined the Food Aid Consultative Group, an advisory panel to USAID and USDA, whose influence was important in writing the 1990 Farm Bill that committed the United States to enhancing food security in the developing world.

The practical and theoretical assumptions made by Africare staff were explored during two trips to West Africa in the fall of 1987, where the proposed Africare approach was discussed with host government officials, with USAID representatives, and with American embassy officers in Chad, Senegal, Guinea, Guinea-Bissau, and Cape Verde. The situation in Guinea-Bissau made that nation appear to offer the greatest opportunities for an inaugural Title II project. On the West African coast immediately south of Senegal, it had about a million citizens and a high population growth rate. Subsistence farming was the main occupation, but agricultural productivity was so low that the country was only 87% self-sufficient in food grain. Periodic droughts, low producer prices, lack of farmer inputs, and socialist economic policies made Guinea-Bissau one of the world's poorest countries. The Africare team that visited Guinea-Bissau learned, however, that the government was in the midst of radical reforms to monetary policies, to pricing and marketing systems, to agricultural programs, and to development goals. These were auspicious for what Africare hoped to do. Africare also received strong encouragement from the American ambassador to Guinea-Bissau, John Blacken, to become a cooperating sponsor of USAID and to open an office. Finally, when President Joao Bernardo Vieira, on a state visit to the United States in the spring of 1988, stopped by Africare House and invited Africare to come to Guinea-Bissau, this new endeavor seemed the way to continue.

The Tombali Sustainable Rural Initiatives Project in Guinea-Bissau provides a good example of the potential benefits of Title II programs to host countries, the collaboration of PVOs with USAID in furthering

American foreign policy objectives, and the methodology of the monetization process. In Guinea-Bissau, there was a food deficit. Rice, an important item in the diet, was being imported by Pakistani, Vietnamese, and other Asian companies, which were paid in foreign exchange. Since the rice that Africare brought into the country would enter under a USAID grant, the Government of Guinea-Bissau did not have to use its scarce foreign exchange or incur more debt in payment. Also important in the arrival of American-donated food was the mechanism of selling it and using the profits. The goal of the project was to encourage private sector investment and growth and to foster economic expansion, especially in agriculture and agro-industry. It was in line with USAID's objective of encouraging entrepreneurship through the Government of Guinea-Bissau's structural adjustment efforts. First, there was to be open bidding for American commodities among the traders of Bissau, the port city, which would stimulate a capitalist competitiveness. The profits would then go to promoting private producer and processor associations in villages of Tombali, the southern-most region. Members were to receive business and management education, access to credit from local banking institutions, and technical assistance in their enterprises.

Africare's new strategy of using Title II commodities in development projects began on July 9, 1990, when the "African Wave" arrived in Bissau with eighteen hundred metric tons of rice. Even before the ship's docking, Africare officials and representatives learned that food resource programs entailed tasks and bore ramifications unlike previous activities. Canvassing the needs of Guinea-Bissau consumers and monitoring price fluctuations on the open market were important in selecting commodities that Africare could monetize successfully. Curtiss Reed, Jr., the Africare resident representative in Guinea-Bissau, and his small staff worked on this weekly. There had to be compliance with the Bellmon Amendment, which was initiated by Senator Henry Bellmon of Oklahoma and became part of P.L. 480 legislation in 1977. It required adequate storage facilities in the recipient country when commodity shipments arrived in order to avoid spoilage and waste. Additionally, cooperating sponsors had to provide proof that importation of commodities would not result in a substantial disincentive to or interference with domestic production or marketing. Storage was not an issue with the rice aboard the "African Wave" because the buyer moved it immediately to his warehouses. Furthermore, the rice was not a disincentive or interference because it accounted for less than 4% of the total quantity of rice imported into Guinea-Bissau in 1990 and only two of Guinea-Bissau's eight regions had produced a surplus for sale. Finding local traders who would bid on the rice was the first real obstacle encountered by Africare. When it presented its initial invitation to bid in February 1990, no traders responded. It was such a new and alien concept that they dubbed it the "National Lottery." They wanted Africare to select and negotiate directly with one trader who would represent all traders interested in purchasing rice. Africare finally conceded and signed a sales agreement with a consortium of five traders headed by Amadou Djabi. Armed with a bank guarantee from the International Bank of Guinea-Bissau that Africare had arranged for the winning buyer, Djabi had his trucks in place when the "African Wave" began discharging its cargo.

Still, there were difficulties. Just over 3% of the bagged rice was lost due to pilferage by dock workers, who were paid such low wages that they expected a personal "allowance" of ten to twenty kilograms of rice per day as a part of work compensation. They themselves were forced to contribute a kilo or two of rice to a container in the guard house as they passed through port security on the way home at night. While the captain of the "African Wave" and his crew tried to prevent theft, they found the number of stevedores too many to control. The Port Authority in Bissau did little to stop the diversion of rice from its intended owner. For the discharge of later cargoes, Africare hired a competent surveying company to oversee unloading and loss was less than 1% of the commodities.

Another critical aspect of monetizing commodities is handling a product whose price is subject to fluctuations on world markets. Although the Africare staff studied these carefully, when the rice arrived in Guinea-Bissau, the world price had dropped to $260 per metric ton, lower than Africare had anticipated. Nonetheless, Africare succeeded in selling the rice for $290 per metric ton due to delayed shipments from Asian competitors and thereby raised $509,214 in Guinean pesos to finance the Tombali project. However, inflation, frequent currency devaluation, and a "gray" or parallel market situation in which the government controlled only 20% of the money supply eroded the value of Africare funds. Harvests were good in Guinea-Bissau in the following year of 1991 and rice was no longer scarce. Africare therefore switched to importing wheat flour and vegetable oil, the latter being particularly suitable because of its higher value than grains and its compactness in shipping. Africare found buyers and was gratified that the number of traders entering bids increased considerably, although it was a continual challenge to organize the bidding process so that dominant merchants like Amadou Djabi, who could buy whole ship loads, were joined by smaller traders who wanted partial lots.

As for Tombali, what were the results? The first change occurred not in the communities of this southern region, but in the capitol corridors in Bissau. It was Africare's success in getting the government of Guinea-Bissau to reorient its position about the role of PVOs in the expansion of the nation's private sector. Since independence in 1973, the government had followed a socialist model of development in which it regulated most aspects of the economy. It expected the Tombali project to be an extension of the state, with Africare implementing it through regime ministries, civil servants, and infrastructure. Reporting was to be to the government's administrative structures. In fact, other PVOS working in Guinea-Bissau before Africare had operated under these conditions and most of them, representing European nations, were comfortable with a socialist environment. Africare insisted on providing assistance directly from the American private sector to the Guinea-Bissau private sector with minimal constraints from governmental agencies. For a year, debate raged within official circles between those who wanted to continue past policies and reformists who called for a more laissez-faire situation that would allow for a market-driven economy to emerge. While the controversy delayed the beginning of the Tombali project, the government's ultimate concession to Africare established a precedent quickly noted by other members of the international donor community, who then applied for permission to take their programs directly to intended beneficiaries.

At the local level, the Tombali project planned to strengthen producer and processor associations by helping their members expand their knowledge of the commercial world. These were groups of fruit growers, horticulturalists, soap makers, craftsmen, rice processors, and fishermen. They were already in existence when Africare proposed its program, but were either in their early stages or were moribund because of government lethargy. One reason to increase their profitability was to slow or even reverse the accelerating rural to urban migration process that was upsetting the socio-economic balance within individual households and within communities. Africare initially selected four of the existing sixty-seven cooperatives for a

pilot phase. It then chose men and women to become business management trainers who went to villages and taught basic principles of
importing and exporting, of accounting, and of improved production
techniques. Soon, the list grew to thirty-nine cooperatives. Finding
sources of credit for the associations slowed their progress at first, but
Africare persuaded SOLIDAMI, a Guinea-Bissau government agency
established to promote, facilitate, and advance the work of NGOs on
sustainable development and microfinance, to expand its service area
to the Tombali region. After a brief trial arrangement with that bureau,
however, Africare decided to set up its own credit system.

One of the benefits of the Africare project to people in the Tombali
region, not just to association members engaged in growing fruit trees
or in horticulture, was in diversification of crops. The government's
emphasis in the past had been on the cultivation of rice for domestic
consumption and on harvesting cashews, peanuts, and palm oil nuts
for export. This dangerous dependence on a few agricultural products
put the population at risk of hunger and the national economy in peril.
Reinvigorated cooperatives coached by Africare business trainers
were soon growing new vegetable, tuber, and fruit species along with
their traditional garden varieties. Other farmers in the communities,
observing the different plantings, imitated their neighbors. The local
diet was improved and a base for activities that could substantially
reinforce food security was established.

Concomitant with Africare efforts was the government's construction of a new paved road from north to south across the Tombali region
that gave many towns greater access to Bissau and to the neighboring
countries of Senegal and Guinea-Conakry. Keep in mind that there
were some villages where no one owned either a vehicle or a donkey
cart. Residents rarely saw a vehicle on a regular basis. Bicycles and
walking were the only means of transportation. As with many innovations, the new road had its advantages and disadvantages for local
people. Legal trading and clandestine and cross-border economic
activities all increased significantly. Farmers and small producers
had easier access to national and regional markets. They could also
exchange rice and other agricultural products for consumer goods
with foreign merchants who came into small inlet ports on the coast.
Cultivators of gardens and orchards had many more outlets for their
surplus than before. Fishermen could smoke or dry what fish that
they did not sell locally and take it to Senegal or Guinea-Conakry
for currency of greater stability than the Guinean peso. Associations

making furniture could expand their sales beyond the immediate locale. These were the winners. The losers were women soap makers in Daruda who, with the new road opening, could not compete with imported soap and blacksmiths in Saltinho who, finding their buckets noncompetitive with imports from Guinea-Conakry, would now have to turn to repairing bicycles and household wares.

In 1994, the first four-year implementation period was extended another four years, but new objectives were added in line with the mandate of a reorganized USAID that Food for Peace activities be monitored and evaluated according to their beneficial effects on the achievement of food security in host nations. Africare was now challenged to strengthen rural credit, to provide community-level infrastructure such as wells, roads, health posts, and schools, and to offer nutrition education and surveillance. It had to carry out a baseline socio-economic survey and gather statistics that gauged progress toward food security. These enhanced goals required an enormous programmatic leap for Africare, including the employment of a much larger Africare staff in Guinea-Bissau and cooperation with Guinean government professionals. They also entailed more external evaluations by USAID and adherence to a wider spectrum of regulations. Just hiring Guinean nationals was a terrific task because of the small number of educated and trained citizens available in the country. Africare was put into a further staffing dilemma with Tombali because local people, especially those already working there, believed that they should occupy the preeminent posts, such as that of coordinator. When Africare concluded that none was qualified and hired an expatriate, a decision contrary to its philosophy of building up the national development capacity, staff morale was affected.

Africare efforts during the second phase of the Tombali project concentrated on the additional objectives of USAID, but their initial implementation was delayed by personnel matters and other circumstances. New staff had to be recruited and trained, especially in the sensitive areas of loan management and nutritional education. The credit coordinator, working with producer and processor associations, faced obstacles in getting them to prepare good applications, to understand the intricacies of a credit system, and to request loans that would enhance or diversify their production rather than their trading activities. Nutrition volunteers, selected by their villages and numbering more than a hundred men and women, were taught improved dietary habits, breastfeeding and weaning practices, hygiene, and preventative health care. Returning home, their target audiences were pregnant and nursing women and families with small children. They found that they had to counter food taboos, persuade people to eat seafood and forest products that they ordinarily avoided, and demonstrate how to substitute cheaper food such as beans in meals for more expensive ingredients like eggs.

Building or repairing primary schools, health posts, well pumps, and roads and bridges or supplying hospital mattresses was a tangible aspect of the Tombali project and Africare achieved good results between 1994 and 1998. All of these improvements were considered in some way as giving the region more food security. One difficulty, however, was the lack of funds to staff schools or health posts once they were constructed, for operational costs were left up to local communities. Africare's work in Tombali was interrupted by the outbreak of a brief civil war in 1998 and although it wished to continue with the project, it withdrew from Guinea-Bissau shortly thereafter. The USAID mission in the country did the same. While not all goals were met, Africare left a legacy of trained national staff, of stronger producer and processor associations, of nutrition volunteers, and of visible improvements to the infrastructure.

The successful launching of the Title II program in Guinea-Bissau coincided with the creation of a competent and knowledgeable Food for Development staff in Washington and in the field. The first food program manager, Katharina Puffenberger, skillfully guided Curtiss Reed, Jr., and his staff during negotiations with the Government of Guinea-Bissau and in arranging for Tombali. She also investigated Guinea (Conakry), Burkina Faso, and Mozambique as possible locations for Title II projects and prepared a comprehensive handbook for training staff overseas and at headquarters. Family commitments later obliged her to exchange her position in Washington for one with USAID in Niger. Her successor, Judy Constable Bryson, came with more than twenty years of experience in sub-Saharan Africa, many of them spent administering P.L. 480 Title I and Title II programs for USAID. Joining Africare late in 1991, Bryson put the Food for Development unit in Washington on a firm organizational footing. She recruited local and overseas employees, led in-house orientation seminars, and held workshops in Africa for Africare country representatives in which they were primed to incorporate food resources in their project proposals. It was she, with the help of overseas staff, who drafted monetization requests for submission to USAID so Africare could expand its Title II operations.

As Africare employees planned for and administered the first monetization programs in Africa, they discovered that their approach to food aid was viewed with skepticism among some charities in the United States. Judy Bryson and Lee Thompson, commodity monetization manager from 1995 to 2005, learned early on that such organizations as CARE and Catholic Relief Services, big recipients of Title II funds, considered food as food, that is, that direct food distribution to needy people improved their food security. These cooperating sponsors denigrated the monetization of commodities through which profits paid for transportation from the American port, handling and storage in the African port, and the costs of a development project as a perversion of Title II's intent. They failed to appreciate the fact that PVO activities in encouraging agricultural productivity and income generation or in energizing domestic markets could be effective in raising sustainable food levels. Their attitude changed in the 1990s, however, as progressively more Food for Peace non-emergency commodities were monetized (nearly 50% by the end of the decade). They then joined other American PVOs in an association of cooperating sponsors called Food Aid Management (FAM) whose central goal was to organize information about the process and to provide guidance through the intricate procedures. Africare staff members were the main contributors to the subsequently published monetization manual that has become the standard reference. Thus, Africare, which had been the upstart new kid on the block, became a go-to authority on the subject.

When Africare investigated whether to become a cooperating sponsor and decided to do so, it necessarily established operational policies and principles based on theory rather than experience. It also held an uninformed view about the full impact of monetization beyond providing funds for certain designated purposes. The challenges of administering monetization programs in Guinea-Bissau and, subsequently, in other nations, however, revealed unanticipated predicaments that required greater organizational sophistication. Their management showed as well that monetization could have far more significance in African countries than Africare staff had realized. The consequence of these new insights was the drafting of formal guiding principles that were instilled in employees in Washington and in the field.

Seared by the loss of 3% of the cargo on its first ship, "African Wave," Africare management adopted the first principle, "Commodities are a valuable asset paid for by American taxpayers. Africare does not lose cargo." It vowed to monitor shipments carefully, to account for all goods on the manifest, and to keep all receipts and papers. It knew that port losses diminished the amount of its working capital, so the message to employees was, "Guard the resources given." Initially, after the "African Wave" disappointment, Africare hired a competent surveying company to oversee unloading, but it soon organized its own team that traveled from port to port and supervised all the steps involved in importing commodities for immediate sale. Another motivation behind the first principle of not losing cargo was the prospect of regular USAID audits. Africare did not want to have to reimburse the funding agency for negligence.

A second principle stated that the mechanism of monetization itself could have a developmental impact in a country through the process of executing the transaction. It had the accumulative value of training citizens of African nations in responding to food emergencies because the experience gained in ordering commodities, getting them off-loaded in ports, and finding traders who would distribute them was equally applicable should those commodities be famine relief. Not only were expatriate involved overseas with monetization, but so were many Africans—PVO employees, government officials, local leaders, and merchants. They, too, learned the system for getting food into the country and to the people. This community participation enhanced the national capacity to manage a disaster. Another positive aspect embedded in the procedure of monetization was training a cadre of local people to deal with port officials in matters of customs and taxes, teaching them how to avoid pilferage and diversion of commodities, and impressing upon them the importance of protecting an employer's assets. Skills and values learned were transferrable outside the workplace.

In the next several years after its initial project in Guinea-Bissau, Africare designed monetization projects for a number of African countries. In Burkina Faso, its technicians planned the rehabilitation of six dams and the construction of 148 wells, some with motor-pumps, for the expansion of irrigated agriculture. Mozambique was just emerging from a civil war and had been devastated by a severe drought. The proposal there was to resettle refugees and displaced persons in the countryside where they could take up farming again.

Somalia, Eritrea, and Chad were also evaluated for the suitability of monetization projects. Most of the proposed interventions were undertaken subsequently, although not all were funded through Title II commodities.

Africare's program to improve maternal and child health and to assure the availability of more food in Guinea, launched in the mid-1990s, marked the beginning of another successful collaboration with a government in its food security strategy. The prefecture of Dinguiraye, in the northeastern part of the country, had the highest level of malnutrition of any region—44% among the general population. Thirty percent of children under five were chronically malnourished (being stunted, which is low height for age, is one indication) and its "hungry season," when households had inadequate food, lasted eight months a year. Initially, thirty districts (official administrative units that have a number of villages in each) were included in the Dinguiraye Food Security Initiative. Twenty more were added after several years, but, beginning in 2000, some districts were "graduated."

Back in 1990, when Africare first considered Guinea for a Title II project, staffers, collecting data on national food needs and market activities, identified vegetable oil as the only suitable import commodity. One obstacle they had faced previously, however, was winning cooperation from traders in Conakry, who were accustomed to importing oil from European dealers and had ties to European bankers. Furthermore, they were not interested in the higher quality and higher priced American oil because local consumers bought whatever was cheapest. In 1996, circumstances were different and a monetization format became viable. Africare designed its sales tender to attract bids from numerous little companies that, buying small quantities, distributed the product widely in rural areas where there were oil shortages.

In its goal of strengthening food security, Africare organized women of Dinguiraye, such as in the village of Tambanoro, into agricultural cooperatives and the women set up community gardens. With Africare-supplied technical support, they used improved seeds and better cultivating techniques. Their group resources enabled them to buy better tools, rent plows, and draft animals for soil preparation, and, instead of putting cinders over their plants to discourage bugs, engage the insecticide spraying services of the Ministry of Agriculture. Africare demonstration gardens introduced new vegetable varieties and carrots, potatoes, and soybeans entered the local diet. One of the biggest needs in the region was improvement in the storage of food. Typically, half of each harvest was lost due to rodents, insects, and rotting. New types of granaries reduced the loss to 10% and improved farmers' potential to hold surpluses for later sale off-season when market prices rose.

The health and nutrition of women and children received even more attention than agriculture during this long-term project. Community volunteer health agents were recruited to implement a nationally recommended health information system. Using it, they attempted to collect, on a monthly basis, specific data on the health and nutrition of all children and mothers in each district. One of the most important indicators was the weight of children up to age three, which gave mothers knowledge about their nutritional status. Utilizing data from this growth monitoring system to identify moderately malnourished children, Africare introduced the Hearth Model program to Guinea in 2000 and implemented it in 110 Dinguiraye villages. Through it, a "model mother" who lived in the same community but had well-nourished children became a peer educator, holding a twelve day session that discussed hygiene, health, child caring, pre-natal consultation, breast feeding, nutritional foods, and diet diversification. She had the assistance of community leaders and residents who encouraged women to attend the workshop and who supplied the majority of the food needed to rehabilitate the targeted children. The community volunteers contributed to the smooth operation of the workshops because of their earlier work in growth monitoring. Being familiar with the goals through the nutrition and health education talks that they had given, they provided "model mothers" with both informational and moral support. The Guinean Ministry of Health was also a factor in the success of the Hearth Model in Dinguiraye. Its health agents vaccinated children and mothers and provided postpartum mothers with Vitamin A. Evaluations of the Hearth Model show that, in the next seven years, not only was there an increase in the number of children who participated in the program, but that, from the beginning, they exhibited weight gain and continued that improvement for at least the next twelve months.

Apart from their work with the Hearth Model program, the community volunteer health agents, of whom there were two for each village, were valuable in other ways for Africare. When they identified malnourished children, they distributed medications and micronutrients. For mothers, they held demonstration cooking classes to show the use of low-cost local ingredients in making a vitamin-rich porridge and to promote the inclusion of peanut butter, ground soybeans, fish powder, and green leafy vegetables in diets. They were important sources of information on family planning, they distributed contraceptives, and they educated local people about HIV/AIDS.

The monetization of Title II commodities in Dinguiraye is an on-going program and over the course of more than a decade significant results have been achieved. The percentage of malnourished among the general population in the original districts has been reduced to 12.7% and the percentage of chronically malnourished among children under five has been reduced to 21%. Instead of there being eight months of food shortage in the region, there are now fewer than six. Food production among members in the cooperatives has increased dramatically, so much so that, some years, they have a surplus of 70% over home needs that they can sell. Consequently, household incomes have risen. An important aspect of this project has been the capacity building that has occurred. Community and district development organizations have formed to analyze local needs and to assume responsibilities with regional government officials in adopting agricultural and health innovations. They design micro-projects and look for sources of external financing. They themselves have become important in offering revolving credit plans to local producer groups, especially to those of women. The citizenry in general has more knowledge about what they can do to improve their lives and, also, what they should expect from policy makers in the national ministries of agriculture and of health. Gradually, community leaders and government staff are replacing Africare employees in providing essential direction in matters that affect their welfare, which has always been an important Africare goal.

In spite of these accomplishments, the people of Dinguiraye face enormous obstacles in their quest for a better life. Some basic problems, whether in dealing with food security or with maternal and child health, can be traced to governmental agencies on which they depend for personnel, equipment, technical support, or supplies that are integral to complete success of the project. Inadequate stocks of essential medicines such as anti-malarials and vaccines, too few materials on which to record data about children, and difficulties in recruiting medical staff for rural areas limit the contribution of the Ministry of Health. Another aspect concerns community health workers: they are unpaid volunteers. First, it is hard to find the required number because of the high illiteracy rate in the region (80%) and, second, they need careful training and close supervision by the national team, which is often tough to achieve, especially during the rainy season. In agriculture, Africare relies on the staffs of the prefectoral department of agriculture and on its counterpart in rural development to provide major technical assistance to farmers. However, these agencies have only a computer or two (and sometimes no electricity) and neither has a vehicle or motorcycle for its field agents, which necessitates that they borrow from the Africare office when they want to travel. Other basic impediments in Dinguiraye are the low level of numeracy, particularly among women, poor soils, uneven and unpredictable rainfalls, lack of general transportation, and unavailability of agricultural inputs.

In Mozambique, where Africare began the Manica Oil Seed Food Security Initiative in 1996, the monetization program differed from those in Guinea-Bissau and Guinea in one respect. It was financed through participation in a PVOs consortium, headed by World Vision, which actually managed the acquisition of commodities and their sale. Wheat became a major import because it is not grown in Mozambique and it easily met requirements of the Bellmon Amendment. Furthering food security was expected through the combined goals of encouraging private enterprise and strengthening household nutrition and health, particularly for mothers and children. Specifically, the plan intended to build a sustainable, small-scale oil seed production and processing industry in a region of Mozambique severely affected by the seventeen-year civil war that ended in 1992. It sought, also, to teach women about wholesome diets and to persuade the entire population to adopt new hygiene practices.

Africare selected five districts with a population of three hundred thousand in the central Mozambique province of Manica, an area that embraces the mountains separating it from Zimbabwe. Agriculture was the dominant economic activity; before independence in 1975, the region was a net exporter of surplus corn, vegetables, fruits, sunflower, and tobacco. A variety of vegetables was grown in gardens with in-field banana and other fruit trees distributed among the rows for erosion control. Animals were used for draft power, transport, and manure. The long civil war following the Portuguese departure ravaged the province and a large percentage of the land that had been cultivated by subsistence farmers was abandoned because of insecurity. (It was estimated in 2001 that less than 30% of the arable land in Manica

Province was being cultivated.) In the postwar era, people resumed the pursuit of their livelihoods with only the hoe and other primitive tools. Their low productivity was compounded by drought and insufficient crop inputs. Nutritional standards suffered because of a concentration on growing corn, which offered greater export opportunities, rather than planting vegetable varieties for home consumption in addition to cash crops. A damaged infrastructure, poor road network, and geographic remoteness put them at a disadvantage in marketing even corn surpluses and in receiving government agricultural services. The province became one of Mozambique's least developed areas.

The idea behind the oil seed project was to encourage small-scale farmers to increase the number of acres they planted in sunflower and sesame and to improve the yield while making it possible for the farmers to produce their own oil or to be able to sell their crops to commercial presses. Forming a consortium in the province with other NGOs involved in the oil sector, with commercial oil enterprises, and with agricultural research organizations was the first step. Together, they could provide extension services to farmers, ascertain the best seed varieties and planting strategies, and pass valuable information to the Ministry of Commerce. Africare sponsored a technical training course for metal workers and engineers of two Mozambican companies in the manufacture of an improved manual ram press and gave village-level demonstrations of this machinery. It sold ram presses itself, usually on a lease/purchase option to individual farmers or to farmer associations. During planting seasons, Africare facilitated the sale of tons of sunflower and sesame seed, primarily through a Mozambican-Zimbabwe company, SEMOC/Seed-Co. There was serious competition, however, from a South African firm, Pannar, which revolved around the type of sunflower seed sold. SEMOC/Seed-Co offered a variety called "Black Record" that produced one liter of oil from every four or five kilos of seed planted. The hybrid that Pannar specialized in reduced the number of kilos needed for a liter to three. Naturally, many farmers selected the hybrid, knowing that it was significantly more expensive than "Black Record," but unaware that it had to be purchased every year whereas the regular strain had a three-year life span. For some farmers, moreover, the actual cost differential was so buried within the intricate contracts they had with a commercial oil pressing company that they could not figure the relative economic advantage of selecting one variety over the other.

Individual farmers and farmer associations that both grew crops and processed their own seeds with new ram presses were better able to calculate their prospects with each seed type, but they, too, were often similarly uninformed about the characteristics of hybrid seed.

In spite of this confusion, Africare surpassed its targets in convincing more farmers to plant sunflowers and in expanding the number of acres under cultivation. Whereas only 4,000 in the five districts of Manica sowed sunflower in 1998, 33,000 did so in 2001. The area devoted to sunflower crops rose from 1,317 acres to 14,250 during the same period. Altogether, Africare leased or sold one hundred and eighty manual oil presses during the first four years of this food security initiative, establishing a strong commercial oils industry in the province.

In the health, nutrition, and hygiene component of the Manica Oil Seed Food Security Initiative, Africare pursued many of the same policies and outreach techniques that it had followed in previous monetization programs such as in Dinguiraye, Guinea, and in direct health programs in Uganda. It tried to inform mothers of preferred methods and foods for infant feeding. In this case, it had to persuade women not to feed newborns porridge and water, which was often not potable, immediately after birth. It had to overcome such traditional beliefs as the efficacy of giving infants wild roots to ward off diseases and those linking baldness to feeding eggs to babies. Africare demonstrations of food preparation failed, however, to draw in enough women to change perceptions and habits about food use. More intense educational messages in the way of posters and informative material were clearly required. Through experience, it also learned the need to build local health posts in order to encourage women to seek help immediately for sick children, the importance of getting husbands involved in nutrition and health activities, and the value of newly installed latrines in bringing a community's attention to better hygiene practices.

Behind Africare's effort to increase household income, food access, and knowledge about food utilization was the assumption that a family's vulnerability to or tolerance for unexpected food shortages was linked directly to its level of prosperity. Data collected by Africare in its baseline studies estimated that, during Fiscal Year 1997, the household income in those five districts of Manica was a low $376, which explained, among other findings, why the malnutrition rate among children under five was 36%. Two years later, reflecting both

Africare's work and overall economic improvement in Mozambique, household income had risen to $477 and that particular malnutrition rate had dropped to 23%. The creation of cooperative rural enterprises and the spread of commercial pressing operations into the area, some firms guaranteeing to purchase farmers' crops before harvest, also contributed to rising affluence. The general expansion of agriculture had resulted in a significant escalation of food access too. Africare learned, though, from interview and observational data that, at least in these five districts of Manica, an increase in a family's income did not necessarily lead to an increase in food security. In fact, the growth of regional commerce tempted families to exchange products generated within the household for furniture, clothing, or restaurant meals available in local markets rather than to conserve them for future needs. For example, instead of keeping home-raised chickens for their own improved diet, they sold them.

The agricultural side of the Manica oil seed program was a great success as more and more farmers, particularly individuals and association members, became small-scale press owners. There remained serious constraints, however. Commercial firms competed with them for harvests with which they sought to augment their own oil production. There was a shortage of working capital and few sources of credit. Getting spare parts even from Mozambican companies was often unpredictable and usually required a trip to a large provincial town, but transportation within the province remained undeveloped. If these impediments did not deter farmers, droughts sometimes set them back.

A second phase, the Manica Expanded Food Security Initiative, built on this first monetization project in Mozambique and kept many of the same objectives, but added a HIV/AIDS component in acknowledgement that the disease increased the risk of household food insecurity. Begun in 2002, it ran until 2007 and included a hundred villages in four districts of Manica province. Instead of its earlier emphasis on sunflower and sesame seed production for crushing, Africare stressed crop diversification and extension services to teach new planting techniques, soil erosion control, and pest management. Helping farmers improve crop storage methods and gain greater marketing skills were also goals. These strategies were successful in reducing the hunger months in these districts from 3.8 in 2002 to 1.8 in 2006 and in raising the gross household income to $522 in 2006, in spite of a severe drought in 2005 and a partial one in 2006. Diets were enhanced by the addition of locally grown vegetables, soybeans, and orange-flesh sweet potatoes.

The nutrition and health section of the second food security initiative in Mozambique was much more intense in its objectives than the earlier program. When Africare staff found that mothers continued traditional practices of infant feeding regardless of apparently understanding the theory behind the new methods, they adopted a variation of the Hearth Model program that had worked well in Dinguiraye, Guinea. In the four districts of Manica, they selected "model families" who gave cooking demonstrations at their houses, illustrated good hygiene practices, and went to local households with malnourished children to follow-up on community acceptance of their suggestions. Although this aspect of Africare's effort proved beneficial to older children and parents, it was less successful in persuading mothers to breast-feed their infants exclusively until four to six months of age. That failure was evident in the high rate of diarrhea in children less than six months old. In fact, a general misunderstanding continued about how to handle the ailment: whether to give the child food and water, the best method of oral rehydration, how long to continue treatment after cessation of obvious illness.

Model families were supervised by Africare-trained community demonstrators who also conducted group discussions about relevant nutrition and health issues and introduced the topic of HIV/AIDS. Working in tandem with other private and governmental organizations that focused on educating the public, they encouraged fidelity and abstinence as well as condom use. They also urged people with symptoms of illness to go to hospitals for treatment and to take their partners with them. The value of model families and of demonstrators was their familiarity with the communities they served and the sustainability they provided to Africare efforts. As in Zimbabwe, however, Africare found that sexually active adults and youth were unlikely to change their habits even when they knew the risk of HIV/AIDS. One common cultural belief among women against which all AIDS activists had to fight was that having sexual intercourse with husbands while they were breastfeeding made their babies sick. Consequently, couples carried out a traditional ceremony called "pitamajuade," which permitted the husband to visit other women. Although it increased the demand for condoms, it is unclear how often they were used. Subsequently, beginning in 2005, Africare expanded its AIDS program in Manica province with services to more than 70,000 orphans and vulnerable children, to caregivers, and to others affected by the disease. The AIDS program remains part of the COPE project that operates also in Rwanda, Tanzania, and Uganda.

Africare's food security program, using monetization of P.L. 480 commodities in Guinea-Bissau, emphasized the strengthening of private food producer and processor associations, with ancillary goals of improved health and expanded infrastructure. In Guinea, Africare focused on the health and nutrition of women and children. Agricultural advancement fit into a broader picture of overall community welfare. The work in Mozambique aimed to improve food security, health, and nutrition through an increase in household income, generated first by oil seed enterprises, and later by multifaceted agricultural activities. Another example of the use of monetization illustrates the valuable contribution that rehabilitating existing roads and constructing new ones can make in boosting a region's food security.

The Uganda Food Security Initiative (UFSI) began in 1997 in the southwestern district of Kabale. Five years later, it was expanded to four more districts. Together, the districts encompassed about 150,000 people living in 144 villages. High population density in the region had resulted in severe land shortage (a typical household of seven persons farmed fewer than three acres) and fragmentation. Land degradation, soil erosion, a steep terrain, and a difficult local environment meant low agricultural productivity and a high level of malnutrition among the population. In fact, 39% of children under five were found to be stunted, the highest percentage in the country.

Africare's goals were to help farmers protect soils against erosion and to increase soil fertility, to increase crop yields while preserving harvests and improving food utilization, to provide year-round road access to communities, and to build the local capacity to assure food security. There were also targets for improving sanitation practices among the households. For ten years, Africare/Uganda imported American wheat to monetize in Kampala, where it was sought by local bakeries because its hardness made good bread. When the wheat arrived by ship in Mombasa, Kenya, 575 miles away, it was taken on Kenya Railways over land via Nairobi, a slow and costly process whose delays often left Africare projects suspended pending buyers' payments. Profit was also affected by unpredictable currency shifts between the time of ordering the commodity and its delivery, as in other countries. Africare received total funding of about $9 million from USAID for the work.

Southwestern Uganda, where Africare decided to make road improvement or construction a high priority, was so bereft of community roads (small roads connecting villages or connecting villages to sub-counties and maintained by the community) that a large portion of the rural population was completely cut off from major regional markets during much of the year, especially during the rainy season. The expression "village track" was more apt than "road" since most were impassable by automobiles. The absence of viable roads—and collaterally of vehicular transportation—was a major factor in the impoverishment of farmers. Not only did they have difficulty getting surplus produce or agricultural products to market, if they had any, but, not knowing consumer demand, they could not tailor their efforts to the cultivation of the most profitable crops. Furthermore, they were handicapped in obtaining seeds, fertilizer, equipment, and other supplies by the distance to urban centers. Improving their accessibility to markets and to agricultural inputs was seen as an important component in elevating incentive and increasing productivity. Enhancing the condition of farmers would promote food security.

Road construction is a collaborative effort involving local and district government agencies, engineers, environmental and agricultural officers, the local population, and, in this case, Africare, which operated with USAID approval. Prospective roads have to be identified and the communities along the routes sensitized. Engineering surveys and impact studies determine the feasibility of their location. Roads, culverts, and bridges are then designed and such equipment as bulldozers, jackhammers, graders, and vibro-rollers must be located within the region or purchased. One of the most vexing tasks is securing the right-of-way and compensating owners with fertile land elsewhere. (The shortage of land in southwestern Uganda made compensation difficult.) Community members must be given a sense of ownership so that they maintain the road once it is rehabilitated or constructed.

Over the ten years of the Uganda Food Security Initiative, Africare completed forty-six miles of road, slightly less than the target, but the positive impact and that of the rest the program exceeded expectations. Among Africare households, the severity of food shortage decreased significantly, in proportion to the length of time they had participated. Africare farmers rented more land, bought more new land, and grew more of most crops than non-participants. They adopted more conservation measures, such as crop rotation and mulching, and had higher crop yields than others. Families enrolled in the Africare project were much more likely than uninvolved people in the community to have well-maintained latrines, clean their food utensils, drink boiled water, wash hands after visiting the toilet, and have a bathing facility. In all five districts, the rehabilitated and new roads led to an explosion of economic activity. New buildings, for both residential and commercial purposes, were constructed. Some housed grain mills, milk cooling centers, grocery stores, butcheries, bars, and restaurants. Food stalls, fresh vegetable markets, quarries, and motorbike shops opened up along the routes. Also important to the communities was the construction of buildings for expanded social services: new schools, health clinics, and a nursery. The roads themselves were a great benefit to farmers, who now could get their produce to market much more quickly than before and who enjoyed a broader consumer base that raised prices for their crops. Traffic counts in the area showed that the number of trucks, motorbikes, and other vehicles increased dramatically. Everyone in the region saw his potential travel time to various destinations reduced and his new mobility more pleasant than before. This was particularly true of patients who could now be taken to medical centers by ambulance rather by hand-carried stretchers or dugout canoes.

The results of Africare's investment in roads have had some imperfections, however. While travel time decreased, the expense of travel increased significantly because fuel costs of motorized transport began rising precipitously in 2003 and showed no sign of abating. There have been other questions about the improved road network for people in southwestern Uganda, aside from the unanticipated financial effect. Its impact on the environment has been particularly troublesome. There have been major problems with increased run-off and erosion, dust, landslides, siltation of water sources, flooding, and destruction of vegetation. Solutions to most of these difficulties lie in constructing more culverts, planting grass along waterways and catchment trenches, planting additional trees, and routine maintenance. However, most communities lack materials and equipment and, more importantly, a will to work collectively toward a resolution. This is a new challenge in community development for Africare, a field in which other PVOs, foundations, and funding sources agree it excels.

Finally, the Rural Enterprise and Agricultural Development Program (REAP) illustrates how monetization of American commodities in South Africa can facilitate the entrance of black farmers into commercial agriculture and black entrepreneurs into agribusiness. Before 1994, black farmers, the majority of the population, were scarcely able to survive on the land because of discriminatory apartheid policies, the absence of financial resources, inadequate agricultural extension services, and a lack of markets in their segregated living areas. The new government in 1994 pursued an agreement with the United States to foster economic and cultural ties between the two countries, resulting in a bi-national commission. The commission's agricultural committee investigated ways that the United States Department of Agriculture (USDA) and the South African National Department of Agriculture (NDA) might cooperate. Subsequently, the NDA staff sought partners to assist it in analyzing rural needs and solutions and then worked with Africare staff to design a proposal for submission to USDA. Known as the Rural Enterprise and Agricultural Development Program (REAP), it was funded late in 1998 with a budget of $9.5 million in crude sunflower and soybean oil for monetization in South Africa. REAP operated under the Food for Progress Act of USDA rather than under USAID's Food for Peace and was the largest USDA program funded up to that time.

Africare chose two districts that before 1994 had been designated as "homelands" for South African blacks. One was Msinga in Kwa-Zulu-Natal Province and the other Nebo in the Northern Province (during apartheid days, it was called the Transvaal, but since 2002 it has been known as Limpopo Province). Both were characterized by poor soils, little industry, and scant infrastructure. In Msinga, most men migrated to such cities as Durban and Johannesburg in search of employment, leaving agriculture almost exclusively in the hands of women. Nebo had the distinction of being located in the province considered the least developed in the country.

The overall design to increase opportunities for black farmers in commercial agriculture and business had at its core a complex set of interwoven requisites. Many of them were fundamentally grassroots organizing and training missions. Others necessitated the physical enhancement of the environment. Some parts of the plan were nebulous in methodology or in measuring achievement. For example, Africare staff proposed turning Msinga and Nebo into rural enterprise zones where production, processing, and marketing were linked, but this goal was conceptually difficult to visualize and involved interactive participants at different stages of activity rather than synchronized with each other. More concrete objectives were to promote sustainable agricultural practices, to provide financial and technical assistance to emergent agribusinesses, and to strengthen such local institutions as farmers' cooperatives. Teaching new skills to master farmers, government extension agents, and cooperative and association managers was another important intention, as was encouraging youth to enter farming. With regard to the infrastructure in Msinga and Nebo, Africare considered an irrigation water supply essential to agricultural improvement and proposed the construction or rehabilitation of dams.

REAP in South Africa got off to a slow and tenuous beginning. Although, initially, it was to be a three-year program starting in 1998, various difficulties—staffing needs, a delay in signing a memorandum of understanding between the governments of South Africa and the United States, problems in assembling steering committees of local citizens—postponed implementation until 1999, effectively limiting the span to two years. By the time of the late 2000 evaluation, only $2 million of the budgeted $9.5 million had been spent. There were definite achievements, but few goals had been met, largely because they were overly ambitious, particularly for such a short project period. Among the findings was a suspicion in South Africa about the mode of funding PVO activities through the sale of U.S. agricultural commodities. Officials feared that it might be a case of dumping goods to the disadvantage of local producers. Another deterrent to success was a lack of harmonious relations between Africare staff on the one hand, and employees in the National Department of Agriculture and the provincial departments of agriculture on the other. Among the misunderstandings was the apprehension of the latter that funding for REAP was coming from their coffers. Internal management and administrative deficiencies were also prominently discussed in the assessment, as was the need for Africare staff to communicate more effectively with South African officials and with their target audience, black farmers. In spite of their belief that REAP was underachieving in almost every aspect, evaluators ended their report on an optimistic note. They concluded that, if Africare overcame the problems enumerated, the program was poised to make much more rapid and substantial progress.

On the basis of the evaluation and with much of the original funding still available, USDA gave Africare a two-year extension to 2002 and later permission for a second phase that ended in 2003. Africare undertook to fulfill as comprehensively as possible the seventy-five recommendations it had received, including hiring more staff, particularly technical personnel, coordinating its activities with South African civil servants, and working closely with local universities on agricultural instruction. It also overhauled its management procedures and it reevaluated the original REAP objectives, in part, with a view of establishing a legacy of tangible physical achievements in Msinga and Nebo. During 2003, Africare concentrated on transferring managerial and technical responsibility for REAP activities to local farmers and authorities. It was the recurring Africare theme of building sustainability into its projects.

During the years 2001 to 2003, Africare, with the help of many partner agencies and beneficiary organizations such as the National African Farmers Union and the Msinga Vegetable Producer Association, completed a wide range of infrastructure improvements in the two districts. It constructed or rehabilitated dams, installed water pumps, laid out irrigation systems, built nurseries, and finished a pack house where farmers brought produce for processing or export. Africare also introduced new technology that enabled users to add value to their agricultural products, such as VitaCow for grinding soy beans into soy milk and efficient equipment for turning peanuts into peanut butter. It did a market survey of commodities likely to have demand and linked the results to the selection of seedlings for reproduction in the nurseries. It supported the establishment of a half dozen agribusinesses and, through the Agribusiness Development Trust that it created in conjunction with the National Department of Agriculture, made it easier for farmers and entrepreneurs to obtain bank financing by standing as a guarantor of loans. All of these actions contributed to transforming the areas from impoverished backwaters into emerging rural enterprise zones, as envisioned in the initial proposal.

The development of human resources within the Msinga and Nebo districts, which was fundamental to the accomplishment of all other goals, centered on training individual farmers, farmers' groups, and rural youth in many facets of agriculture and agribusiness. This was done through workshops dealing with elements of improved cultivation, maintenance of irrigation systems, the use of computers to track marketing conditions, and good farm management practices. Gradually, black farmers in Msinga and Nebo became aware that they could have more control over their lives than previously and that the national government must respond in a timely manner to their economic plight. Supporting their political activity were those men and women engaged in commercial farming and agribusiness who wanted favorable circumstances in which to prosper. The result was a combined rural demand for government support at many levels, with beneficial agricultural policies and programs. Africare's contribution was to initiate the overall plan, to organize and inspire farmer groups, to help government agencies become proficient in the execution of long-term development strategies, to provide training and technical assistance, and to make black farmers more self-sufficient and independent as they pursued a livelihood in agriculture. The REAP project, although only five years in length and operating in only two districts of South Africa, is an example of a coordinated, multifaceted effort that brings together public and private interests. Its ultimate success now lies in the hands of participants.

During the twenty years that Africare has employed monetization of commodities, it has had to adjust to significant changes in emphasis in the U.S. Food for Peace program that USAID administers. The most recent ones result from reduced congressional appropriations for P.L. 480, caused in part by the expense of American fighting in Iraq and Afghanistan and by dwindling food stocks for export. The new policies also reflect an effort to remove distinctions between emergency and development programs, one intended to be short-term for a surprise hardship and the other long-term with goals to ameliorate conditions behind chronic food insecurity. USAID further wants to concentrate its activities in a smaller number of countries. Consequently, it has drawn up a priority list of twelve nations, all but two in sub-Saharan Africa, and it now requires that every monetization proposal include plans for food distribution. Recognizing that HIV/AIDS victims often are already malnourished and that their communities become even more vulnerable to food insecurity as a result of the epidemic, USAID is determined to increase their resilience to the threat of hunger. It has also joined food relief with nutritional education, which it had long espoused, as a means of strengthening HIV/AIDS households. Since it has always been Africare's philosophy to focus on severely malnourished children and on groups of people affected in some way by HIV/AIDS, it can continue with its traditional programming in nutrition, while adding the new component of food distribution. It has even qualified for PEPFAR funding for this.

The practical consequence for the Africare Food for Development staff in Washington is the need to design projects more creatively than before. After all, Africare has never been enthusiastic about direct

149

food distribution. This was the distinction that Lucas and Kennedy established when they first discussed becoming a cooperating sponsor with USAID. Even more important now than before are the following considerations in evaluating prospective recipients: Is there a food need? Can it be met through a food program? Will Africare have a competitive advantage to other organizations? Will a food program complement our other efforts in the country? Another big question is, "How can we work through indigenous organizations to distribute food discreetly?"

Africare's first response to the new USAID directive, beginning in 2005, was to link food distribution to projects in Burkina Faso and Rwanda. These were nations where it was already engaged in a number of development activities, including those helping HIV/AIDS carriers. The objective was to provide people living with AIDS and those affected by the virus, such as household members and peer educators, with supplemental food products in order to improve their nutritional status. Zondoma Province in Burkina Faso and Nyamagabe Province in Rwanda were the areas selected, the first with an estimated 2% HIV prevalence and the other with an estimated 8% prevalence rate. The only requirements for citizens to participate were that they reside in the area, that they provide proof of HIV/AIDS infection, and that they join a HIV/AIDS association.

In both nations, Africare coordinated a wide range of formats that sought to educate the public about HIV/AIDS while distributing food rations to people affected by the disease. It encouraged behavior change and communication through voluntary counseling and testing (VCT). It used mobile VCT and cinema units, youth centers, and peer education to raise awareness. In Rwanda, Africare built eight public health VCT centers and offered health insurance to each person receiving commodities. Implementation of the COPE model has also been important. The Burkina Faso program had many more components than its counterpart in Rwanda because nearly 40% of the population in Zondoma Province, dominated by subsistence smallholder households vulnerable to land erosion and erratic rainfall, suffered from some form of food insecurity. Improvements in nutrition, agricultural and animal production, water availability, and micro-finance were seen as having a direct impact on families upset by HIV/AIDS.

One big difference in Africare's experience in Rwanda and Burkina Faso was in the method of distributing food. In Rwanda, Africare established twelve distribution sites, as identified by community members, where people with the disease came, showed their identification card, and claimed a monthly household ration of bulgur, corn soya blend, and vegetable oil. In Burkina Faso, however, the level of stigma attached to infected residents was so high that Africare gave the food rations to HIV/AIDS associations, which then distributed them to individuals. They received bulgur, lentils, soy flour, and oil.

Early evaluations of the distribution programs, although based largely on anecdotal evidence, pointed to successes as well as to the need to rethink certain practices. There were many improvements reported in the physical condition of people living with HIV/AIDS. They had gained weight, had more stamina for working in their gardens, and were responding well to medical treatment. If talking publicly about the disease is an indication, a slow reduction was taking place in stigmatization and awareness was growing in the communities. Africare found, however, that there was a disturbing anomaly in the actual method of food distribution and consumption. First of all, a household of one person received the same ration size as a household with fifteen members and, as in much of Africa, all family members shared food, regardless of its source. Many of the intended recipients, consequently, were not receiving sufficient rations for themselves. Another factor was family dynamics. There was no way for Africare to know whether the food was divided according to who was ill or according to gender, birth order, age, or family position.

In most of its development activities, Africare has stressed income generating opportunities, but one deficiency detected in these programs was an absence of such planning for people living with HIV/AIDS. Of course, the subject was complicated by the factor of illness and the uncertainty of what jobs patients might be able to perform. Nonetheless, Africare considered it a worthwhile area to investigate for later monetization programs. A final question raised by preliminary evaluations concerned the contents of the ration package itself. The specific types of food handed out had never been evaluated for optimal effectiveness and many recipients complained that some rations were foods that were unknown locally. For example, in Rwanda, bulgur was so unfamiliar to them that they had to experiment with ways to prepare it. A related concern had to do with nutritional education. When people living with HIV/AIDS visited health centers, they were given the standard nutritional advice offered to the general population; they did not receive information tailored to them. One suggested

151

solution was to implement a modified form of the Hearth program with cooking demonstrations of both healthy locally grown food and unfamiliar food that would bolster the diets of the ill.

Of all the strategies that Africare has undertaken during its forty-year history, none has been as institutionally challenging as the monetization of commodities for the financing of development projects. Many ventures were complex multi-million dollar commitments in nations with poorly functioning governments, low in bureaucratic capacity and overwhelmed by the immensity of the task. They required negotiations with many more agencies and businesses in the United States and overseas than other programs. They necessitated coordination and supervision of diverse aspects at an intense level. Yet, as a result of its competency and positive results, the Food for Development unit in Washington was so successful at getting funding from many governmental sources that, for a time, there was jealousy among other staff members. It seemed to them that one segment of the Africare operation was getting all the attention. Gradually, as the annual budgets show, there has been a restoration of balance in program activities and, within Africare headquarters today, that source of tension appears to be absent.

7

Encouraging Democracy and Good Governance

The promotion of civic education and the extension of political liberty have been understated, but intentional, goals of many Africare programs throughout much of its existence. It informally encouraged democratic principles in communities of the Sahel as early as the mid-1970s. For example, in the Integrated Rural Development project at Seguenega, Upper Volta (Burkina Faso), Village Development Committees were formed to allow the whole spectrum of local citizens to engage actively in tackling health and water issues. This took much more effort than planners envisioned, but it was a learning experience. Over the years, Africare subtly injected a participatory managerial style when it organized men and women's cooperatives in which members worked together, pooled resources, and shared results. It also formatted a governing structure for recipients designed to give them a sense that they had "bought into" the objectives. While cooperatives were natural in farming, they were important in fishing, too, as in the Kafue Flats of Zambia where the group determined who would receive loans, and in such activities as the producer and processor associations in Tombali, Guinea-Bissau. The methods by which democratic values were introduced in rural settings were informal adjuncts to a larger process of achieving economic goals. What Africare undertook later had purely political dimensions.

The first formal effort aimed at this type of influence came through the South Africa Career Development Internship Program, launched in 1989, with a grant from IBM Corporation. Other corporate donors later contributed and USAID, in 1990, awarded Africare $1.5 million under its "Training for Disadvantaged South Africans Project." This was an opportunity for Africare to help the struggling country while adhering to Bishop Walker's insistence that no aid be given to the apartheid government. Professor Z.K. Matthews, a prominent black

South African academic and political activist at Fort Hare University, who earned an M.A. at Yale University and studied at the London School of Economics, but returned to South Africa to mentor such students as Oliver Tambo and Nelson Mandela, stood as a role model for Africare staff. The plan targeted the estimated two thousand South African students enrolled in American colleges and universities. As South Africa neared transition to majority rule, Africare intended to build a corpus of men and women trained to such a high level in their specialties that they were likely to assume leadership roles in the new society. The goal was to place fifty interns during the first year and varying numbers in successive years for four to six months in public and private sector positions, according to their professional interests. The additional extracurricular opportunity aimed specifically at instilling participants with principles of western business management and government. The on-the-job experience in American corporations and organizations would give post-baccalaureate graduates a practical view beyond the academic and theoretical one of the classroom.

During the seven years that Africare arranged internships, more than four hundred black South Africans were placed with such American giants as Bristol-Myers Squibb and Texaco, with public institutions such as Washington, D.C., public schools and the University of Pittsburgh, and with social service groups, like the Black United Fund of Texas. A particularly appropriate posting with the American Civil Liberties Union made a law graduate an intern advocate for prisoner rights. Africare not only established links between students and their assignments, but held supporting conferences and workshops to address the unfolding tableau of South African life and the workplace circumstances likely to confront them. Early on, it incorporated "Confidence, Assertiveness and Coping" seminars into its framework. Conflict resolution and networking techniques were prominent topics. Of the four hundred participants, nearly all returned to South Africa and were successful in finding mid- to upper-level jobs in their fields. For those in business, their practical experience was a big factor in winning over prospective white employers. Many interns ultimately became corporation executives, but many achieved distinction through government or other non-business service. Positions such as membership on the Commission for Human Rights, clerking for the Constitutional Court, and deputy director of the Johannesburg Civic Theatre illustrate the diversity of their career paths. Every field of human endeavor—business, private sector development, law and human rights, government service, social change, health sciences, and education—benefited from the employment of Career Development Internship Program alumni. An important factor in the success of the interns was that they were among the most talented black South African graduates of U.S. institutions of higher learning and, hence, almost destined to rise to the top of the managerial and professional ranks in the new South Africa.

In December 1992, Africare opened an office in South Africa by stationing a country representative in Johannesburg. Its strategy focused on human resource development, strengthening local indigenous institutions, and improving water access and primary health care in rural areas. With the nation preparing for its first democratic elections in April 1994, Africare could immediately take additional steps to encourage constructive political change. Rather than holding seminars and workshops affiliated with the Career Development Internship Program just in the United States, it offered some in South Africa and broadened the guest list. In January 1994, Africare began a program called "Training for Governance in the New South Africa," financed by USAID. It invited political candidates for premierships (a premier is equivalent to a U.S. governor) and their top aides to Washington for briefings by several American governors and their staffs on the duties of governing, on state finance, and on personnel management. After the election, successful candidates in some provinces and their transition teams received training in South Africa on fiscal and legislative procedures. More than five hundred South African political leaders and civil servants were beneficiaries of the practical information offered to them through the governance program.

Contemporaneously with its efforts to promote brand new democratic institutions in South Africa, Africare undertook the goal of helping other African nations in their shift from one-party regimes to more representative political rule. Benin, on the west coast, attempted the establishment of a popularly-based administration and market economy after its seventeen year-old Marxist government was voted out of office through free elections in 1991. With a grant from USAID in 1994, Africare began a seven-year program to promote democracy and to improve governance. The purpose of the Benin Indigenous NGO Strengthening project (known as BINGOS) was to reinforce civil society by encouraging local NGOs to participate in the identification of community needs, in the mobilization of citizens at the grass-roots level, and in self-help remedial activities. Many of these organizations

155

were of recent origin and all were fragile. The leadership possessed sketchy knowledge about program development, proposal writing, fund raising, and financial management. It needed instruction in such key principles as diversity, transparency, and accountability.

Africare began by selecting twenty-three local NGOs operating in both urban and rural areas to participate in pilot training sessions. They had sundry objectives, from tackling health and family planning issues to creating village solidarity groups for political action. Two examples are the "Association for the Protection of the Consumer and the Environment of Benin" and the "Association of Beninese Women Lawyers." Through group workshops on such important topics as administration, project planning, and evaluation, Beninese leaders acquired information to become professional in their activities. They also made visits to the sites of other NGOs. A particular need was to strengthen all aspects of dealing with money. One of the first sessions brought together NGO accountants who were honed in the skills of financial management and control, bookkeeping, and budgeting. In the belief that participating NGO leaders would better assimilate the principles taught to them if they could apply the knowledge in a practical way, Africare funded many of their new proposals. The consumer protection group mentioned above launched a campaign to inform city residents of their rights and of "smart" shopping practices. It distributed a leaflet with ten cartoons depicting confrontational situations that advised customers of their best response. Another NGO gave entrepreneurial and managerial training to unemployed youths, with those completing the course receiving loans to begin micro-enterprises. The Network for Peaceful and Transparent Elections allied many groups into a coordinated effort to monitor Beninese elections. Africare also gave support to a think tank with even broader political aims, GERDDES (Research Group on the Democratic, Economic and Social Development of Africa), that is now active in twenty-five African nations. Headquartered in Cotonou, Benin's largest city, it publishes its members' manuscripts and issues press releases stating its opinion of such political events as recent military coups in Togo and Niger.

Not all of the selected NGOs wished to comply with stringent Africare requirements, however. Over the period of the project's life, some left the program, but others joined, so that, by its end in 2000, ninety-five had been helped. Those participating gained in organizational strength and improved internal operations. They increased credibility with donors and development partners by establishing a

Beninese Code of Conduct for NGOs. Moreover, the effort of many participating NGOs to assist fledgling grassroots groups in becoming agents for the promotion of good governance and political democracy in their communities was a significant offshoot of the BINGO project. These were called "Relay NGOs." To sustain the goals and objectives of the BINGO program, the Network of Beninese NGOs for Democratic Governance was established in 1999. Its mission is to strengthen civil society through activities that raise community awareness, advocacy, and civic education.

Burundi, in central Africa's Great Lakes region, was another nation with a tenuous hold on democratic government in the early 1990s when its presidents were assassinated and civil war erupted between the Hutus and Tutsis, the dominant ethnic groups. For more than ten years, murder and brutality decimated the population. Survivors huddled in regroupment and displacement camps within Burundi, where they were still often vulnerable to attacks from mobs, or entered refugee camps in neighboring countries. Africare began activities related to encouraging civil society in 1995 with a program in the Burundi capital, Bujumbura, on Lake Tanganyika, that it called "NGO Support and Strengthening Project." The NGO sector in Burundi at this time was almost a new phenomenon. Many organizations had sprung up as a result of the political crisis and most directed their activities toward humanitarian assistance, such as reducing the rates of preventable and curable diseases or increasing food security. Africare objectives were to train them in internal management, peaceful conflict resolution, and participatory project development. One of many Burundian NGOs receiving institutional support from Africare was the Mutualist Self-Help Organization for Reconstruction and Development (ARD). Its purpose was to promote cooperation in self-help efforts within local communities most affected by political strife, the goal being to redirect attention from ethnic hatred to a shared assault on poverty.

In 2001, Africare decided to shift its work from the urban setting of Bujumbura to two rural areas, the adjacent provinces of Gitega and Karusi east of the capital at the geographic core of the nation. These regions had a high number of displaced persons, a high rate of poverty, and among the highest population densities of Burundi. Calling the program its "Strengthening Civil Society Organizations Project," Africare also added literacy, micro-projects, and rehabilitation of social infrastructure goals. Even though the first phase lasted only three years, the results were propitious for continuing the effort throughout the decade, which Africare did. During that initial period, the target of building human capacity at the local level through training leaders of civil society organizations and the community had limited success. More than three thousand attended the five-day workshops and were taught the fundamentals of participatory organizational management and the skills necessary to the efficient operation of their groups. They made contacts with other associations and the women especially became bolder in expressing their opinions. However, the length of the training was insufficient to establish the principles involved. Too often, just the president and the treasurer attended and did not train their members, and Africare employees did not follow-up on the effectiveness of their work.

The importance of expanding literacy cannot be overstated, for findings from other parts of Africa show it to be the most important element in building community capacity. For the twenty-five hundred people, mostly women, receiving literacy training in Gitega and Karusi, it meant being able to participate in the national debate about the high rate of illiteracy and to spread community awareness about such pressing matters as HIV/AIDS and peaceful conflict resolution. Another goal, sponsoring micro-projects, resulted in more than a hundred micro-projects being financed during the initial three years. They encouraged diversification of economic activities from the traditional sectors of agriculture and livestock-rearing and some, existing within displaced persons' camps, gave a sense of hope and a means of livelihood to these uprooted Burundians. The outcomes of the micro-projects were typical of private enterprises involving diverse objectives and independent actors. The Dushirehamwe fish farm association in Gitega province, formed in 1999 with twenty-three members (nine men and fourteen women), received a grant from Africare in 2002. All aspects of its project were well-organized, from having a duty roster to holding twice monthly meetings to discuss issues. It was so successful that, in the next year, participants were able to finance on their own a second fish farm. In contrast, the Dushigikirabatwa Association in Karusi province, established in 2002, had twenty-five members (twelve men and thirteen women) whose executive committee had no power and who were under the domination of two teachers at the local commune college. A year after receiving its grant, only 40% of the money could be accounted for, but the group's treasury was almost empty. Africare evaluators concluded that, with increased awareness in communities of possibilities for funding support, some speculators arose with the sole motivation of assembling associations to exploit the opportunity.

Social infrastructure refers to public buildings and other edifices that facilitate the functioning of communities and give benefit to the population as a whole. Many house service-providers that offer citizens opportunities for advancement or ameliorate inequality. Burundi had suffered nearly a decade of civil war when Africare moved to the interior of the country in 2001. The rehabilitation of the infrastructure was seen as a way of promoting cohesion in society and of encouraging cooperation between the government and the public. The construction of a new magistrate's court in one commune, after it had been destroyed ten years previously during the war, was a notable achievement. The reconstruction of two classrooms and the renovation of four others in a local primary school was another. A nutrition center was rehabilitated, latrines were built for an ethnic minority, and a commune college was repaired. All of these additions and many more unmentioned additions contributed to an improved quality of life in these two provinces.

In spite of the considerable success attained during the first phase of the effort to strengthen civil society organizations in the Gitega and Karusi provinces, Africare had to confront external factors that impeded its work and sometimes even undid what had been accomplished. Politicians within the country continued to wrangle over the future government. Peace accords, reached with help from mediators across Africa, were made and broken. Fighting disrupted the countryside and dispersed the population even farther than before. Rival forces stole goats and other animals from micro-projects. They damaged and then looted new staff houses at a health center. Regular field visits by Africare staff to participating associations became impossible. Because of the increased insecurity of the region, training of community leaders could not be decentralized. Instead, all participants had to journey to workshops at a central location in the city of Gitega, the second largest in Burundi, which entailed additional expense. Africare, bearing all the costs, was forced thus to reduce the size of the group invited.

The second phase of this program began in 2003 with non-governmental Africare funds and a grant from USAID. There was also technical support from Strategies for International Development, an Arlington, Virginia, outfit that specializes in developing the competence and sustainability of NGOs, and from ActionAid International/Burundi. The latter charity, founded in Great Britain, but now headquartered in Johannesburg, also collaborated by underwriting some HIV/AIDS activities. Burundi, after a decade of civil war, was a broken nation faced with the rehabilitation of its physical and human components, the reintegration of society, and the repatriation of refugees and combatants. Limiting the number of NGOs participating to thirty-eight, Africare brought together a diverse collection of organizations. Many worked directly with HIV/AIDS carriers, with orphans, or with households headed by children and the elderly. Others targeted displaced or repatriated people while some focused on households without land. The challenge of illiteracy in the community received attention from several NGOs.

Instead of funding NGO activities directly, as in Bujumbura, or financing citizen association micro-projects, as during the first phase in the Gitega and Kirusi provinces, Africare now concentrated on teaching NGO leaders the distinctive characteristics of designing, implementing, funding, and evaluating effective programs. It was a realignment of emphasis of which the goal was to assist Burundi NGOs in achieving autonomy.

Preliminary results of this second phase in Gitega and Kirusi illustrate the difficulties attending the transfer of functional knowledge from outside, foreign professionals to executives of largely volunteer agencies in other countries. On the subject of strategic planning, the NGOs benefitted greatly from thinking about their organizational structure and mission, but often failed to comprehend sufficiently the external political, economic, socio-cultural, and technological environment in which they operated. Sometimes they mistook an increase in the number of staff for an indication of their effectiveness. Most NGO members had no previous experience with writing project proposals. What they prepared in the past were usually incomplete and without formulated objectives, indicators, or clarity of action. The workshops offered by Africare helped most NGOs to master this prerequisite to success, yet there remained the problem that they did not research prospective donors sufficiently to tailor their projects to donor interests. Moreover, instead of lobbying new donors, they still focused on Africare as a possible source of funding or on those organizations with whom they were already familiar. Nonetheless, there was a significant level of achievement in just several years and capacity building among the NGOs did take place.

Burundi's neighbor, Rwanda, likewise suffered from civil war and genocide after the assassination of its president in 1994. Africare had been involved in refugee assistance (refugees from Uganda) and in environmental enhancement in Rwanda for more than a decade. After peace was restored, USAID chose the organization, due to its experience in civic education elsewhere, to carry out an $8 million project to develop participatory democracy. The goal of this Local Governance Initiatives project (LGI) was to assist the Government of Rwanda in devolving development responsibilities of the regions down to local government authorities, who, in turn, would canvas citizens about perceived needs, particularly in the infrastructure, and possible solutions. At the heart of the program was the hope that, through uniting on the issues, establishing priorities, and suggesting a plan of action, members from different ethnic and political backgrounds would reconcile. An added feature of USAID funding was the allocation of $80,000 to every participating community for infrastructure improvement.

Implementation of the project was undertaken in thirty communes of five prefectures containing high degrees of vulnerability and poverty, but adequate security to operate. After recognizing that the Rwandan population, at the grassroots level, was unaccustomed to participating in decision-making or proactively pressuring political leaders for improvements, Africare concentrated on training elected officials at the District level on principles of participatory community development. In a cascading pattern, those trained were to teach the tier of officials beneath them, who then mentored the next down, and so on until the new methods were instilled in cell representatives at the village. Simultaneously with instruction were identification of development needs and establishment of priorities. This information went back up the ladder to District headquarters. Here, Africare technical staff studied the proposals for feasibility and budgetary compliance. Those approved were sent to the Africare country office in Kigali and, finally, scrutinized by USAID for meeting established environmental preservation standards before funds were disbursed.

While the intentions of the Local Governance Initiatives project were admirable and there were measurable results in terms of infrastructure completion in many communes, there were deficiencies in the operation of the program, in the outcome, and in long-term consequence. One of the most serious overall flaws was the short duration of LGI. From its inception in 1997 to its conclusion in 2001, it was in actual operation only thirty months and included a size-able area of Rwanda. A much longer time was necessary to acquaint government officials and the populace with unfamiliar political methods and for them to internalize the principles of participatory democracy. In hindsight, Africare employees realized that, rather than concentrating on building the capacity of elected officials from the District level down, a better strategy would have been to work more directly with the population. This, of course, would have required far more time than the project allowed them. A related consideration was the goal of promoting reconciliation among the different ethnic and political factions of Rwanda. Thirty months proved far too few to accomplish much along those lines. Another flaw in LGI was a de-sign that centralized decision-making in the Africare country office staff and, even more importantly, in USAID, with its ultimate power to fund only proposals that met environmental protection standards. It was too bureaucratic. Local Africare staff had to refer all matters to headquarters in Kigali. The whole system was such an inefficient and time-consuming process that there were cases in which com-munity development projects were not fully funded by the time LGI ended.

The questions of long-term benefit and of sustainability are also raised by the Africare experience in Rwanda. The Local Governance Initiatives project was funded by USAID at the request of the Rwan-dan Ministry of Local Government and Social Affairs. Once foreign assistance ended, the national government became responsible for continuing community projects. Even during LGI, there was some doubt about the commitment of officials in the capital, who, claim-ing limited government financial resources, occasionally did not pay salaries to civil servants in the local administrative structure. The demoralization of these civil servants resulted in poor work per-formance and sometimes accounted for delays in disbursement of funds for projects. In these cases, the consequent disillusionment of citizens with the participatory process had its beginning at the cen-tral government, but Africare's project design contained no means of influencing it and no follow-up strategies to continue the progress made in the prefectures. Furthermore, the District officials trained, as well as those lower in the governmental hierarchy, were elected. New local government elections in 2002 produced a fresh roster of political figures, and the absence of any plan for perpetuating Africare capacity building left them without the knowledge or experience acquired by their predecessors. The sustainability of Africare's achievement was thus jeopardized.

Recent small examples coming from Guinea, Niger, and Chad illustrate further the diversity of Africare activities in this field over the years. The first was part of the Dinguiraye monetization food security program in Guinea that aimed to improve the health and nutrition of women and children. A survey in 2003 found that, of the 191 women canvassed, 74% did not have birth certificates, 92% did not have copies of their marriage certificates, 77% did not know how to obtain a national identification card, and 92% did not hold an identification card. Without the latter, they could not travel freely, vote during presidential or other elections, or open a bank account. Africare began implementation of the Dinguiraye Rights of Women program in collaboration with the local Department of Health and with COFEG, an association of more than forty women's NGOs. It trained community-based volunteers in such subjects as human rights, the Guinean fundamental code of law, and the importance of having a national ID card as well as other documents. By the end of the one-year drive, it had enabled a thousand women participants in the monetization program to receive their IDs and copies of their marriage and birth certificates. Initial results seemed small, but the importance of these civil rights for women was now established within the region and there were avenues by which ideas could be advanced.

Niger is a second case that shows the range of Africare attempts to promote democracy and good governance. Upon achieving independence from France in 1960, the people of Niger elected a prominent and respected politician, Diori Hamani, as their first president. He soon outlawed opposition parties and created a single-party authoritarian regime. The Sahelian drought crisis and corruption charges led to a military coup in 1974, after which Niger was controlled by a series of colonels who slowly acquiesced, by the early 1990s, to popular demand for a national conference that would write a new constitution and prepare for general elections. Political parties, civic associations, unions, and student groups sprang up to participate in the debate. The civilian government elected in 1993 ended up as an unworkable coalition that was replaced in 1996 with another round of military rulers. A further coup in 1999 resulted in the promulgation of the fifth constitution since 1960. New presidential elections brought to power Tandja Mamadou, coincidentally born in Maine-Soroa, and he ruled fairly successfully until 2009, when, facing compulsory presidential term limits, he bypassed the legislature and the judiciary to hold a national referendum on the extension of his service. Labor strikes, political opposition, and international approbation culminated in another military coup in February 2010.

Throughout Niger's political turmoil and even after it lost its patron, Diori, Africare continued its programs in agriculture, health, and well construction. In 2000, with repeated funding from the National Endowment for Democracy, it began coaching indigenous NGOs, particularly those promoting civil society and women's rights, in successful methods of grassroots political participation. Africare's usual format was to hold a succession of workshops on democracy and good governance in which representatives from NGOs learned what were considered the essentials of NGO operation: democratic and transparent management, conflict resolution and nonviolence, and lobbying procedures. Whether or not NGOs working solely with women were the targeted groups, Africare stressed the importance of including women in the democratic process and of reducing gender inequality. NGOs selected at the beginning of the program came from Niamey and the interior of the country, but by mid-decade, Africare began concentrating on those in the northern region of Agadez where a Tuareg rebellion, famine, and Muslim fundamentalism had undermined government stability. NGOs here were seen as particularly valuable in countering Tuareg feelings of marginalization and in decentralizing the monolithic political power that for years had fueled public disaffection. Progress toward these goals was halted in 2007 with a renewal of war between Tuareg militias and the Nigerien army. President Tandja declared a state of emergency while NGOs attempted to help civilians needing food, shelter, and medical assistance. Heavy downpours of rain and flooding in August added to the human misery, worsened by the inability of international aid agencies to reach many parts of the north because of landmines.

Nearby in Chad, the nation's political history and trajectory were remarkably similar to those of Niger. It too received independence from France in 1960 and in the mid-1970s began experiencing military coups, insurgencies, coalition politics, and destabilizing foreign incursions into the country. Government massacres of civilians and clashes with rebel groups, some advocating democratic objectives, contributed to the chaos. From among the generals, there arose in late 1990 Idriss Deby, who, under pressure from many political factions within the country and from France, held a national conference in 1993 to discuss the creation of a pluralist democratic regime. This was the catalyst for the founding not only of political parties (legalized in 1992), but of voluntary associations representing social, religious, human rights, development, gender, and specific inter-community issues. The first presidential election held in accordance with the 1996 constitution resulted in a victory for Deby, who has since been reelected twice after a national referendum of Chadians in 2005 abolished presidential term limits. In spite of the apparent stability in Chad's leadership, the nation is actually extremely fragile. Thousands of refugees entering Chad from Darfur in neighboring Sudan have become not only a burden on the government, but a source of ethnic conflict. There are also refugees from the Central African Republic on the southern border. Moreover, armed opposition groups and widespread banditry within Chad uproot citizens, adding to the number of internally displaced persons. In this current situation, the Government of Chad has declared a state of emergency.

Africare is attempting to do in Chad what it is currently doing in Niger: increase grassroots participation in civil society by strengthening non-governmental organizations. With grants from the National Endowment for Democracy, its first task has been to identify groups seeking to address tolerance, peaceful cohabitation, and democracy issues from among the many groups with more parochial or personal ambitions. Africare found that most NGOs in Chad are organizationally and financially weak. Seldom do they have an office or staff and their internal governance sometimes is itself undemocratic. Yet, they are the best means by which to establish communication between their constituencies and the country's policy makers. From a category of NGOs that it designated as "developed" in its baseline survey, Africare selected ten for capacity building. Their representatives were tutored in procedures for running NGOs, such as participatory decision-making, long range institutional planning and development, project design, and financial management. They were further trained in the use of conflict resolution and cross-cultural interaction techniques. One feature of the program that Africare used with NGOs in Niger that was even more important in Chad was the sub-granting of funds to the groups in order for them to gain experience in implementing projects encouraging dialogue on democracy and good governance topics within their communities.

Related to these efforts in Niger and Chad to strengthen civil society has been a move since 2001 to build solar-powered radio stations in rural communities of northern Niger, one of Africa's most isolated regions. As recently as 2000, Niger had only one state-owned telephone company, one state-run internet service provider, and state-owned radio and television stations. In a switch of policy, however, the Government of Niger began opening up these enterprises to competition and further chose to promote rural radio networks as an important development tool. It gave stations authority to broadcast local and world news and weather as well as information about democracy and civil rights, health, agriculture, and women in development. Africare immediately recognized not only the potential in setting up broadcasting facilities, but the advantages of enhancing them with other applications. Africare radios were equipped with solar-powered television and two-way communication, the first important in permitting the showing of visual material about such subjects as HIV/AIDS and the second linking not just all Africare radios, but giving Africare staff in Agadez immediate contact with the country rep in Niamey. With a view toward sustainability of the radio network, an important part of Africare's work has been to ensure community participation in decisions regarding programming, station management, and governance. Once Africare completes its installation and early operation, all responsibilities belong to local citizens. Organized into radio associations, they must also maintain the equipment and find income-generating activities to pay the costs heretofore assumed by Africare.

8

Refugee Assistance and Emergency Relief

A primary cause of human misery in sub-Saharan Africa since the mid-twentieth century has been uneven and unpredictable rainfall, accentuated by prolonged droughts. The effort to understand whether this is a new environmental threat or the continuation of age-old patterns requires the historical reconstruction of African climate variation. This relatively new field of academic endeavor, however, is thwarted by the absence of data other than that provided indirectly in histories, archives, local chronicles, the journals of travelers and settlers, or from geological evidence. Whereas what we know about the African climate in the distant past is more speculative the farther back we go, information about the nineteenth century and more recent decades gives a better picture due to material provided by a great number of ship captains, missionaries, colonists, foreign government officials, and European visitors to sub-Saharan Africa. It helps to put contemporary episodes into a context that demonstrates the cyclical nature of environmental activity. It contributes to recognition that drought is a periodic, recurring event that will probably always threaten African nations. It establishes the need, now that meteorological science has shown that natural phenomena explain the origins of drought, for African and overseas agencies, governmental and private, to establish warning systems with the goal of forestalling future food crises.

One example from history that illustrates African climatic variations comes from missionary journals and other documentary sources of Europeans traveling in southern Africa in the nineteenth century. From these, we ascertain that the enormous area known today as Botswana had significant rainfall swings. There were major droughts in every decade from 1820 until 1900. Conversely, with one exception, there were periods wetter than normal in every decade from 1810 to

1900. The prevalence of dry spells, emphasized more by witnesses than wet phases, fueled a debate within the British scientific community over the eventual desiccation of Africa. For evidence, these scholars and prominent arm-chair travelers relied on the correspondence of David Livingstone and other London Missionary Society members who, as they established mission stations farther and farther to the interior of southern Africa, recorded information about the weather. While even the careful collection of data by Livingstone, himself an advocate of the concept of long-term desiccation in Africa, failed to convince skeptics and has never received empirical scientific support, his observations provided testimony to the inevitable cycles of drought over a very large region. Livingstone, as he subsequently explored the southern half of the African continent, did report famine at different locations in the 1850s and 1860s. However, it was not the result of rainfall failure, but of tribal warfare or disease.

Another example from the historical record also illustrates cycles of dry and wet years in a large geographical area as well as the fact that drought does not necessarily lead to famine. In the early nineteenth century, the population of northern Somalia, mostly herders and fishermen, had a symbiotic commercial and labor relationship that sustained their subsistence even during periods of drought. At such times, pastoralists moved their herds around and hoarded their livestock. Everyone practiced conservation measures and, when necessary, gave up what for them were luxuries, such as drinking coffee. There was no famine. During the second half of the century, however, as the pattern of recurrent drought continued, the word became synonymous with famine. The explanation for this change of fortunes lies in the emergence of a new economic emphasis by the ruling African group, the Majeerteen. As early as 1800, ships, such as those of the British East India Company sailing from Bombay via Aden to Suez, regularly wrecked off the Horn of Africa, where crews were murdered and goods were looted by the Majeerteen. Slowly, as the chiefs built up their economic and political power, certain lineages became stronger than others. The next step was consolidation of most authority into the hands of one lineage and its perpetuation by shipwreck loot and taxes on merchandise entering coastal ports. The Majeerteen sultans by mid-century, after agreeing to humane treatment of shipwrecked sailors, set out to increase their wealth by encouraging trade in livestock, gum, incense, and myrrh with ship captains from Muscat, Bombay, and Aden. Ignoring ecological consequences, they pressured pastoralists to build up their herds and by other measures upset the fine economic balance between herders and fishermen. Their policies were profitable to some elements of the population, but left one group, pastoral people, particularly vulnerable to rainfall shortages that continued every decade or so through the rest of the nineteenth and into the early twentieth century. The droughts of 1868 and 1880, when there were great famines, stand in marked contrast to that of 1840-43 when one English visitor reported seeing fat goats, immense flocks of sheep, and large herds of horned cattle.

The extensive work of scholars attempting to reconstruct the climatic history of West Africa has shown that the Sahel has also experienced cycles of drought and above normal rainfall. The relatively dry first half of the nineteenth century was succeeded by a return in about 1860 or 1870 to conditions significantly wetter than any in the twentieth century. After 1900, there were seven periods of reduced rainfall in seven decades, including a severe drought in 1913 and the 1968-74 droughts. Famine ensued from many of them.

The message from this limited review of historical literature is that sub-Saharan Africa has natural fluctuations in rainfall and societies must minimize the deleterious effects of drought through careful management of their resources. It has been the goal of Africare, with support from various agencies of the United States Government, such international players as United Nations High Commissioner for Refugees (UNHCR), private foundations, and individual donors, to link development with relief, believing that handouts are a dead-end street unless victims of environmental catastrophes possess the means and a strategy to go forward. After its initial life-saving efforts in the Sahel in 1973, it began planning long-term programs to help the nomads and farmers there reconstruct their lives and livelihoods. These programs really launched Africare as a development agency and it steadfastly tries to maintain the distinction that it works with refugees as an extension of development programs rather than existing as an emergency refugee organization that extends it operations to development.

Drought has been but one of the menaces disrupting African nations in recent times. Warfare between countries and civil unrest within countries have dislodged citizens from their homes and destroyed their often meager assets. These conflicts have been common causes of famine, as in earlier centuries. Joining with the UNHCR and the Lutheran World Federation to aid the Zambian Government in settling a tide of refugees escaping wars in neighboring countries was Africare's first experience with this type of refugee. Subsequently, it sent advisors to Somalia to help it cope with the refugee crisis ensuing from a conflict with Ethiopia over the Ogaden. Victims of environmental catastrophes and of foreign and civil wars have been the principal beneficiaries of Africare humanitarian efforts, but those affected by random misfortunes, such as Nigerians living near a munitions depot explosion, have also received emergency assistance. Since the 1990s, Africare has responded to the growing threat of starvation among a whole new group of Africans: those touched in some way by HIV/AIDS.

Africare did not start out to be an aid group and it is not one, per se, but it has worked with American governmental agencies, multinational relief bodies, and private foundations on almost every natural and man-made emergency in sub-Saharan Africa since the early 1970s. This has been a major segment of its operations, as financial statements attest. The opportunity to join in life-saving measures across the continent was not only consistent with Africare's statement of purpose, but valuable to it in an economic sense. While Africare has the philosophy of going where it sees a need, it must nonetheless have sound financial underpinnings, as all charities, and the overhead payment to participants built into relief budgets, varying from 5% to 20% of direct line items or even more, contributed significantly to the organization's income. In some early years, the budget category labeled "relief and refugee assistance" accounted for 20% to 25% of program services. Hence, the ad hoc nature by which Africare sometimes committed itself to new ventures and opened offices in far-flung African nations resulted not just through a combination of American foreign aid decisions and appeals from African governments, but also through shrewd calculations of funding. For example, Kevin Lowther, regional director for southern Africa, in a 1993 memorandum to C. Payne Lucas and Joe Kennedy, repeatedly enumerated how much money would be generated in overhead if Africare expanded its fledgling program in Angola. It should be said at the same time, however, that federal and international requests for Africare involvement or approval of its proposals were based on recognition of its past effectiveness and its immediate availability. Correspondingly, Africare had the institutional flexibility and adaptability to be in-country rapidly.

The frequency of droughts in sub-Saharan Africa since the founding of Africare in 1970 highlights the place that famine relief and emergency assistance have assumed in Africare's operations. Between 1970 and 2004, fourteen nations reported drought more than ten times. Their names are familiar and the list includes Somalia, Ethiopia, Zimbabwe, and all six of the Sahelian countries. If the total number of nations affected by drought is counted during that period, the figure ranges from one in 1986 to thirty in 1983. The 1983-84 droughts were more severe and caused more incidents of famine over a greater part of sub-Saharan Africa than that of the Sahel from 1968 to 1974. Other peak years were 1992 and 2001. Again, beginning in 2005 and continuing to the present, severe drought in a band across West Africa from Niger to Sudan and southward through Kenya to the tip of Africa has brought hunger to millions of people. In many countries, the effects of drought have been exacerbated or even surpassed in human suffering by warfare of some type. It is an unfortunate truth that African nations are less able to meet their food needs now than they were earlier, in part because of increasing populations, in part because of the controversy over genetically modified seeds and other agricultural inputs, and in part because of additional factors.

Experts have different definitions of the word "famine," but most generally agree that it refers to extreme incidents of starvation and associated diseases that result in unusually high mortality from a lack of food. It is simplistic to say that there is any one cause. Drought is certainly a foremost explanation, but it is often compounded by pestilence, as in the 2005 invasion of locusts in Niger, by the presence of civil strife, or by disease, such as a high rate of HIV/AIDS infection. Regarding the actual mechanism of famine, scholars debate two main theories. One, the supply side theory, attributes widespread hunger to a decline in the availability of food stocks within a country through droughts, floods, or population pressure and adherents to this belief advocate the development of drought-resistant species, better food storage, and related improvements in agriculture. The other approach is called the entitlement or demand side theory. By it, rural people, the majority of the population in sub-Saharan Africa, have low and unstable incomes dependent on a fragile environment. As drought deepens, large numbers of them lose purchasing power and are unable to pay market prices for food. Farmers have no crops to sell, herders sell their livestock or see it die, and agricultural laborers become unemployed. Families begin to dispose of household goods and garden equipment. The next step often is for family members or whole families to leave their homes for other areas, inside or outside the country, where they might survive. In the meantime, established traders in towns are benefitting by being able to buy up commodities at depressed prices and holding them for higher profits later. Many entitlement theorists argue that, with the fundamental problem being the inequity between the social classes and the marginalization of the poor, more democratic and stable governments would lessen the risk factors for famine. They are less concerned about a country being self-sufficient in food production than in ensuring access to food by the vulnerable.

After delivering emergency relief to drought victims in the Sahel in the 1970s and while continuing the effort in some of the six nations in successive decades, Africare crossed the continent to Ethiopia, where famine prevailed, in 1984. Parts of the country had suffered intermittently from rainfall shortages for a decade, but even more important than the environmental situation in explaining hunger was the political. Emperor Haile Selassie had been overthrown in 1974 and replaced by Colonel Mengistu Haile Marian, who, seeking revolutionary transformation of Ethiopian society, militarized the economy, set up large state farms, and denied government support to the majority rural population. More than 40% of the country was controlled by guerrilla forces representing autonomous movements in the northern provinces of Eritrea and Tigray. In war-torn areas, whether guerrilla-dominated or government-controlled, armed troops had reduced agricultural sufficiency through the requisitioning of peasant food, disruption of markets and transportation, and military conscription. A Relief and Rehabilitation Commission, established in 1975 in response to the 1973 famine, tried to alert Western nations to the increasing starvation during the first nine months of 1984, but was met with skepticism, particularly when the regime spent enormous sums of money celebrating the tenth anniversary of the revolution in September. No effective relief action, domestic or international, was taken until foreign media, such as BBC, publicized the plight of Ethiopian citizens. By late fall, the overseas donor community began shipping grain and supplies to Ethiopia.

For the United States, which had withdrawn development funding and had been phasing out its USAID Food for Peace Program (P.L. 480) since Mengistu aligned Ethiopia with the Soviet Union in 1974, it was a difficult decision whether to supply emergency assistance in spite of the left-leaning, hostile government or to pursue President Ronald Reagan's strategy of supporting anti-communist opposition.

The Administration soon concluded that food could be a political weapon and allocated money for food deliveries. Recognizing that the Mengistu government wanted to distribute aid only to its internal allies and for strategic, regime-strengthening purposes, the United States insisted on certain conditions that would ensure the integrity of the program, the distribution of food to needy people in all areas of the country, and the avoidance of corruption. The World Food Programme (WFP) and American NGOs, many of them already with a track record in different regions of Ethiopia, were the means chosen to carry out the American mandate. Hence, Africare, along with Catholic Relief Services, Save the Children Federation, World Vision, Lutheran World Relief, and other American charities, became part of the international effort to alleviate suffering in a desperately poor, politically fragmented nation.

Africare opened a field office in Addis Ababa in December 1984, and appointed a country representative who, with his staff, worked with the Relief and Rehabilitation Commission and other organizations. One of the most controversial issues concerned which areas of Ethiopia would receive food aid, specifically whether the central government would allow commodities to reach insurgent territory where famine was the most severe. This was never resolved satisfactorily, for 80% of American aid went to Mengistu, who used it to placate the urban population and his soldiers, groups most capable of toppling him. Under intense international pressure, he finally allowed a few American groups to operate in the northern war zones and Africare was one of them. A major center of Africare activity was the city of Mekele, capital of Eritrea, where feeding shelters were set up for Ethiopians fleeing distant famine-stricken villages. Africare distributed blankets (at an altitude of 6800 feet, the area was very cold at night), cooking utensils, clothing, tents, oral rehydration salts, and some food commodities. An Africare volunteer medical team dispensed treatment and medicines through a field hospital. Two other sites of similar Africare assistance were Amatare, also in Eritrea, and Kat-bare, south of Addis Ababa in Shoa.

To supplement the financing it received through its agreements with U.S. Government agencies to participate in Ethiopian relief, Africare mounted a fund raising campaign in the United States. One mass mailing enclosed postcards addressed to "Field Workers in Ethiopia" that recipients were to return with personal messages and, it was hoped, donations. Monetary contributions flowed into Africare headquarters

173

from private citizens, local chapters, churches, and civic groups. Even cities joined in the effort, as in January 1985, when Aspen and Snowmass, Colorado, raised $200,000 with a sponsored competition called "Africare, We Care: Not a Trivial Pursuit" and other activities. Corporations and businesses also gave. Private foundations, such as the Lilly Endowment, awarded sizable grants. Many business firms furnished in-kind gifts. Member companies of the Pharmaceutical Manufacturers Association of the United States donated medicines. Levi Strauss and Co. gave 217,000 units of new clothing.

The worst part of the Ethiopian famine was over by the end of 1986. The United States gave $282 million in relief aid in 1985, over half of all that Ethiopia received, $156 million in 1986, and lesser amounts thereafter. Reversing its policies on development financing for unfriendly countries, the Reagan Administration supported passage in Congress of the 1985 African Famine Relief and Recovery Act, which authorized funds for water projects, small-scale agricultural projects, emergency health care, and similar activities—all the types of programs that Africare had been doing since 1971. Moreover, the new legislation applied not just to Ethiopia, but to any African country affected by food supply problems during 1984 and 1985.

In Ethiopia, Africare swiftly switched its focus from helping people in feeding shelters to attempting long-term solutions through well-drilling, irrigation systems, and agricultural inputs. It was soon able to apply its development skills to a new area of Ethiopia. Although neighboring Sudan, which shared a long border with Ethiopia, also experienced a short, but less intense famine in 1984, its real troubles began with efforts in 1983 to overthrow Jaafar Nimeiri, who had assumed power in 1969. Political turmoil and civil unrest continued after his downfall in 1985, causing large numbers of the population, particularly those belonging to non-Arab ethnic groups in the south, to escape across the border to Ethiopia. The World Food Programme, UNHCR, and UNICEF established refugee camps as early as 1983 and a very large one, with at least 150,000 permanent residents, was set up at Itang in the Gambella region of southwestern Ethiopia. Africare undertook the improvement of the water system for the Itang camp, which consisted of eight villages of mainly Nuer-speaking people, in 1989. It drilled wells and erected storage tanks for them, installed pumps, and created a distribution mechanism, all with the purpose of improving sanitation and health. When Africare worked at Itang in 1989 and 1990, the refugees were all Sudanese. In May 1991, after the fall of the Mengistu government and the attacks on Itang, camp residents moved en masse back to southern Sudan.

Civil wars across the African continent during the decade of the 1990s were often the primary generator of refugees, internally displaced persons, food insufficiency, and health threats. A major conflict occurred in Angola. Just as Africare finished its effort among refugees from civil strife in southwestern Ethiopia in 1990, the Office of U.S. Foreign Disaster Assistance asked it to assist orphans and displaced persons there. Civil war had been raging in Angola since the Portuguese granted it independence in 1975, but a peace accord between the main contenders for power, the MPLA and UNITA political movements, was being arranged and was indeed signed in May 1991. The fighting, with MPLA being supported by Cuba and the Soviet Union, and UNITA receiving war materiel from the United States and South Africa, had ravaged the country from its Zairean to its Namibian borders. Schools, health centers, public buildings, and water points were now in shambles. Aside from the thousands of civilians killed, families had been uprooted from their farms and scattered. There were both orphans and children separated from their parents wandering the countryside. Many of them made their way to towns where there was some hope of food and shelter. It was these young individuals that Africare initially helped by supplying mattresses, blankets, eating utensils, and food commodities to orphanages where many youths arrived. Other early activities in Angola were offering vaccinations to mothers and children and helping displaced families begin again with seeds, farm tools, and household goods.

Africare's entry into Angola for crisis relief turned into a long-term presence and the organization has been well-received in spite of the shifting policies of the American government. The May 1991 peace accord soon broke down and civil war continued until 2002. At one time, UNITA controlled 70% of the country; later, MPLA ruled 60%. One-third of Angola's population of twelve million was displaced during the twenty-seven years following Portuguese rule. Africare, engaged in both UNITA-held communities and in government-dominated areas, sometimes found it difficult to persuade both sides that its assistance was evenly split between them. As the war subsided in the late 1990s, Africare added reconstruction and development programs to its emergency aid projects. It provided agricultural education in the best methods of seed multiplication and livestock and edible oil production, landmine education and clearance, and

175

infrastructure repair, in addition to offering vocational training for street children in Luanda and other cities, facilitating the reintegration of UNITA combatants into civilian life through resettlement and retraining, and giving health care to internally displaced women and children. Both categories of activities continued into the twenty-first century. Through the World Food Programme, ChevronTexaco Company, Archer Daniels Midland Company, and other donors, Africare distributed food to internally displaced persons and malnourished children in many Angolan districts. Polio eradication and malaria prevention drives were supported by the Bill & Melinda Gates Foundation, USAID/CORE group, and ExxonMobil Foundation. American and international governmental agencies, as well as such private firms as Cabinda Gulf Oil and Citizens Energy Corporation, funded agricultural training, improvements, and innovations. Wells, an Africare specialty, were paid for by the African Well Fund and the Office of U.S. Foreign Disaster Assistance.

It is highly likely that Africare and other American charities will become much more engaged in Angolan development than they have been, for the U.S. State Department has come to recognize the strategic value of friendly relations with the essentially one-party government of Jose Eduardo dos Santos, head of the MPLA. In 2008, Angola surpassed Nigeria as Africa's top oil producer and its economy is one of the fastest growing in the world, thanks to oil production, which contributes about 85% of GDP. To the consternation of the United States, Chinese companies have been awarded contracts to rebuild the infrastructure and, additionally, China has become an important trading partner. The Angolan government, one of the most corrupt in the world, has yet to turn much attention to questions of poverty, inequality, and economic diversification, however. Improving agriculture is essential because Angola's urban population, now 57% of the total as a result of large migrations from rural areas during the civil war, and its heavy dependence on imported food (half of the country's food supply) provide opportunities for here-to-fore subsistence farmers to prosper and to build national food security. It would also help reduce Angola's serious unemployment problem.

Offering seeds and tools for vegetable gardening to refugees from many of Africa's civil and national wars had the effect of augmenting relief aid while imparting a measure of hope for the future. It also fostered self sufficiency and economic independence. Africare did this in Somalia, Liberia, Sierra Leone, Angola, and other countries. Near

Jalalaqsi, Somalia, a town of 15,000 located one hundred and fifteen miles northwest of Mogadishu, 80,000 refugees had sought safety from internecine wars in the region. Africare, in one project, helped sixty refugee women and their families establish a thirty-three acre vegetable garden that produced, in addition to other crops, more than a thousand bushels of corn the first season. Additional refugee sites in Somalia likewise came under the Africare mantle.

When Liberia fell into civil war in 1989 as dissidents under Charles Taylor attacked the Samuel Doe government, more than seven hundred thousand Liberians, mainly of Doe's Krahn ethnic group, fled to neighboring West African countries. Africare collaborated with the refugee aid coordination committee of the Government of the Ivory Coast to manage a thousand acre vegetable gardening project in the Ivorian prefecture of Guiglo bordering Liberia where 132,000 refugees congregated. Local chiefs decided on the selection of vacant land for farming, and government agricultural agents distributed cutlasses, hoes, rakes, and other implements to individual families for land preparation. Once the plots were ready, agents offered a seed selection that included okra, tomatoes, eggplant, cabbage, and onions. Forty-six tons of fresh vegetables were harvested during the one-year project and although some refugees repatriated during that time, Africare estimated that 16% of the refugee population had benefitted by its end in late 1992. In fact, total production so far exceeded expectation that there was a need to provide more post-harvest storage facilities, to find more outlets for marketing, and to think of alternatives usage of the crops. The difficulties of reaching this level of success should not be overlooked, however. The first major issue was acquiring land for the gardens. There seemed to be unlimited space available in the prefecture, but land tenure and ownership were communal and passed on from generation to generation. Family history was conveyed in stories of land usage. Additionally, as customary, local chiefs, allocating territory to newcomers, tended to assign marginal areas or ground several miles distant from villages to the refugees. Then, there were invasions of grasshoppers and unpredictable weather, both detrimental to good crop yields.

Sierra Leone was also consumed by civil war in the 1990s. A Revolutionary United Front (RUF) army of disgruntled radicals entered the eastern part of the country from Liberia in September 1991, and quickly showed the inability of the government to defend the population. Although control of diamond production was popularly thought to be the basis of the conflict, there were long-standing political and economic grievances that had given birth to opposition groups within the country. RUF counted on their support, but its brutality, recruitment of children into the military, and widespread devastation of the countryside caused civilians to flee. Rebel armies stretched over about half of Sierra Leone at times and once even reached the suburbs of Freetown, the capital. The United Nations and African regional political monitors were mostly ineffective in arranging ceasefires or settling the military stalemate. In 2001, with the help of UN peacekeepers, a civilian government regained power over the entire country and the war ended. As many as 75,000 citizens may have been killed during the decade and 500,000 displaced. Many people, especially children, became amputees, for RUF had a predilection for chopping off hands and limbs. Girls were targeted for the sex trade and women were often rape victims.

Emergency assistance to displaced Sierra Leoneans was the first program undertaken by Africare during the civil war because of the increasing stream of people flowing into provincial capitals from rural areas. Beginning in 1991 with day-care for children, a project financed by Alpha Kappa Alpha sorority, it soon expanded its operations to supplying the uprooted with food and medical relief. These initial steps were supplemented incrementally during the decade as Africare, in cooperation with American and international agencies as well as private donors, turned from emergency response to developmental activity. It offered technical advice and agricultural inputs to displaced farm families, particularly those in eastern and southern regions most affected by the fighting. It helped displaced women learn income-generating skills such as blanket weaving, soap making, and tie-dying. It rehabilitated damaged health clinics and it trained health workers and traditional birth attendants. Moreover, it emphasized health and sanitation when it rebuilt old wells or drilled new ones and constructed latrines.

Africare's participation in Sierra Leone relief encountered unforeseen difficulties and illustrates the risks that charities must assume when they enter war-torn nations. The first episode was the disappearance of an American expatriate Africare employee, his Sierra Leonean driver, and his Sierra Leonean landlord in October 1992, when RUF forces overran the town where they were living. The American and the driver were part of the Sierra Leone Red Cross Society's food distribution program and they were "invited" to see the rebel base seven hours away. Off they went over torturous roads in the Red Cross Land Cruiser, followed by the landlord in his BMW. For five weeks they were harangued by the rebels because the Red Cross was not delivering assistance to Sierra Leoneans behind enemy lines. Meanwhile, C. Payne Lucas, with only a report from the landlord's daughter, who witnessed the abduction, and from a village chief, who saw the two vehicles heading upcountry, urged the U.S. State Department and the embassies of West African nations in Washington, D.C., to pressure RUF for their return.

The second unanticipated disruption of Africare service in Sierra Leone came during a lull in fighting between government troops and RUF rebels when international organizations—prematurely, it turned out—began planning for the transition to peace. Africare was heavily involved in health and agriculture activities sponsored by the United Nations Development Programme, the European Economic Community, and USAID, but in May 1997, a military coup overthrew the elected government and brought all work to an abrupt end. Ten months later, the earlier politicians reinstalled, Africare was able to continue its programs. Unfortunately for Africare, for development agencies (whether public or private), and most of all for the citizens of African nations who need assistance, what happened in Sierra Leone is common where there is political unrest. For both Liberia and Angola, as examples, Africare announced in several annual reports during the 1990s that the civil war was over and that it would again pursue projects for the reconstruction and development of the nation. Subsequent issues all too often rued the fact that fighting had resumed.

For the last fifty years, international relief agencies, private charities, and foreign governments have witnessed the continuous flow of refugees and internally displaced persons produced by the interconnected political turmoil of three contiguous nations in central Africa: Sudan, Chad, and the Central African Republic. Mutinies, coups, secessionist movements, civil and foreign wars, and repressive regimes, both civilian and military, have made this region a cauldron of trouble. Seldom, however, do most citizens in the West learn about the problems of these distant nations or have any comprehension of the human suffering stemming from them, unless the condition is so egregious that some humanitarian group, celebrity, or news forum cries an alarm. The 1984 famine in Ethiopia is a case in point and the current situation in Sudan, where the plight of refugees from Darfur began receiving world-wide media attention in 2003, is another.

However, the effects of civil unrest in the Central African Republic and in Chad, which are significant, have received scant notice. Little has been written about what it means to the Government of Chad to house dozens of refugee camps inside its eastern and its southern borders. Almost nothing has appeared in print or in television reports about the movement of refugees into host countries and the local social-economic consequences of their relocation.

Political instability characterized Sudan long before tensions in Darfur broke into hostilities, in fact, from the time of independence in 1956. Two civil wars between the Arab-dominated Islamic-inclined military governments in Khartoum and the non-Arab, non-Muslim ethnic groups in the South from 1970 to 2000 resulted in millions of displaced persons within Sudan and of refugees fleeing to the neighboring countries of Ethiopia, Uganda, and Kenya. Millions more died as a direct result of the conflict or as a consequence of the attendant famine. Just as the brutal war between North and South came to a negotiated settlement early in the twentieth-first century, long-simmering hatreds among a complex mixture of ethnic groups in Darfur, the western region of Sudan about the size of Texas, exploded into a vicious battle of reprisals that left no man, woman, or child unaffected.

The word "Darfur" in Arabic means home or abode (dar) of the Fur, the principal ethnic group (since all people in Darfur are black, distinction among them is designated by ethnic group) who, as sedentary agriculturalists, have occupied the climatically-desirable and rich land in the south-central part of the region since before recorded history. They are non-Arab and their language is unrelated to Arabic. To the west of them are other non-Arab groups with their own languages, an important one being the Zaghawa, a pastoralist group divided by the Sudanese-Chad border. Non-Arabs share Darfur with two other major ethnic categories: Arabs and West Africans. Arab nomads began migrating into the northern and southern sections of Darfur about five centuries ago and through intermarriage acquired African physical characteristics. They kept their Arabic languages and emphasized their unique Arab identity. As herders of camels in the north and of cows in the south, they moved seasonally in search of grass and water. The West Africans were agriculturalists from nations currently called the Central African Republic and the Democratic Republic of the Congo. Except for the Fur, most of Darfur's present population of perhaps ten million people (the last census was in 1973) came originally as transients or migrants, but, whatever its population's origin, language, or racial heritage, it is all Muslim in its religious faith.

The territory of Darfur, far from Khartoum, has been loosely administered by a central government, whether colonial or independent, for nearly two hundred years since Egypt, itself a province of the Ottoman Empire, wrested its control from autonomous sultans in the early nineteenth century. The marginalization of Darfur became particularly striking in the decades of the 1970s and 1980s as drought worsened and the region became militarized through wars in neighboring Libya and Chad. Shortages of rainfall in certain parts of Darfur prompted pastoralists to move into central agricultural areas and this happened at a time when farmers, encouraged by improving urban markets, were increasing the amount of land under cultivation. Simultaneously, some agriculturalist ethnic groups, affected by drought where they lived outside the core zone, migrated into it, also adding pressure to established agricultural interests. It became a battle for resources—land, water, and open spaces—exacerbated by the historic rivalry between Arabs and non-Arabs. The central government, not acknowledging that drought and famine existed in Darfur, ignored the growing tension among the population.

Contributing to the environmental aspect of a downward spiral toward civil war in Darfur was Sudan's involvement in the political affairs of neighboring states. Chad received its independence from France in 1960 and, like Sudan, has experienced a North-South division as well as military coups during most of the fifty years since. A Libyan-backed coalition government in the 1980s tolerated Libya's temporary occupation of the northern third of Chad, but succumbed in 1990 due to the persistent challenges of Idriss Deby, a Zaghawa, who used Darfur as his base to attack the incumbent general. Not only were there Libyan troop movements through Darfur during the decade, but also Libya-armed Arab paramilitary groups with AK-47s and grenade launchers, and the distribution of propaganda about the rights of Arabs being trampled by the "African" regime in Chad and the "blacks" of Darfur. While Arab ethnic tribes were receiving weapons and being politicized, the Fur and other non-Arabs likewise were arming themselves and forming militias in response to the flood of Arab refugees from Chad with their animals into their traditional homeland. In the 1990s, the racial divide in Darfur increased. Though there were efforts to disarm militias and assign political power proportionately to different segments of the population, the government's decision to create its own pro-Arab militia, the *janjaweed*, known as the "demons on horseback," worsened the situation. The Fur and the Zaghawa, both non-Arab in composition although growing rivals for the same natural resources, then created the Darfur Liberation Front, which in 2002 began attacking government posts in retaliation for *janjaweed* killings, cattle rustling, devastation of the landscape, and forced Arabization of village names. The Darfur war had begun and thousands of people, mostly women and children, turned west to cross the desert into Chad.

More than a year passed before the United Nations High Commissioner for Refugees (UNHCR) sent representatives to investigate reports reaching the outside world and then an emergency response team of specialists in security, logistics, the legal rights of refugees, and other subjects flew from Geneva to Abéché, a four-hour drive from the Chadian-Sudanese border, to size up the situation. As a consequence of their observations and decisions, they opened the first U.N. refugee camp at Farchana, about forty miles inside Chad, in January 2004, with 148 women, children, and elderly people. It was designed to accommodate 8,000 refugees, but ultimately housed 20,000. In subsequent years, the UNHRC opened eleven more camps in eastern Chad for Sudanese refugees, from Oure Cassoni, opposite northern Darfur just three miles inside the national boundary, to Goz Amer in the south. Their estimated number at the end of 2008 was 268,000, while the total number of persons displaced in the region as a result of war since 2003 is two million, including an estimated one hundred thousand Chadians.

Africare began assisting refugees from Darfur in 2005 when it took over the management of Gaga camp, newly established by the UNHCR in eastern Chad. Most of the nearly two hundred new arrivals came from other refugee camps where water supplies were running low or were isolated refugees escaping border areas where *janjaweed* raiders stole their livestock and threatened their lives. Gaga had not only a river nearby, but four boreholes, and theoretically could handle 30,000 people. Gradually, as refugees were transferred from overpopulated camps, relocated because of insufficient water resources, or sought refuge from the mounting attacks of militias, rebels, and bandits, it sheltered about 20,000 Sudanese, half of them children under the age of fourteen. Africare's first tasks at Gaga were to provide for the rudimentary needs of people who typically fled their homes with only the clothes on their back. It put up tents and built wells. It distributed food provided by the World Food Programme. It furnished blankets, mats, kitchen utensils, and jerry cans. With the intention of protecting the environment, it gave out improved wood-burning stoves called "Save 80" (interior parts were stainless steel and the stove conserved 80% of the fuel ordinarily needed to cook a meal) or helped residents construct mud wood-saving stoves and supplied firewood. In the hope that camp members would become self-sufficient in food and earn some income, Africare offered improved seed, such as millet, beans, and okra, and gardening tools. Four hundred and fifty acres of land were under cultivation at the end of 2008. Both refugees and local residents were offered vaccination services for their animals and two hundred single women received six hundred sheep to begin herds. Nurseries were established to produce thousands of seedlings for anyone nearby who wanted them. Africare staff organized training sessions in agriculture, livestock, environment, water, and sanitation.

However, things have not been all rosy at Gaga or at the other eleven UNHCR camps designed for Darfuri people. In May 2009, an Amnesty International research mission, after touring Gaga and meeting with camp leaders and other residents, expressed dismay at its findings. The first category of concern was the physical environment. Water was in extremely short supply, tents were worn out, and there were complaints of insufficient food rations. Even more serious was the lack of security. Women and girls were most affected because they were vulnerable to threats, beatings, and rape by armed bands when they left the camp to seek additional firewood and water or to visit markets. Although a new Chadian police force had been posted in eastern Chad under the auspices of the UN to protect refugees and displaced persons, it viewed its mandate as so limited as to be nearly worthless to them. More disturbing to Amnesty International representatives than the physical conditions at Gaga were the psychological. They detected a sense of despair, a feeling among the refugees of being trapped. It stemmed partly from inadequate safety and from restlessness after several years of nomadic life, but a major factor originated in the limited education available for Gaga children. There was a good primary system and, in the four years of camp operation, a large number of children had completed the grades. However, there was no additional schooling for them once they reached the age of about thirteen. Many youths believed that there was no future for them in Gaga and, hence, were ready recruits for militias and other armed groups, both in Chad and in the Sudan. A socio-economic problem unmentioned by the Amnesty International account was the increasing tension between farmers and herders over land, grazing areas, wood, and other resources in the region because of the sudden settlement of large numbers of refugees. This historic competition accentuated ethnic rivalry between Chadians and Sudanese.

Although this single, unverified report, albeit by a reputable organization, must be weighed for what it is, the conditions uncovered at Gaga were not surprising to the relief community because of their similarity to what was happening elsewhere in eastern Chad. In some camps, the availability of water was so limited that, in hindsight, observers said that the sites should never have been chosen. Several had no source of water themselves, but depended on water pumped out of wells in towns and trucked miles across the desert. Shortages of food were considered understandable, since much of it was brought over land through Libya; official storage facilities were often looted, and aid workers suffered carjackings, armed robberies, kidnapping, and murder. The level of violence against camp residents, again especially women and girls, was at least as great at the other UNHCR camps as it was at Gaga. In many cases, it was worse. Being closer to the Sudanese border, the locations were thoroughfares for rebels, militias, and bandits. Some were infiltrated by political dissidents who recruited residents and children for their forces, claimed food rations, or created havoc. Occasionally, camps became victims of fighting themselves, as when Sudanese government planes dropped bombs on rebel positions near Oure Cassoni in May 2009, killing or wounding six Chadian civilians and destroying the cattle of some refugees.

Darfuri refugees have added just one more pressure point on the fragile Chadian government in recent years. Another comes from the nearly 60,000 refugees who have entered the southeastern section of Chad from the Central African Republic (CAR), most since the latest coup of 2003. Although, like other French colonies, the CAR received its independence in 1960 with a constitution and all the paraphernalia for democracy, it has experienced fifty years of revolving door governments, from a monarchy to military regimes to elected civilian administrations. Coups, attempted coups, mutinies, and election irregularities have kept the populace in a state of constant turmoil and with labor unrest, economic malaise, and energy crises, the country remains one of the poorest in the world. Throughout years of political upheaval, citizens have fled to such adjacent nations as Cameroon or even Sudan, but now the flow is greater and it is mainly northward into southern Chad because of continued fighting between the CAR government and rebel forces in upper CAR. Also, the UNHCR refugee camps that were erected quickly across the border, coincidentally at the same time as in eastern Chad, are a lure.

Months before General François Bozizé overthrew the elected president of the CAR in March 2003, citizens responded to the growing unrest of their region by moving into Chadian border villages and towns where they slept on the streets and drew water from local wells. Most had only the clothes on their backs. Wealthier ones had sleeping mats and cooking pots, but like everyone else, had nothing to eat. By mid-March, UNHCR officials estimated that there were 30,000 refugees, primarily around Gore, where Chadian troops harassed them so much, including the attempted abduction of women, that they were ordered to stay out of the area. Bozizé's failure to cement his control over CAR subsequently led to a general lawlessness and almost anarchy in the northern part of the country. Rebel factions, bandit gangs, and government soldiers pillaged food, burned villages, raped girls, kidnapped children, and murdered civilians. In spurts of hundreds or thousands, according to the level of violence, villagers sought refuge in southern Chad from 2003 onward. The UNHCR ultimately established four large refugee complexes, three close to its base in Gore and one eighty miles inside the border at Moula. The great majority of newcomers were farmers and the rest were herders.

The three camps near Gore—Amboko, Dosseye, and Gondje—are usually collectively called by the one name, "Gore," and at the end of 2008 they hosted more than 33,000 refugees from CAR. Africare began managing them in 2006, a challenge magnified by their location in lush malarial forests and amplified by a long rainy season. The organization distributed food, constructed buildings for staff, schools, and administration, and set up demonstration plots of various crop species for seed multiplication. It trained host community farmers and refugees in improved agricultural techniques. Looking forward, Africare plans to implement many of the strategies that it has used elsewhere in Africa to promote food security and economic opportunities for refugees. But, speaking of the future raises the question of whether the overall goal of the UNHCR is to repatriate most of the 60,000 CAR refugees in Chad or to integrate them into Chadian society.

Most aid officials believe that refugees the world over want to return home once peace has been restored in their countries and that the uprooted will take back with them new skills and knowledge for a better life. However, given the political history of the CAR in the past fifty years, the programs that Africare and other agencies are doing to raise the level of health, income, and community welfare, and the frequent intermarriages, it seems likely that many refugees will remain in Chad. There are major problems created by their settlement in the area, however, and most have to do with competition for natural resources. Because of its thick forests, much of the land of southern Chad is not usable for agricultural or animal purposes, causing a land shortage. Consequently, in Gore, each farm family has less than a half acre to cultivate, although agricultural extension agents believe that it needs an acre. (When the UNHCR established its new camp at Moula in 2008, it granted each refugee family an acre.) Herders, such as the semi-nomadic Muslim Peul, finding that space near the camps is occupied, must take their cattle miles away to graze. They also sometimes have confrontations with farmers, both local and refugee, when their animals stray into growing crops. Not only are refugees competing with the local population for land, but they are gathering so much firewood that deforestation and related environmental damage has occurred.

One unforeseen circumstance that arose around Gore was a growing conflict between local people and refugees because the refugees were seen receiving WFP handouts, Africare agricultural inputs and training, veterinary services, and other benefits unavailable outside the camps. While this was not entirely true—in 2006, 695 host community farmers and 1,400 refugees were trained in improved agricultural techniques, for example—the perception persisted and the UNHCR, in 2008, expanded its programs in southern Chad to impoverished local villagers. Now, development goals for everyone are replacing the shorter term focus on refugee survival.

Repatriation of refugees from the camps of eastern Chad to Sudan is also a UNHCR goal, but in light of circumstances in both countries, seems unlikely to occur in any significant number. One prerequisite for repatriation is the settlement of demands by numerous insurgent groups controlling different regions of Darfur. Their factionalism, suspicions of the central government's motives and intentions, and accusations of continued genocide impede efforts by the international community, including the United States, to negotiate a peace agreement. Furthermore, before refugees will move back to their homes in Darfur, they must see it as a place where life is viable. Politically,

Sudan is undergoing potentially cataclysmic changes. Not only must refugees calculate conditions locally, but nationally. Other factors concern how refugees will live back in their villages without the supplied clean water, education (though limited), and health care of the camps. Another major worry both for them and for everyone else in Darfur is the prospect that the United Nations peacekeeping force in Darfur (UNAMID) and Chad will withdraw and leave the security of citizens in hands previously proven as unworthy. Humanitarian organizations working in the region share this apprehension. As difficult as their upheaval has been, many Darfur refugees may elect to remain in a new land rather than face starting over in their uninviting country of origin.

9

Transition and Challenge

Africare entered the twenty-first century as an organization facing impending change. The small core of skilled ex-Peace Corps personnel who had served in managerial positions for twenty-five years or more had recently retired or sat on the verge of retirement. It was well-known in Washington that C. Payne Lucas, the charismatic president since 1971, contemplated retirement, as much as he hated the thought. Lucas was the rainmaker. Lucas was the political master who could call politicians, CEOs, ambassadors, lobbyists, journalists, and just about anyone else in Washington to discuss legislation, advocate policy positions, wrangle more government funding, or get publicity. As the boss in the office, he was never happier than when there was a "crisis" and all was turmoil within the building, contributed to considerably by his own behavior. Staff meetings were characterized by energetic exchanges of opinion and for a time Lucas kept a "thug's list" of country representatives and other overseas workers who had not submitted reports on time, did not follow procedures, or were otherwise thought deficient in their job performance. His management style emanated not from business school manuals, but from a take-charge approach first tried on young, impressionable Peace Corps volunteers. He was very particular about decorum and office appearance. Employees, for example, were forbidden to have beverages or food on their desks and messiness was not tolerated. Yet, there was a soft side to Lucas. He never could fire anyone. His solution to having an unsatisfactory staff member at Washington headquarters often was to offer a second chance by sending him or her abroad as a country representative, administrative assistant, or other resource person. After completion of a one or two-year contract, the reprieved employee did not return to Africare in Washington. It took some disastrous experiences for Lucas to realize that he was not doing the individual or the organization any good by being indulgent toward first-time failures.

The driving forces of C. Payne Lucas—and what made his leadership of Africare effective—were his passion for the needy of Africa and his desire to create an African American institution for African development. The first contact Lucas had with Africa came in the early 1960s when, as a soon-to-be-unemployed intern for the Democratic National Committee in Washington, he got a job as a desk officer for Togo at Peace Corps headquarters. Subsequently, he was sent to Togo as a field representative and the experience of being for the first time in a country where blacks were in charge inspired him to consider what was possible in post-colonial Africa. His next Peace Corps assignment was as country director in Niger and he later served as the regional director for all of Africa. In his positions with the Peace Corps, Lucas talked to the presidents of African nations, to national health ministers, to local officials responsible for development projects, and to Americans attached to U.S. embassies and such agencies as USAID. He traveled widely, especially in Togo and Niger, following up on the activities of Peace Corps volunteers. The need he saw remained in his heart. In fact, the compassion he felt probably accounts for the one weakness of the Africare administration that Lucas acknowledges: the incapacity to say "no." An example of this is a visit to Uganda with Alan Alemian, regional director for East Africa, where they visited a girls' school and found that many students did not have the $50 yearly tuition. Impulsively, he promised assistance, but then had to return to Washington and raise money for them.

And Lucas could raise money. He held audiences, from schoolchildren to foundation directors, in rapt attention by the emotions he expressed and by his animated, colloquial speaking style. He was an expert at telling heart-rending stories of villagers overwhelmed by adversity, but he was just as good at inspiring listeners to believe that they could bring new life and hope to those people. Since he frequently toured Africare projects, he could describe in vivid detail the beneficial effects of a new well, a new clinic, or additional agricultural resources in an African community. He enjoyed boasting how the residents of areas were so happy with Africare's work that they put up special displays for his visit. Other Lucas qualities that augmented his passion and emotion were his stamina and indefatigable nature. He was a whirlwind of activity: overseeing the Africare office, keeping close ties with members of the Black Caucus and with other national legislators, meeting with donors and potential donors, hosting celebrities from Shirley Temple Black to Desmond Tutu, getting corporate sponsors for the Bishop Walker dinner, speaking annually to dozens of groups around the United States, and traveling extensively in Africa. Passion, emotional connectivity, the ability to deliver the message in personal terms, and energy made Lucas a natural spokesman for African causes.

The other driving force for Lucas was his goal to create an organization through which African Americans could identify with Africa and connect to their heritage. He wanted them to get interested in Africa, to start talking about Africa, and to be part of a movement to save Africa. This was one reason why fundraising initially targeted black congregations. Lucas claimed, with some hyperbole, that $100 from a black church involved more people than $50,000 from a white church. At the beginning, he was actually concerned that too many whites might become supporters and, subsequently, as shown already, Africare was warned that its heavy dependence on funding from white groups and foundations jeopardized its relationship with African Americans.

Lucas was also convinced that competent African Americans working in Africa had a competitive advantage to white Americans because they gave Africans pride. In actual fact, early overseas employees in supervisory roles were mostly white, but through deliberate measures they did contribute to the process in African nations of bringing up an educated workforce that could assume managerial and technical duties. Lucas believed, too, that a black organization with black employees in African countries removed suspicion that they were connected with the U.S. Central Intelligence Agency and avoided problems of cultural confrontation. There is no evidence to support the former claim and the latter can be disputed by numerous accounts of disagreements in field offices over application of government labor laws, by lawsuits against Africare by former field staff, and by experiences of some of Africare's expat employees. Nonetheless, these assumptions guided Lucas in his drive to create a purely African American development organization.

In great contrast to Lucas was Joseph C. Kennedy, who retired in 1999 after serving as director of international development for twenty-eight years. His quiet demeanor was the opposite of Lucas' bull-in-a-china-shop personality. The two men seemed to have a symbiotic relationship, so much so that both could work at headquarters for several days without talking to each other. One long-time Africare observer commented that Kennedy was Lucas' alter-ego: "C. Payne *was* Africare. He took the chances, sold the idea. Joe made things operational." It was Kennedy's job to manage the overseas program, including supervising regional directors in Washington and overseeing field offices abroad. He approved the choice of projects, reviewed grant proposals, examined project expenditures, and studied progress reports and evaluations. In addition to this enormous work load, Kennedy traveled months at a time in Africa to judge the administration of Africare grants, meet with government officials, and give encouragement to field staff. Kennedy had a reputation for selecting the most remote villages for Africare projects because of the belief that they were the most needy and the least likely to receive aid from elsewhere, but visiting them often necessitated several days of torturous travel and camping in the bush. Kennedy also tended to favor smaller projects because they were less complicated and complex than such giant undertakings as the Integrated Rural Development job at Seguenega, Burkina Faso.

In his African travels, Kennedy was often among the first representatives from aid and development organizations to witness shocking conditions attending a new famine, civil war, or natural catastrophe. His search for plugged wells in the Sahel in 1974 and his observations of the devastating drought in Ethiopia in 1985 are examples of first-hand information he shared as he spoke in churches, schools, and many venues about Africa's plight and potential. This was a point always emphasized by Kennedy, Lucas, and other Africare personnel who gave public speeches: Africa is a land of potential. Kennedy was also secretary of the Board of Directors and responsible for recording the minutes of Board and executive committee meetings. He continued in that position after his retirement. Ever careful to protect Africare's image, Kennedy reveals no controversies, no disappointments, and few details other than those publically known in his rendition of general meetings, although he concisely acknowledges disagreements within the executive committee.

While Lucas and Kennedy possessed very different personalities, there were great similarities in their outlook and policy orientation. They were both very conservative. This was good in financial matters, particularly in the early years when they were cautious in hiring staff and committing Africare to new projects. (Later, Africare nearly went under due to slack financial management.) Employees proposing different modes of operation could expect rejection of their ideas, especially from Kennedy, who saw himself as the guardian of the true

Africare. Lucas and Kennedy were both cautious in regards to new directions in their organization. Other areas of agreement between the two men were on the employment of Africans to run big Africare programs and the hiring of women as country representatives. On both of these issues, their attitude changed over time, but for the first twenty years of Africare history, it was mostly expats who supervised multi-million dollar in-country projects and mostly men, occasionally an African, such as Sahr Tongu in Burkina Faso, who were appointed country reps. The thinking of Lucas and Kennedy on Africans in top management positions stemmed from a desire to prevent the Africanization of the organization and from the reality that, at that time, there were few Africans in their home countries with the experience to manage vast, complex projects. Their reluctance to post women as country reps can be explained on several levels. It was partially due to gender insensitivity common at that time and was also based on knowledge that the customary male dominance in African societies might present obstacles to women in supervisory roles. The latter proved true, testified to by some women who confronted sexism during their assignments.

Lucas retired as president of Africare in June 2002 (his title had been changed from executive director sometime earlier). He was sixty-eight years old and a forty-year veteran of American efforts to assist sub-Saharan African nations. There was great apprehension among Board members, employees, donors, relevant U.S. government officials, and friends of Africare as to who could fill such big shoes as the ones Lucas would leave. There were questions as to whether a past or present staff member or a Board director might be suitable. There were the issues of gender and of race. Did Lucas' successor have to be a man? Did he have to be black? The Africare Board selected a USAID insider, Julius E. Coles, who had spent twenty-eight years in the Foreign Service and had retired from his government position in 1994 with the rank of Career Minister. In the interim between 1994 and 2002, he had been, successively, director of Howard University's Ralph J. Bunche International Affairs Center and director of Morehouse College's Andrew Young Center for International Affairs. While with USAID, Coles was mission director in Swaziland and Senegal. He had worked in two other African nations, Liberia and Morocco, as well as in Vietnam and Nepal. Because of his connections to USAID, some Africare observers thought that this was a move to secure more federal funding. Others believed that, because of Coles' age—sixty—he was only a stop-gap until a better candidate came along. The consensus was that he would be a transitional leader and he was, serving as president through 2009.

Coles and Africare faced a very difficult transition. Lucas was a bigger-than-life figure who was synonymous with the organization, who personified it. Where Lucas was boisterous, easily accessible, and sought attention, Coles was reserved, gave the impression of inaccessibility by hunkering down in front of his computer screen with his back to the door, and moved almost unnoticed through the building. Lucas was so emotional that he sometimes cried when employees left. Coles was cool and matter-of-fact. Everyone in the office knew that much of Lucas' shouting and berating one day might be transformed into a love-fest the next, but rumors that Coles had a hair-trigger temper worried them.

These factors of personality and style were superseded in importance by the problems that Coles saw in Africare management. The first had to do with the administration of overseas programs, grouped according to three geographic regions, each with a director. Coles believed them to be individual fiefdoms, with no cross-fertilization of ideas. Every division had its own procedures and policies, such as in personnel matters, where the manager decided salary scales, bonuses, and vacation time. He wanted a more professional organization, beginning with overhauling and standardizing the operational format at this top level of employees and moving through the rest of the staff. However, to bring more coordination and cooperation among regional directors, it was necessary to reduce the authority of individual bosses. The practical hurdles of this feat were accentuated by the presence of Lucas and Kennedy in the shadows, who, though retired, objected to lessening their role.

Far more serious when Coles took over than the issue of improving Africare's professionalism was that of its financial standing. He quickly learned that Africare was not as solvent as he thought. Its outstanding debt was $2.9 million and its financial reports were two to three years behind. Coles fired the Africare finance director, replaced the auditing firm, and hired an outside consultant to decipher the records. What emerged was a situation originating with a USAID $7.4 million letter of credit from 1980 to 1994, of which $2.9 million could not be accounted for, and another letter of credit from 1994 to 2002 for which there also was no accountability. There were other creditors in addition to USAID.

It seems to have been a case in which Africare management lacked the skills necessary to administer the escalating budget and did not recognize the magnitude of the problem it was creating by neglecting the fundamentals. Through the 1980s, Africare's revenue stream had crept up slowly from several million dollars to $15 million in 1993. That year, the first of the new Clinton administration, there was a great leap in income. Africare broke the $25 million line and, with rapid expansion, it soon had $35 million annually at its disposal. Africare leaders became aware of greater fiscal responsibility and enhanced accounting oversight through a report of the finance director to the Board of Directors in December 1993. He told them that the United States Government had become more sophisticated in its auditing requirements and that the Office of Management and Budget (OMB) had recently enacted procedures that increased the scope of audit work. He concluded, "We must make sure that we have proper documentation and authorization for all transactions. We must assure reports are prepared and submitted on a timely basis and that our internal control systems are in place." Most Board members apparently had scant knowledge of actual financial operations, but Lucas, in particular, seemed to disregard the warning and the finance official himself evidently did not heed his own advice.

There is one possible partial explanation for this state of affairs and it is grounded in the complexity of the system. Africare had many projects funded by various donors and federal agencies running simultaneously in different countries. It found it necessary occasionally to "borrow" money from USAID projects to keep the others going, but because of weak internal financial controls, Africare field employees lost track of the money trail. Not knowing how much funding for a project they had used or how much was left, they spent more than was allocated, leaving Africare with a cost overrun that it had to absorb. The intricacies of these interwoven financial dealings proved too great to keep straight.

The total cost for closing this episode, including the bookkeeping investigation, was $9 million and it required using more than half of the endowment fund, much to the opposition of Lucas and Kennedy. In an executive committee meeting, Kennedy argued that it took Africare thirty years to accumulate the money, but now most of it was going to be spent in a year. To avoid such financial disasters in the future and to restore Africare's credibility, Coles put tighter controls over field office staff, insisted on prompt fiscal reports and more transparency in overseas business transactions, and audited major country programs. He installed a new field accounting system and acquired new accounting software. He recruited a professional management team to supervise all aspects of the organization's financial affairs.

When Coles accepted the presidency of Africare in 2002, Lucas and the Board charged him to take it to the next level by increasing its size and its programs substantially. Africare, at that time, had field offices in twenty-six countries and a budget in the $40 million range annually. The new goal was to expand operations to thirty-five or forty nations and to double or triple financial resources to $80 or $100 million annually within the next decade. In fact, at the end of Africare's fiscal year in June 2008, it had total revenues and support of $46 million and worked in twenty-three countries. The real story of the organization's vitality lay, however, in the tally of its overseas commitments. While the accumulated value of project grants, contracts, and donations for the period of 1970 to 2002 was $446 million, the figure rose to $826 million under Coles, an increase of $380 million. The big sectors where Africare intensified its program were in health, particularly in malaria prevention and treatment, and in water resources/sanitation. Of the fiscal 2008 budget, $20 million went to this combined category, illustrating more concentrated attention to familiar activities in nations where it already had a presence.

Increasing the Africare budget and multiplying program commitments has been one of the most controversial issues in Africare history, not in themselves as goals, but in the source of money and the nature of sponsorship. It dates back to the mid-1970s when Africare, struggling to become a development organization supported mainly by African Americans, failed to raise funds concomitant with its ambitions. In reality, the gift from Lorraine Watriss and a small grant from USAID in 1973 to deliver goods to drought victims in the Sahel saved it from oblivion. Lucas immediately acceded to the idea of seeking federal grants, as they were then called, on the grounds that the money came from American taxpayers and that Africare would use it well. At headquarters, however, there were staff members, including Joe Kennedy, who opposed the new linkage, believing that the organization would lose its independence and that it would become mired in reporting and auditing requirements. Some of the same employees today complain that PVOs with government funding have lost a lot of their individuality and no longer include knowledge from extensive consultation with villagers in their proposals ("we find out what USAID wants done; we write the proposal"). Other participants in the debate argued that Africare had no alternative option because it had no other way to sustain itself. Slowly, USAID became the dominant force as it financed big integrated rural development projects such as Seguenega in Upper Volta. In 1980, it provided 80% of Africare's revenue. In subsequent years, the percentage has had wide fluctuations from 34% (1986) to 75% (1993). When Coles arrived at Africare, 68% of its financial resources derived from governments, American and African. One of his major goals was to reduce that heavy dependence; he succeeded somewhat by lowering the figure to 62% in fiscal 2008. Taxpayer dollars were augmented with those from such private sources as the Gates Foundation and such large corporations as Exxon. Coles also reorganized the development office, remodeled the Web site, and inaugurated a new marketing campaign to rekindle interest among Americans—not just African Americans—in the cause of Africa.

The lack of financial support for Africare by the black community that forced it to rely heavily on USAID has prompted a great deal of arm-chair speculation about Africare's strategy of fund raising, the ability of Black Americans to give monetarily to the organization, and even the interest or commitment that Americans, black or white, have to helping Africa. One Africare Board member said that it was disgraceful that Africare is as dependent on USAID money as it is—disgraceful, she said, not for the organization, but for the people who should be supporting it. She did not offer reasons as to why they did not. Another regretted that fellow Board members had not given Lucas adequate support and mourned the death of that great fund raiser, Bishop Walker. Some observers blamed Lucas for not adopting their ideas. The best explanation, however, lies in American history. Lucas was running counter to it.

When Lucas, in 1971, began to plan a charity run by African Americans and supported primarily by them, he saw Africare benefiting from new political and social energies that had emerged from a seventy year drive for full civil rights in the United States. What he overlooked as he surveyed possible funding sources is that American philanthropy has distinct characteristics that determine who gives and who gets. The pattern and evolution of benevolence show marked racial differences, historically, that reflect for African Americans a pre-Civil War society of slave and free blacks and a post-Civil War society of Jim Crow segregation and discrimination. From colonial times, the major focus of American philanthropy, particularly in the black community, has been religious organizations, chiefly the Christian church. Black Americans, until at least the 1960s, additionally directed their donations almost exclusively to several other types of community-oriented causes: local humanitarian needs, establishment of schools and commercial enterprises, and movements for social and economic betterment. The only non-domestic interest to which they contributed was to foreign missions, mainly through the African Methodist Episcopal Church. White Americans were also parochial in their giving, but there was a wider scope that included such fund raising campaigns as those for the war for Greek independence in the 1820s and relief efforts for starving Armenians during World War I. A primary explanation for the attention of white Americans to European events was the linkage of specific immigrant groups to their countries of origin. For Black Americans, however, there were no nationalistic feelings of group identity or allegiance to specific areas of the African continent. The challenge that Africare faced as a charity appealing to African Americans was to entice them to look beyond black philanthropy as a local mechanism for survival, mutual assistance, and self-help to aiding strangers of their own race an ocean away.

Formal black philanthropy outside the church began in Boston when Prince Hall, a free black local businessman who was probably born in the Caribbean and fourteen other free blacks joined the local Masonic lodge in 1775. Later, in 1784, they formed their own branch, which ultimately became known as African Grand Lodge #1. From Boston, black masonry spread to Philadelphia, where the renowned Episcopal priest Absalom Jones established a lodge, and to other cities. A fundamental principle of Masonic orders is providing charity in local communities and Prince Hall's group took interest in the plight of freed slaves and their families. As black lodges were established in Providence, New York, Philadelphia, and elsewhere, they likewise concentrated on ameliorating the conditions under which free Negroes lived.

In the same vein as the Black Masons, other secular charities arose before the Civil War to address the problems of African Americans. Many were mutual benefit associations such as the African Society of Mutual Aid and Charity in Boston, the Baltimore Society for Relief in Case of Seizure, and the Phoenix Society in New York. Their goals of improving housing, education, job opportunities, legal assistance, and a myriad of other facets of life stretched the resources of members and supporters. In some cities during the nineteenth century, homes for aged black women were established by black and white benefactors. The spirit in all cases was one of helping neighbors, friends, and perhaps even needy strangers within the local community, just as a family would give assistance to kin in difficult times.

After the Civil War, societal changes resulting from often uprooted former slaves and the uneasy transition in the lives of the black population as a whole magnified the importance of community-centered charities. Added to the turmoil was the slow accretion of state and federal legislation that limited the civil rights of African Americans and discriminated against them socially and economically. New charities now combined improved human welfare and political activism in their programs. Several groups that rose in response to these circumstances have been mentioned earlier (the National Association of Colored Women and the National Association for the Advancement of Colored People), but an influential fraternal order that challenged segregation while it fought for civil rights and equality of educational and economic opportunity was the Improved Benevolent and Protective Order of the Elks of the World, better known as the Black Elks. Organized in 1898 in Cincinnati, Ohio, its members stressed such community service as eradicating illiteracy among African Americans and later gave college scholarships to black students. The IBPOEW became a worldwide institution whose brothers included Booker T. Washington, W.E.B. Du Bois, and Thurgood Marshall.

To these black charities tackling domestic issues were added many more in the twentieth century—The United Negro College Fund, The Links, and United Negro Appeal among them—but African American philanthropy, particularly after 1960, was dominated by organizations engaged in extending civil rights to minorities. Just a few of them besides the NAACP were Congress of Racial Equality (CORE), Student Nonviolent Coordinating Committee (SNCC), and Southern Christian Leadership Conference (SCLC). Black Americans were now solicited to support Freedom Rides, sit-ins, boycotts, and marches for the passage of full voting rights legislation. Financial participation in these activities transcended the narrower aims of their previous charitable giving but offered potential benefits to them. The "foreignness" of the distant appeal was thereby compensated for by the prospect of the reward. Africare, in contrast, had the problem that its only incentives for black donors were psychological and intangible: self-actualization in affirming an African heritage and the personal satisfaction of doing good.

Bridging the different eras of black philanthropy was the missionary movement, the only link that African Americans had to the world outside the United States before the Spanish-American War, with the exception of those who knew participants in the colonization drive of the mid-nineteenth century. Between 1820 and 1980, from 250,000 to 350,000 Americans served as missionaries in Africa, but no more than 600 were black. More than half of those went to Liberia and only about half of the 600 anywhere in Africa were sent by black church boards. African American churches believed that they had a special relationship and a special obligation to Africa and Africans, but their limited financial resources spread among two dozen missionary societies kept activities minimal. Obviously, black missions were too insignificant to provide Africare a favorable backdrop in communities, for there was little, if any, knowledge of foreign religious endeavors. Africare worked hard, particularly in the 1970s and 1980s, to raise money from congregations and was somewhat successful, but it was always competing with those whom members considered the most important recipients of their charity, their own needy.

Just a brief review of African American philanthropy illustrates that Lucas and Africare were fighting tradition when they expected a great groundswell of black support for an organization with the almost abstract goal of helping African people on a continent thousands of miles away. There is only one other long-standing national African American charity that might be compared to Africare today, but its differences are significant. It is Opportunities Industrialization Centers International (OICI), established in 1970 in Philadelphia by Leon H. Sullivan, pastor of Zion Baptist Church. OICI was an offshoot of OIC of America, whose goal was to provide job training and skills for disadvantaged inner-city black youth. The international branch initially declared its mission as offering assistance to local citizen groups in other countries, particularly African, who wanted to create their own skills development programs for underprivileged youth. Over time, it expanded it activities to conflict management, food security and agriculture, health and nutrition, microenterprises, capacity building among local NGOs, and other societal needs. Where it differs most from Africare is in its geographical scope, its outreach mechanism, its budget size, and its funding. During nearly forty years of existence, it has worked in about twenty-five countries on four continents. Currently, it has operations in just four African nations. Its financial statement for the latest year available, fiscal 2006, ending in September, shows that more than 90% of its $8 million budget is funded through federal sources.

A new age of black philanthropy emerged in the 1990s as religious organizations, still the focus of giving, expanded their community-oriented programs in conjunction with government agencies and as individual African Americans prospered during an era of American economic growth. Churches and faith-based groups, with state and local funds, now began to sponsor summer camps, substance abuse programs, and HIV education and prevention activities, and to dispense welfare. The new class of ultra-wealthy donors centered its charity mainly on domestic activities of benefit to Americans, specifically those in the black community. When giving to foundations, setting up personal foundations, joining boards of large charities, sponsoring fundraisers, and donating to individual charities, it looked for opportunities where it could have an impact on cultural enhancement, educational objectives, medical breakthroughs, and social change.

Black philanthropy appears scarcely more interested in the plight of Africans today than it did in 1971 when Lucas begged African Americans to go one step beyond the Afro and the dashiki. There are notable exceptions, however, all connected to black celebrities. Some lend their voices in support of international agencies seeking to help refugees or children, examples being Danny Glover for UNICEF and Jamie Foxx for the Global Fund that fights AIDS, malaria, and tuberculosis. Others show their concern for African poverty by sharing their wealth. Oprah Winfrey is the best known for this and her biggest contribution has been the establishment in 2007 of the $40 million Oprah Winfrey Leadership Academy for Girls in South Africa. Before that, she joined Bono and other celebrities in promoting a line of clothing and gadgets whose profit will benefit the Global Fund. One African American charity of recent vintage with goals similar to those of Africare is Save Africa's Children, founded in 2001 by Bishop Charles E. Blake, pastor of the 24,000 member West Angeles Church of God in Christ in California. This small faith-based fund supports orphans of AIDS victims in twenty-one sub-Saharan African nations and AIDS research. Its Web site publicizes the names of its celebrity backers, from Denzel Washington, who has given a million dollars to the group, to Natalie Cole, Kanye West, Louis Gossett, Jr., Courtney B. Vance, and Gloria Gaynor. Aside from private donors to Africare, to Save Africa's Children, and to several miniscule new organizations and from a handful of black entertainers, actors, and business people, African Americans are not engaged in Africa's dilemma. The paucity of their participation accentuates the unique role that Africare, over forty years, has played in trying to persuade them to donate to a cause far from their homes and of no material benefit to themselves.

Another conundrum in Africare's history is why it has such a poor record in retaining employees, especially at its Washington headquarters. Lucas bragged that youngsters came in as apprentices and went on to enrich other organizations, but in fact, many revolving-door staff members were already established in their careers when they came to Africare and they departed for better positions. Often, they left angry because of their perceived treatment, the lack of advancement opportunities, low pay and minimum benefits, or the belief that their talents were not being utilized. Lucas' volatile nature could certainly offend anyone accustomed to conventional business behavior, and country reps, applying unfamiliar national work laws and Africare procedures, had a special set of circumstances to challenge them. The bureaucratic structure in Washington was a narrow pyramid with Lucas and Kennedy at the top, three or four regional directors on the next level, certain other officers roughly equivalent to them sharing the same platform (finance, management, fund raising, and such), and then a broad base of workers ranging from young professionals aspiring to careers in public service to secretaries. There was slim chance for upward mobility, even for regional directors and other officers. If they wanted to get ahead, they had to leave, but that does not explain entirely the loss of gifted personnel. Africare was always known for its low pay, both for employees in the United States and in foreign countries. Lucas told them that part of their compensation was the satisfaction of their work, their love for their job. There was no workers' pension plan until the 1990s, when a plan was at last suggested by Bishop Walker before his passing.

The high turnover in personnel continued during the administration of Julius Coles. Unlike Lucas, Coles knew how to fire unsatisfactory employees, a survival tactic he says he learned early in his civil service career. Through his culling and through resignations and retirements, fifty-four (60%) of the ninety expatriate staff working in Washington and in the field left Africare between 2002 and 2009. Coles sought to replace it with a more experienced and qualified roster through salary increases and a pay structure competitive in the job market. He also changed the retirement plan from a less desirable defined benefit plan to a defined contribution plan and established savings plans.

The issue of salaries for overseas African staff was complicated by the requirement that Africare comply with national labor laws regarding minimum wages, retirement funds, and severance. Newly assigned country reps typically began by getting a compensation plan from the American Embassy in their country that compiled sample salaries paid by PVOs, missionary groups, local governments, and private businesses. They faced difficulties in actually using the information because the local population considered an American PVO to be rich. They were also at a disadvantage in competing with large international agencies and governmental bodies that had reputations for paying better than small charities. Sometimes these obstacles were overcome by a prevailing community belief that it was more prestigious to work for Americans than for other foreigners or for their own nationals. A more insidious salary difficulty originates in the Africare procedure for tailoring project proposals to the requirements and wishes of prospective donors. When the proposal is submitted to a foundation, private corporation, government agency, or other funding source, it has a detailed budget that includes salaries for the in-country staff, equipment and supplies, transportation, overhead, and other costs. Once grants or contracts are awarded, unhappiness arises among the national staff because it discovers that different programs and projects pay a different range of salaries for the same positions, according to the budget approved by the funding institution. Hence, an accountant overseeing a health program may earn an income substantially more or less than an accountant working in the next office on agriculture.

Related to the uncoordinated pay structure is the Africare policy of giving its field employees, at all levels and including American expatriates, just one-year contracts. There are sound reasons for this. All programs and projects are designed for a specific, limited time, sometimes for three or five years, but frequently for shorter periods, with the possibility of extension. There have been unusual circumstances when programs were terminated short of the target date. Many employees, notably the in-country staff, are hired to carry out particular jobs linked to an individual program or project. When the project is finished, they must qualify for another position in order to remain with Africare. There is also the possibility that civil unrest, coup d'états, or wars will force Africare from a country, in which case it does not want to be liable for lengthy contracts with its erstwhile employees. Given the uncertainties of its overseas operation, Africare avoids long-term personnel commitments, but many employees consider Africare's contractual arrangement a detriment both in their private and professional lives. They complain that getting a mortgage or loan for a home or a car is difficult because lenders want them to have a secure income. They are reluctant to enter into long-term financial commitments, not knowing their future at Africare. Some staff members observe that one-year contracts do not encourage a strong attachment to the organization or to planning ahead. To staunch the criticism of one-year contracts, particularly since African nationals are increasingly managing multi-million dollar projects and are steadily replacing American expats as country reps, Africare recently has formulated a comprehensive procedure for them to use when they approach lenders, but so far there seems to be an inconsistent understanding of the document.

There are questions relating to Africare history whose answers can never rise above the level of anecdote and opinion. One of them is whether the organization used personality and race to flourish in Washington. While all observers characterize Lucas as highly political, there is no agreement whether he kept Africare middle-of-the-road during Democratic and Republican administrations. His links to Sargent Shriver, Hubert Humphrey, Charles Rangel, Jr., and other prominent Democrats were well-known, but Republicans controlled the Oval Office for twenty of his thirty-one years at Africare. The evidence of escalating revenue in the 1980s and of influence in the Reagan and first Bush White Houses supports the belief that Lucas charmed politicians on both sides of the aisle. Prevented by its charter from overt political activity, Africare did not have lobbyists on Capitol Hill, as some charities did. Nevertheless, Lucas called legislators, congressional aides, officials in government departments, and undersecretaries with great frequency. He liked to meet them socially, too, the favorite watering hole being the Cosmos Club. Such hobnobbing bolsters critics who claim that Africare got its money because of who it knew rather than what it did.

Far more consequential than using personality to achieve success in Washington is exploiting race to benefit an organization. Some people with connections to Africare—ex-employees, former USAID officials, individuals now affiliated with rival PVOs and contractor groups—allege that it cultivated the image of itself as an African

American charity deserving special consideration when it submitted proposals to prospective donors, carried out projects and programs, and had its work evaluated. The word "arrogant" came up repeatedly in interviews, with the respondents believing that Africare projected an over-confident attitude of knowing what it was doing. They pointed out that Africare received non-competitive grants for a while and complained that, even when it competed with other organizations, it relied on the old boy network rather than playing by the rules. At USAID, some employees tended to allow policy irregularities to pass by with the remark, "Oh! That's Africare." Critics contend that Africare was not very business-like and did not hire the best people. Moreover, it was as politically-oriented overseas as in Washington. One retired USAID mission director bitterly recounted an experience that lost him his posting in West Africa. On the advice of his staff engineers, he had rejected an Africare proposal for the country where he served. Africare officials went over his head to the American ambassador, resulting in his reassignment and the proposal's approval. This individual continues to support Africare, but that is questionable among Africare's severest detractors who say that, behind its behavior vis-à-vis other PVOs, USAID, and big donors, there is the implied threat, "Don't mess with us. We're African American."

Africare apologists—these include representatives from all three groups mentioned—maintain that the organization worked from an uneven playing field when it began seeking foundation and government funding in the mid-1970s. Africare had to fight harder for support than other charities and it had to be better than other charities to get respect. Defenders further argue that, although considered a minority contractor by USAID, it had to jump more hoops than larger, more established charities. In assessing proposals, reviewers were more likely to complain that an Africare budget allowed for too many cars or too many staff members than they were to criticize a CARE entry, for example. Another type of discrimination against Africare was the inequitable manner in which USAID restrictions were upheld. Cynically believing that Africare would get the money anyway, USAID employees did not release the organization from some onerous requirements that they frequently lifted for other PVOs, such as the necessity of buying only American-made goods. That Africare was such a small charity also worked against it because foundations and government agencies like to deal with entities they know and these are mostly big firms doing big projects. Africare concentrated on grassroots activities in the countryside—vegetable gardens, clinics, community wells. Building up a favorable reputation was a slow process. Compounding the problem often was the absence of sophistication in Africare proposals, resulting from its lack of experience and ignorance about what was expected in a good presentation. Proponents insist that this could have been remedied with coaching.

Almost all Africare observers, both inside and outside the organization, agree that Africare has been severely challenged to staff itself with a full roster of competent employees, particularly in its overseas offices. Various explanations have been offered. One is that, with its emphasis on being an African American charity whose employees were black, Africare was headhunting among a population cohort that had better options with other domestic and international institutions seeking to integrate their staffs. Another blamed reliance on ex-Peace Corps volunteers, who might be hired, it was alleged, for $2 million projects even if they were unqualified. A third reason had a lot to do with how the new employees were nurtured once they signed their contracts. One critic charged that on-the-job training was largely non-existent and that, as a consequence, "a lot of these kids in the field don't know what they don't know." Aside from these suggested causes were practical considerations. Low salaries and limited employee benefits discouraged desirable prospective applicants and certainly figured in staff satisfaction. Finding men and women with the required language skills was an enormous obstacle to filling vacancies since many Africare projects were in non-English speaking countries. An Africare trait that made it the response team sought by UNHCR or by other relief organizations in a crisis also contributed to its problem of sufficient staffing abroad. That was the reputation for program flexibility, which meant that it could be on-ground, in-country within days of an alarm. Africare did this by reassigning workers from other field offices and hiring new temporary staff members, often with minimum experience, to fill gaps.

The issue of adequate staff numbers and competency also raises the question as to whether the basic problem stemmed from indiscriminate commitment to too many overseas projects and programs. When Africare was reincorporated in Washington, D.C., in May 1971, it listed its purpose as assisting in the improvement of the health of the African people through a number of means and in harmony with the environment. Lucas expected its work to be limited to West Africa. Two years later, its only activity was Kirker's hospital and outreach program in Diffa, Niger. The subsequent opportunity in mid-1973 to participate in Sahelian drought relief gave Africare its first chance to illustrate to federal agencies, foundations, and private citizens its institutional capability. Its focus on three basic features of rural life—water resources, health, and agriculture—represented feasible building blocks for a young organization. In its first decade, from 1970 to 1980, Africare remained close to its programmatic objectives, but went from involvement in one nation, Niger, to ten, six whose language was French. Moreover, they were scattered in four large regions of the continent. Another dramatic geographic expansion came in the 1980s when Africare doubled its reach to twenty countries and began working in three languages other than English. The types of undertakings broadened, too, but they were small side projects complementing established goals. Africare continued to pursue grants and contracts in additional countries, hitting a peak in 1996 with twenty-eight. Altogether, there were four official non-English languages spoken in them.

This enormous proliferation of discrete projects in multiple languages across most of sub-Saharan Africa over twenty-five years, precipitated particularly by the accelerating needs of relief assistance and world health, resulted in an extension of goals to accommodate new donor emphases and funding opportunities. Africare's mission manifesto has always been fluid, with some organizational objectives being added and some being dropped from official communications over time, but a recent statement on its Web site that "Africare programs are in the following broad areas: health and HIV/AIDS, food security and agriculture, water resource development, environmental management, literacy and vocational training, microenterprise development, civil society development, governance and emergency response" illustrates how wide a net Africare came to cast in seeking grants and contracts. It seemed to be more of a shotgun approach to African development than one focused on the three original aims.

The changing composition of Africare interests abroad was first visible in the early 1990s as annual reports began to mention projects that intended to teach conflict resolution and human rights, encouraged microenterprise development, sought to strengthen the indigenous NGO network, and promoted principles of democratic governance. Africare also added such educational programs as teaching literacy and vocational skills to orphans and displaced children in Angola, another non-traditional activity. (The monetization program is omitted here because it enhanced food security.) The costs for many of these new initiatives, however, were lodged within old categories of the annual budget, whose percentages remained similar to those of earlier periods, and therefore did not draw attention to how Africare programming was evolving.

The explanation for Africare's unceasing quest for greater and greater overseas involvement during its history is two-part: first, for humanitarian reasons, as Lucas admits, it could not say "no"; second, being dependent on non-private, restricted funding, which came primarily from the American government and international agencies, for a large percentage of its revenues, it could not say "no." Consequently, it had to apply for contracts and grants designed to further the development objectives that financial backers, in consultation with African governments, decided upon. There were occasions, too, in which foundations or corporations had big ideas that they were willing to fund and even though Africare might not have the in-house expertise to carry them out, the temptation was too great not to latch on to the opportunity. Hence, Africare quickly acquired assignments all over the continent. In some instances, there was only one project in a nation, but it still required expat staff (often with foreign language fluency), vehicles, an office, and supervision from Washington.

Another factor that accentuated staff deficiencies, both in number and quality, was the growing diversity in the type of projects. An emphasis on food, health, and water resources forced employees to have multiple competencies and knowledge bases, but once Africare stepped outside those fields, country reps and others faced an even steeper learning curve. While specialized managers were hired in Washington to direct the HIV/AIDS and monetization units, there was no commensurate enlargement of the supervisory staff at headquarters to advise country reps. Joe Kennedy remained as director of international development. There were three or four regional directors, depending on how the continent was divided at the time. Although some junior assistants were added, senior staffing was the same in 1996 as in 1983, whereas the revenue had climbed from $6 million to $36 million. Africare maintained positions in twenty-eight countries for several years after 1996, but then slowly contracted to twenty-one, where it stood at the end of Coles' tenure. Contrary to the charge he received from Lucas and the Board when he became president in 2002, Coles consolidated operations and limited them to nations where they paid for themselves rather than expanding them merely because of the opportunity they offered Africare. He returned the organization to its earlier focus on a narrower definition of health, water, and agriculture and increased funding within those three areas for which Africare first became known.

Besides rethinking how broadly it wants to be spread geographically and programmatically in Africa, Africare management has a number of other fundamental issues facing it. One is concern about its financial strength. The uneven and unpredictable nature of public support and revenues for Africare operations from its beginning in 1970 put the organization perpetually in a vulnerable position always a step away from disaster, as one veteran employee remarked. The idea of a safety net in the form of an endowment fund became reality in 1983 with an individual gift of $25,000. However, this was the year that Africare began a capital campaign to renovate the Morse school and, shortly thereafter, the drought in Ethiopia became a focus for fund solicitation. Increasing the endowment had to wait, but the need became more apparent during the decade as Africare began to experience budget deficits. In 1987, there was a shortfall of $662,000, expanding to $2 million in 1989, and nearly as much the following year. The main explanations for this problem were Africare's liability for administrative overhead not covered in private donor projects and its inadequate pool of unrestricted funds that could be applied to emergencies, cost over-runs, and such. Not only would an endowment enhance Africare's asset base, but interest from it would be available for expenses.

The real effort to establish an endowment began in 1990 when Africare launched the "Campaign for Africa" with the goal of raising $20 million by 2000. The Ford Foundation led it with a $2 million challenge grant and,during some years thereafter, the Board of Directors allocated sizable chunks of cash from the program budget (in error, as it turned out, and the money had to be restored). The fund achieved its greatest size in 2004 with $14 million. It proved its great value to Africare when the "rainy day" that Lucas always feared materialized in the necessity to repay USAID unaccounted-for project expenditures. In addition to providing Africare with a measure of financial security, the endowment contributed annual income particularly treasured because it was unrestricted in its usage. For example, the 1995 financial statement reported accumulated interest from the endowment of $647,841, and for the four years of 2000 to 2003, interest and dividends totaled more than $3 million. Coles made rebuilding the fund a priority and in 2009 it stood at $12.5 million.

Another issue for Africare management is its future leadership and its organizational structure. C. Payne Lucas automatically became executive director in 1971 and Joe Kennedy, the only other paid employee, naturally took the second position as director of international development. Other staff members were added according to function as the need for their services arose: bookkeeper, accountant, project designer, secretary, fund raiser, and so forth. Everyone reported to Lucas, although Kennedy had a special relationship and latitude with him. It was essentially a two-man operation. As Africare grew in size, there was little commensurate evolution of a supervisory hierarchy that had responsibility for staff under it. Lucas did hire Elton King in 1988 as director of management services at Africare headquarters and for years he served as confidant and troubleshooter. He had retired after a lengthy Peace Corps career and residence in many African nations. Among his many contributions to Africare were the authorship of a new policy manual for overseas staff and special missions to field offices where personnel problems were interfering with their work. Upon Kennedy's retirement in 1999, Lucas renamed his position "Senior Vice President," but the duties remained essentially the same. His choice for the job, regarded as a dynamic development pro and possible heir, stayed only two years, leaving a vacancy that gave Coles the opportunity to name his own second-in-command. He selected Jeannine Scott, who began her career at Africare shortly after graduate school by writing donor proposals and later serving as country representative in Senegal. Coles considered her his chief of staff and seemed comfortable sharing a broad executive role.

Related to leadership at the top is the issue of perpetuating a stable core of middle level managers at Washington headquarters who oversee diverse projects in the different regions of Africa, monitor field offices, and direct health and monetization programs. Africare was blessed during its first quarter century and more with dedicated, long-serving employees: Robert Wilson, Alameda Harper, Alan Alemian, Kevin Lowther, Carolyn Gullatt. All had Peace Corps backgrounds and, together with Lucas and Kennedy, they shared an ethos and a purpose. Today, the composition of the second generation supervisors is quite different. Several are ex-Peace Corps, but the majority has no commonality in its work experience. The men and women come from the finest American graduate schools and possess enviable résumés.

They are perhaps even more qualified than their predecessors to do their respective jobs. There is the nagging worry, though, that attitudes, times, and values have changed from the early days and that the spirit of the founders is being lost in the competition for professionalism.

At the beginning of 2010, with the retirement of Julius Coles, the Africare Board of Directors entrusted leadership of the organization to a man from the universe of big development money. Darius Mans, holding a doctorate in economics from the Massachusetts Institute of Technology, came with more than twenty years of employment with the World Bank, starting as an economist and ending as Director of the World Bank Institute, the research arm of the parent body. He had also served as project implementer in Mozambique and had provided consulting services to Angola after the end of its civil war. Immediately prior to his arrival at Africare, Mans was the acting CEO of the Millennium Challenge Corporation, an agency within the State Department announced by President George W. Bush in 2002 to give development aid grants to poor countries for economic and political reforms. Throughout his career, Mans has worked with organizations that deal in billions of dollars and advise foreign governments on mega-sized projects. Africare, in contrast, has never had a budget over $60 million. It is a big change for him to adapt his thinking, strategy, and goals to the modest, narrower objectives of a small charity.

Mans began at Africare during a time of introspection, of operational analysis, and of contemplation about future growth. The organization celebrated its fortieth anniversary during 2010. Looking over those years of effort to persuade the American people, particularly in the black community, to join a humanitarian cause, and to create development projects to improve the lives of Africans, there are obvious questions. How successful has the organization been? What good has come from the more than a billion dollars expended? How much of the Africare-supplied infrastructure—wells, health clinics, teacher housing—still exists? How much follow-through is evident from workshops, training sessions, and demonstration fields? What has been the sustainability rate of the thousands of projects? Who really benefited?

Many of these questions can be answered more anecdotally than statistically. Africare knows that it has not been as successful as it should have been in engaging the American people in supporting a private effort to help Africa. It has not gotten its story out sufficiently. Of the billion dollars in projects all over sub-Saharan Africa, there are several kinds of evidence besides local lore to support the view that thousands of people and hundreds of communities have been direct or indirect beneficiaries. Africare archives are filled with reports from field workers of the application of new skills, new technologies, and new methods in everyday activities. Achievements in reducing malnutrition and vulnerability to food shortages, improving infant and maternal health, and dozens of other efforts fill not only the pages of Annual Reports, but literally thousands of staff summaries. Regarding the Africare-supplied infrastructure, much of it is known to still exist, but the problem of tracking it all down is compounded by the fact that, once built, it is handed over to local communities that may or may not have maintained it. The human factor in workshops and training sessions and the temporary nature of demonstration fields make their impact also difficult to assess, as it would be in the United States and elsewhere. Sustainability of a project is hard to gauge too. For each, Africare aimed at achieving realistic goals within an allotted time and then turning responsibilities over to local participants. Continuation of the program thereafter depended on them and their resources. Often, as with women's vegetable gardens, the effort lived on. There were other cases, as with road building in Uganda, in which local people were uncooperative and progress stalled. Parenthetically, it should be added that proponents of foreign aid programs sometimes complain that bureaucrats are impatient with results, that they want to see success at the end of a three-year or five-year project, failing to realize that the full contribution of the work may not be evident for fifteen or twenty years. Finally, the question of who really benefited can be answered only indirectly. Africare, known all over sub-Saharan Africa by governmental agencies, is sought for a wide range of needs. Its positive reputation as a development organization implies that it has fulfilled the purpose that the founders enunciated forty years ago. Furthermore, a concrete honor that indicates its place in providing African assistance is the prestigious acknowledgment of Africare's leadership as an African charity through its selection by President Barack Obama to share a portion of his 2009 Nobel Peace Prize money. (With it, Africare launched the Obama Water Project in Ghana in September 2010, to give clean water and decent sanitation to households in three communities.) These actions by African governments and by the American president signify appreciation of Africare for a job well-done since 1971.

Upon assuming office in January 2010, Darius Mans began his work with an organizational analysis. Rather than focusing initially on the processes of structure and staffing, he asked "What business are we in?" He immediately challenged the Board of Directors to develop a strategic plan, saying to the members, "Take a blank sheet of paper. Imagine what you want Africare to be in the twenty-first century, not what it was these past forty years—but what you want it to be." With the strategic plan in hand, he commanded senior staff to draft an operational plan. Mans is keen on management and on strengthening Africare as a charity run with the attentiveness of a successful business. Every program area has been evaluated according to the competition (what other charities are engaged in the work?), Africare's strengths and weaknesses, and whether that particular endeavor is a growth business. Additional considerations have been Africare's core competencies, the funding interests of USAID and other foreign aid sources, and possible participation in partnerships. One thing Mans learned in this assessment was that Africare did not have a single water specialist on staff, although development of water resources has always been a main focus. He found gaps in other technical areas, too, but instead of planning to add more personnel, he broached the prospect of working with land-grants and Black colleges. Looking at his senior management team, Mans concluded that he needed to streamline its organizational structure to match more closely the functions of the new strategic plan. Consequently, he eliminated the grouping of programs according the geographical area of Africa in which they were located and, hence, an arrangement whereby regional directors were responsible for a vast array of projects within each, regardless of their diversity.

Looking forward, Mans is following the two strategic plan priorities for Africare set by the Board of Directors: to become the premier NGO working in Africa, and to become the leading voice speaking on Africa within the United States. The first requires performance and money. Resources must be shifted to core competencies and an overseas accounting system, more precise than any previous one, must be installed to inform Africare executives instantly of the exact status of any project in Africa. Human capital is also crucial in performance, and here Mans identifies an important imperative as the new president of Africare. He must unite the staff behind a common mission. As mentioned earlier, there remain a few Peace Corps veterans, but Africare House is a United Nations of employees of varying nationalities and ethnicities. The problem of turnover continues as well.

The funding of Africare programs has been difficult from the beginning and during most of its history, Africare has been alarmingly dependent on USAID. Mans is determined to alter that relationship. He has a strong incentive to wean Africare from USAID because the big federal agency is doing more work and projects in-house. There are not only fewer contract opportunities for Africare to seek, but there is greater competition for good employees as USAID seeks more Africa experts. Africare has also been the recipient in the past of large awards from such foundations as Ford and Rockefeller, which now consider Africare to have "graduated" beyond their scope of benevolence. Mans believes that Africare can replace support from these types of foundation with money from new wealthy Dotcom companies if it does a better job of telling its story about achievement and capacity. One idea for doing this is to create a Business Development Unit, which some PVOs have. It would look for business, spot opportunities, and work with staff to develop strong technical proposals. In this way, there would be coordination rather than a haphazard, scattered approach to supporting the program. The proliferation of charities since 1970 makes it mandatory that Africare becomes more professional in its approach to fund-raising.

Africare wants to become the leading voice speaking on Africa within the United States. This is likely to be much more difficult to attain than becoming the premier NGO working in Africa because it requires access. Mans complains that, in the American media, only a few old voices are consistently consulted. Gaining access to broadcasting and newsprint executives is part of the problem. Another is that, as a charity, Africare is restricted in its statements to non-political issues, which narrows its range of subject matter. While, for example, it can alert the American public to conditions in Darfur refugee camps, it cannot express an opinion on the management of the Darfur conflict by the Sudanese government. A larger obstacle is of a lack of attention in the United States to African affairs, except for key, often tragic, events. Even major newspapers scarcely have one piece a week within their pages about sub-Saharan Africa. Among broadcasting companies, National Public Radio is an exception in its coverage, having several correspondents resident there. At the moment, possessing only its Web site, Africare clearly has a challenge.

A related subject that Mans has yet to address is gaining the financial support of the African American community and making the American people constituents. C. Payne Lucas, Joseph Kennedy,

Clyde Richardson, and others at the founding visited black congregations wherever they could get an invitation. They successfully solicited money from the boards of major religious denominations, black and white. They received donations from black sororities and fraternities, labor unions, civic groups, and clubs. In the late 1980s, however, as USAID contracts multiplied, Africare leaders paid less attention to private funding opportunities that required speeches, travel, and personal contacts. They came to rely on the Bishop Walker dinner, remunerative at least in part because of corporate sponsorship, as a substitute for private financing, but it has never had the effect of reaching the average person outside Washington, D.C. Although Julius Coles tried to renew interest in Africare work at the community level, the organization remains so unfamiliar in most of the United States that it will take a major effort to tap its roots again. Africare has a heritage and it has filled a niche in American society. Unless it reclaims those assets, it loses the distinctiveness that enabled it to survive for forty years and it becomes just another development group. Americans of all races and ethnicities are open to supporting an African American charity. The challenge for Africare is spreading its story and message.

The question that Mans posed to his Board of Directors—"What do you want Africare to be in the twenty-first century"—is applicable not only to this one organization, but to all government agencies and all charities, world-wide, that are providing development assistance to sub-Saharan Africa. It implies in perpetuity, that Africare will continue to exist forever. Is it conceivable that one day, before another forty years has passed, Africans, having overcome economic and social obstacles, will truly take command of their domestic affairs and declare an end to foreign aid? Hardly any individual in the aid community, internationally, nationally, and locally, seems to envision such a time. Among the few voices speaking of putting aid out of business in a generation or two is that of Bono, whose glowing account of individual African success stories appeared in a 2010 Op-Ed piece of *The New York Times*. From his travels, he senses the coming end of the usual donor-recipient relationship and of the "old, dumb, only-game-in-town aid." In its place, he sees smart aid that considers such factors as accountability, transparency, measurable results, adherence to the rule of law, and the use of trade, investment, and citizen input. While his is the optimism of a celebrity outsider, he is, nonetheless, reaching for that day when Africans can feed, clothe, and care for themselves. Mans should make that goal more explicit.

215

Inherent in Mans' question is another disturbing fundamental issue. Has foreign aid become such an industry that the patient must not be allowed to get well? It is a sad fact that, were the mechanism of foreign aid dismantled, there would be a serious disruption of recipient and donor societies at all levels. As the military cannot afford peace, so it seems that the world cannot afford the cessation of poverty. That success in Africa has been so elusive is not an indictment of development organizations, private or governmental—and certainly not of Africare, which was founded with noble objectives and plodded on through years of struggle—but acknowledgment of the magnitude of the task. The physical size of Africa and its unique climatic features complicated the effort to plan and implement programs such as in agriculture. The absence of roads, vehicular transportation, and telephones stymied aid workers who tried to publicize a new health service or well-baby clinic in rural communities. The conflicting approaches of international participants, ill-conceived projects, uneven cooperation by host governments, practical problems of administration, civil disturbances, and natural disasters were all deterrents to the achievement of healthy, prospering societies.

It seems likely, then, that Africare and similar groups will continue to participate in helping the African people during the next forty years, but if Bono is right, with adjusted roles and as minority players in governments that seek specific technical assistance. While Africare may have to change the nature of its involvement, the idealism of its founders can still be a guide on a continent often overcome by the realities of hardship.

Bibliography

Primary Sources

African Development Fund. *Appraisal Report, Integrated Rural Water Supply and Sanitation Project for Ntchisi and Mzimba Districts, Republic of Malawi.* Report. N.p.: African Development Fund, 2001.

African Development Fund. *Republic of Rwanda, Rural Water Supply and Sanitation Programme, Appraisal Report.* Report. N.p.: African Development Fund, 2003.

Africare. *Annual Reports.* Washington, D.C. 1974-2009.

Africare. Archives. Washington, D.C. 1971-2010.

Africare, Board of Directors. Minutes. Honolulu. September 14, 1970.

Budget, First Africare Program. April 17, 1971.

Cable. Diori Hamani to William Kirker. Niamey. November 24, 1970.

Cable. William Kirker to Diori Hamani. Honolulu. 28 October, 1970.

"CHAD: Humanitarian Profile No. 2—2006/2007." ReliefWeb.int. www.reliefweb.int (accessed February 13, 2007).

"Correspondence." Diori Hamani to William Kirker. December 2, 1970.

"Correspondence." William Kirker to Family. Various dates.

"Correspondence." William Kirker to Maitouraré Gadjo. October 9, 1970.

District of Columbia, Recorder of Deeds. "Articles of Incorporation of Africare." May 4, 1971.

Exec. Order No. 8802, 3 C.F.R. (1941).

Food Aid Management. *Monetization Manual, A Guide for Title II Cooperating Sponsors.* Washington, D.C.: Food Aid Management, 1999.

Gray, Jeff. *Africare Benin Annual Report*. Report. Cotonou: Africare, 1996.

Hazelhurst, Sherry, and Derek Milner. *USDA Forest Service Technical Assistance Trip, Watershed Assessment of the Ugalla Landscape*. Report. Washington, D.C.: Government Printing Office, 2007.

International Fund for Agricultural Development. *IFAD strategy paper on HIV/AIDS for East and Southern Africa*. Strategy Paper. www.ifad.org/operations/regional/pf/aids_5.htm (accessed January 19, 2007).

LeBreton, Ginette. "Refugee relocation operation in southern Chad rushes to beat the rainy season." Unhcr.org. http://unhcr.org/cgibin/texis/vtx/search?page=search&docid=42caa9354&query=refugees,%20chad (accessed July 5, 2005).

Metropolitan Washington, D.C., Chapter of Africare. Papers. 1981-1990.

Neve, Alex. *Amnesty Research Mission to Chad: 29 April-13 May 2009*. Report. http:www.amnesty.ca/blog2.php?blog=chad_mission (accessed 2009).

"New influx of 1,000 refugees from Central African Republic to southern Chad." Unhcr.org. http://www.unhcr.org/43da42b14.html (accessed January 27, 2006).

Nigeria. Federal Ministry of Health and Federal Ministry of Education. *National Workshop on Education and Planning for the Prevention of AIDS and Drug Abuse, Final Report*. Badagry: Government of Nigeria, 1988.

"Presidential Medal of Freedom Recipient Rev. Leon Howard Sullivan." Medaloffreedom.com. www.medaloffreedom.com/Leon-HowardSullivan.htm.

The Queen's Medical Center, Honolulu. "Slide showing of infectious diseases, people and customs in Niger, Africa." Memorandum. September 21, 1970.

Redmond, Ron. "Chad receives new refugee influx from Central African Republic." Unhcr.org. http://www.unhcr.org/cgibin/texis/vtx/search?page=search?search&docid=43f5b0c54&query=refugees,%20southern%20chad (accessed February 17, 2006).

Redmond, Ron. "Chad/Sudan: Flight both ways; Central Africans move away from border." Unhcr.org. http://www.unhcr.org/cgibin/texis/vtx/search?page=search?search&docid=44082b964&query=refugees,%20southern%20chad (accessed March 3, 2006).

Redmond, Ron. "South Sudan: Repatriation from Central African Republic complete." Unhcr.org. http://www.unhcr.org/cgibin/texis/vtx/search?page=search?search&docid=461f67102&query=car%20refugees (accessed April 13, 2007).

Research Group on the Democratic, Economic and Social Development of Africa. "Statues." Gerddes.org. www.gerddes.org.

State of Hawaii, Department of Regulatory Agencies. "Charter of Incorporation [for Africare]." September 11, 1970.

State of Hawaii, Department of Regulatory Agencies. "Petition for Charter of Incorporation [for Africare]." September 10, 1970.

"Subject of the Discussion: Freedom for Women in the Farchana Refugee Camp [Eastern Chad]." N.p. June 10, 2008.

Uganda. Ministry of Gender, Labour and Social Development. *National Orphans and Other Vulnerable Children Policy*. Kampala: Government of Uganda, 2004.

"UNHCR rushes to transfer refugees to new camp in southern Chad." Unhcr.org. http://www.unhcr.org/483c17764.html (accessed May 27, 2008).

"UNICEF providing vital aid to refugees in southern Chad." Unicef.org. http://www.unicef.org/infobycountry/chad_49886.html (accessed June 4, 2009).

UNICEF. "The Return to Southern Sudan of the Sudanese Refugees from Itang Camp, Gambela, Ethiopia." August 31, 1991.

United Nations High Commissioner for Refugees. *Republic of Chad, Working Environment*. UNHCR, 2007.

United Nations. Office for the Coordination of the Humanitarian Affairs. "Eastern Chad: Refugee camps populations (as of April 08)." N.p. May 19, 2008.

United States. Department of Agriculture. Evaluations of Africare Projects. 2000-2004.

United States. Department of Agriculture. *US Food Aid Programs Description: Public Law 480, Food for Progress and Section 416(b)*. www.fas.usda.gov/excredits/FoodAid/Title%201/pl480ofst.html (accessed November 4, 2004).

United States. Department of Commerce. Bureau of the Census. *The Social and Economic Status of Negroes in the United States, 1970*. Washington, D.C.: Government Printing Office, 1970.

United States. Department of State. The United States President's Emergency Plan for AIDS Relief. *About Pepfar*. www.pepfar.gov/about.

United States. Department of State. "U.S. Pledges Help for Refugees in Chad, Central African Republic." Press release. America.gov. http://www.america.gov/st/washfileenglish/2007/March/200703201442231EJrehsiF0.321789.html (accessed March 20, 2007).

United States. Department of the Treasury. Internal Revenue Service. Form 990, "Return of Organization Exempt from Income Tax." 2000-2009.

United States. Government Accounting Office. *International Food Security, Insufficient Efforts by Host Governments and Donors Threaten Progress to Halve Hunger in Sub-Saharan Africa by 2015.* Washington, D.C.: Government Printing Office, 2008.

United States. United States Agency for International Development. *Audit of USAID/West Africa's Management of the P.L. 480 Non-Emergency Monetization Program in Burkina Faso.* Dakar: USAID, 2007.

United States. United States Agency for International Development. Development Experience Clearing House (DEC). *Evaluations of Africare Projects.* Washington, D.C., 1985-2009. http://dec.USAID.gov/.

United States. United States Agency for International Development. Foreign Affairs Oral History Collection. *An interview with Judy C. Bryson.* Arlington, VA, 2005.

United States. United States Agency for International Development. West African Regional Food for Peace Office. *Impact of USAID/FFP-Funded Programs on Smallholder Household Food Security in Burkina Faso.* No. 3. 2009.

U.S. Congress. Senate. Foreign Relations. *Chad and the Central African Republic: The Regional Impact of the Darfur Crisis. Hearing Before the Subcommittee on African Affairs of the Committee on Foreign Relations.* S. Doc. Washington, D.C.: U.S. Government Printing Office, 2008.

World Food Programme. "Update on WFP Operations for Refugees and Internally Displaced Persons (IDPs) as of 1 March 2007." 2007.

World Health Organization/UNICEF. *A Snapshot of Sanitation in Africa.* Technical paper. Durban: WHO/UNICEF, 2008.

World Refugee Survey. "Statistics for Chad, 2008 Summary." World Refugee Survey. www.worldrefugeesurvey.org/index.php?title=Chad.

Secondary Sources

Abbott, Philip. *Overview of the 2007 USDA Farm Bill, Food Aid & the Farm Bill.* Publication. West Lafayette, IN: Purdue University, 2007.

Adelman, Carol C., and Nicholas Eberstadt. *Foreign Aid: What Works and What Doesn't.* Washington, D.C.: American Enterprise Institute for Public Policy Research, 2008.

Adelman, Carol C. "Global Phianthropy and Remittance: Reinventing Foreign Aid." *Brown Journal of World Affairs* XV, no. II (Spring 2009): 23-33.

"Africa: Africare and Water for All Join Forces to Foster Healthier Schools and Communities." All.Africa.com. www.allAfrica.com (accessed March 11, 2009).

"Africare—Improving rural Food Security in Dinguiraye." USAID.com. www.usaid.gov/gn/news/2003/030411_foodforpeace/africare-indinguiraye.htm (accessed February 5, 2007).

Alden, Chris. "From Neglect to 'Virtual Engagement': The United States and Its New Paradigm for Africa." *African Affairs* IC, no. 396 (July 2000): 355-71.

Amin, Julius A. "The Peace Corps and the Struggle for African American Equality." *Journal of Black Studies* XXIX, no. 6 (July 1999): 809-26.

Atlanta Daily World. "Black Organizations Support to 'Africare' Increasing." September 29, 1988.

Axe, David. "AGRICULTURE-CHAD: Farmers, Herders Collide in Southern Refugee Camps." Inter Press Service News Agency. http://ipsnews.net/print.asp?idnews=43129 (accessed July 9, 2008).

Axe, David. "U.N. Refugee Agency Expands Chad Aid to Local Population." *World Politics Review*, July 11, 2008. http://www.worldpoliticsreview.com/article.aspx?idnews=2418.

Axe, David. "'With the Right Methods, You Can Be Self-Sufficient.'" Inter Press Service News Agency. http://ipsnews.net/print.asp?idnews=43162 (accessed July 12, 2008).

Ball, Erica L. "African American Philanthropy." Philanthropy.org. www.philathropy.org/publications/.../african_american_paper.pdf (accessed n.d.).

Bariagaber, Assefaw. *Conflict and the refugee experience flight, exile, and repatriation in the Horn of Africa.* Burlington, VT: Ashgate, 2006.

Barrett, Christopher B., and Daniel G. Maxwell. "PL480 Food Aid: We Can Do Better." Global Policy Forum. http://globalpolicy.org/socccon/hunger/relief/2004/12031foodaid.htm (accessed December 3, 2004).

Bono. "Africa Reboots." *The New York Times*, April 18, 2010, WK12 sec.

Bratton, Michael. "Academic Analysis and U.S. Economic Assistance Policy on Africa." *Issue: A Journal of Opinion* XIX, no. 1 (Winter 1990): 21-37.

Brown, Carolyn M. "America's Leading Black Philanthropists." *Black Enterprise*, August 2005.

Carson, Emmett D. "African American Philanthropy." www.cof.org/files/Documents/Publications/Cultures.../bibafam.pdf.

Carson, Emmett D. "Valuing Black Benevolence." *Foundations News*, May/June 1990.

Case, Ben. "Sudan: Civilians under Siege in Refugee Camps." Inter Press Service News Agency. http://ipsnews.net/ (accessed July 14, 2009).

Center on Philanthropy and Civil Society, The City University of New York. "African American Philanthropy Literature Review." CPCS—Philanthropy.org. www.philanthropy.org/.../AfricanAmericanLitReview.final._000.pdf (accessed 2003).

"Central African Republic: Refugees Pouring into Chad in Dire Need of Help—UN." AllAfrica.com. www.allAfrica.com (accessed February 6, 2009).

"CENTRAL AFRICAN REPUBLIC-CHAD: Forgotten refugees face epidemics, food cuts." IRIN. www.irinnews.org/Report.aspx?ReportId=59420 (accessed June 22, 2006).

"CENTRAL AFRICAN REPUBLIC-CHAD: Fresh violence, rape drives thousands of Central Africans across border." GlobalSecurity.org. www/globalsecurity.org/military/library/news/2005/08/mil-050802-irin03.htm (accessed August 2, 2005).

Cepeda, Susana. "Ethiopia: A Humanitarian Mission." *Sane World* XXIV, no. 3 (March 1985).

"CHAD: Re-assessing the aid footprint." IRIN. http://www.irinnews.org/Report.aspx?ReportId=87343 (accessed December 7, 2009).

"CHAD: Refugees waiting for HIV services." IRIN. www.alertnet.org/thenews/newsdesk/IRIN/215650513df776faa858a171f0b569d5.htm (accessed March 10, 2008).

Cobb, Jr., Charles E. "United States and Africa; 'Where do we go from here?' Summit delegates ask." AllAfrica.com. www.allAfrica.com (accessed February 20, 2000).

Collier, Paul. *The bottom billion: why the poorest countries are failing and what can be done about it.* Oxford: Oxford University Press, 2007.

Conner, Will, and Ralph Blumenthal. "Solar Flashlight Lets Africa's Sun Deliver the Luxury of Light to the Poorest Villages." *The New York Times*, May 20, 2007, A8 sec.

Consortium for Development Relief in Angola. *Development Relief Program, March 2003 to December 2005, Results Report.* Report. N.p.: Consortium for Development Relief in Angola, N.d.

Cutler, Peter. "The Political Economy of Famine in Ethiopia and Sudan." *Ambio* XX, no. 5 (August 1991): 176-78.

Dalsimer, Isabel P., Ralph H. Faulkingham, and William H. Rusch. *Evaluation of AID Development Program and Support Grants to Africare.* Washington, D.C.: General Research Corporation, 1978.

Dash, Leon. "Sahel Quest for Water is Slow, Costly." *The Washington Post*, May 16, 1981, A10 sec.

Dealey, Sam. "The U.N. Shares Blame for Darfur Atrocities." *U.S. News & World Report*, January 26, 2009. http://www.usnews.com/blogs/sam-dealey/2009/01/26/the-un-shares-blame-for-darfur-atrocities.htm.

Devarajan, Shantayanan, David Dollar, and Torgny Holmgren. *Aid and reform in Africa: lessons from ten case studies.* Washington, D.C.: World Bank, 2001.

Devereux, Stephen. "Why does famine persist in Africa?" *Food Security* I, no. 1 (February 2009): 25-35.

DeVries, Danny. "Choosing Your Baseline Carefully; Integrating Historical and Political Ecology in the Evaluation of Environmental Intervention Projects." *Journal of Ecological Anthropology* IX (2005): 35-50.

Doctors Without Borders. "Food and Shelter Urgently Needed for Central African Republic Refugees in Chad." Press release. Doctors Without Borders. www.msf.org/ (accessed March 18, 2003).

"Dorothy Height Biography." Thehistorymakers.com. http:///the-historymakers.com/biography/biography/asp?bioindex=546.

Doyle, Leonard. "US Food Aid is 'Wrecking' Africa, Claims Charity." *The Independent/UK*, August 17, 2007. www.commondreams.org.

Du Bois, W.E.B. *The souls of black folks*. New York: Dodd, Mead, 1961.

Dugger, Celia W. "African Food for Africa's Starving is Road-blocked in Congress." *The New York Times*, October 12, 2005, A4 sec.

Durrill, Wayne K. "Atrocious Misery: The African Origins of Famine in Northern Somalia, 1839-1884." *The American Historical Review* LXXXXI, no. 2 (April 1986): 287-306.

Easterly, William, and Nancy Birdsall. *Reinventing foreign aid*. Cambridge: Mass., 2008.

Embassy of the United States (Malawi). "Ambassador Bodde Launches PlayPumps." Press release. (accessed February 16, 2009).

Endfield, Georgina H., and David J. Nash. "Drought, Desiccation and Discourse: Missionary Correspondence and Nineteenth-Century Climate Change in Central Southern Africa." *The Geographic Journal* CLXVIII, no. 1 (March 2002): 33-47.

Endfield, Georgina H., and David J. Nash. "Missionaries and Morals: Climatic Discourse in Nineteenth-Century Central Southern Africa." *Annals of the Association of American Geographers* LXXXXII, no. 4 (December 2002): 727-42.

Favor, J. Martin. *Authentic Blackness: the folk in the New Negro renaissance*. Durham [N.C.]: Duke University Press, 1999.

Flint, Julie, and Alexander de Waal. *Darfur: a short history of a long war*. London: Zed Books, 2005.

Foley, Jonathan A., Michael T. Coe, Marten Scheffer, and Guiling Wang. "Regime Shifts in the Sahara and Sahel: Interactions between Ecological and Climatic Systems in Northern Africa." *Ecosystems* VI, no. 6 (September 2003): 524-39.

Forgey, Benjamin. "Morse School's Admirable Revival." *The Washington Post*, March 5, 1988, B1,2 sec.

Gamarekian, Barbara. "His Pitch is Hunger; His Market, the World." *The New York Times*, November 29, 1984, B16 sec.

Gasman, Marybeth. "Trends in African American Philanthropy." Onphilanthropy.com. www.onphilanhropy.com/site/News2?page=NewsArticle. (accessed March 3, 2006).

Gerber, Dan. "USAID Project Strengthens NGOs in Benin." *African Voices*, Fall 1995.

Glantz, Michael H., and Richard W. Katz. "Drought as a Constraint in Sub-Saharan Africa." *Ambio* XIV, no. 6 (1985): 334-39.

"Global: Monetised food aid under scrutiny." IRIN. www.irinnews. org/Report.aspx?ReportId=74257 (accessed September 12, 2007).

Haas, Peter M., John A. Hird, and Beth McBratney. *Controversies in globalization: contending approaches to international relations.* Washington, DC: CQ Press, 2010.

Haile, Menghestab. "Weather Patterns, Food Security and Humanitarian Response in sub-Saharan Africa." *The Royal Society, Philosophical Transactions: Biological Sciences* CCCLX, no. 1463 (November 29, 2005): 2169-182.

Hanson, Stephanie. "Angola's Political and Economic Development." Council on Foreign Relations. www.cfr.org (accessed January 21, 2008).

Harr, Jonathan. "Lives of the Saints, International hardship duty in Chad." *The New Yorker*, January 5, 2009.

Harrigan, Jane. "Supply side famines: The case of Malawi 2001-02." Lecture. www.docstoc.com/docs/16041498/Supply-side-famines_ The-case-of-Malawi-2001-02.

Hassan, Salah M., and Carina E. Ray. *Darfur and the crisis of governance in Sudan: a critical reader.* Ithaca: Cornell University Press, 2009.

The Hilltop. "Sorority Raises $47,000." November 20, 2007. www. thehilltoponline.com.

"History of the National Urban League." National Urban League. www.nul.com.

"History of the PlayPumps Water System." www.Waterpumps. org.

Hunt, Erica. "African American Philanthropy: A Legacy of Giving." Twenty-First Century Foundation. www.21cf.org/pdf/LegacyOf Giving.pdf (accessed 2003).

Hutchinson, George. *The Harlem renaissance in black and white.* Cambridge, Mass.: Belknap Press of Harvard University Press, 1995.

Jacobs, Sylvia M. "African Missions and the African American Christian Church." In *African American Experience in World Missions*, 30-47. Pasadena, CA: William Carey Library, 2003.

Johnson, Douglas H. *The root causes of Sudan's civil wars.* Bloomington: Indiana University Press, 2003.

Joseph, Richard A. *State, conflict, and democracy in Africa.* Boulder, Colo.: L. Rienner, 1999.

Kerr, Ricahard A. "Fifteen Years of African Drought." *Science* CCXXVII, no. 4693, N.s. (March 22, 1985): 1453-454.

Kissi, Edward. "Beneath International Famine Relief in Ethiopia: The United States, Ethiopia, and the Debate over Relief Aid, Development Assistance, and Human Rights." *African Studies Review* XXXVIII, no. 2 (September 2005): 111-32.

Koponen, Juhani. "War, Famine, and Pestilence in Late Precolonial Tanzania: A Case for a Heightened Mortality." *The International Journal of African Historical Studies* XXI, no. 4 (1988): 637-76.

Krauss, Bob. "Isle Group Asks Help for Africa." *Honolulu Advertiser*, December 3, 1970, A-4 sec.

Legge, David R. "Beating Drums for Africare." *The Washington Post*, October 16, 1972, B3 sec.

Levine, Michael L. *African Americans and civil rights: from 1619 to the present*. Phoenix, Ariz.: Oryx Press, 1996.

Lewis, Jane J. "Dorothy Height." About.com. http:///womenshistorylabout.com/od/civilrights/p/dorothy_height.htm?p=l.

Longmyer, Kenneth. "Black American Demands." *Foreign Policy*, no. 60 (Autumn 1985): 3-17.

Lucas, C. P. "Black Pride, Black Action." *Vital Speeches of the Day* XXXV (1968): 505-08.

Lund, T., M. H. Rahman, S. R. Boye, L. Johansen, and I. Tveiten. "Evaluation of Africare Food Security Initiative in Nyambumba, Uganda." *Journal of Innovative Development Strategy* II, no. 1 (April 2008): 10-17.

"Making Value-Added Food Products in Mozambique." USAID. http://africastories.usaid.gov/search_details.cfm?storyID=347&countryID=15&sectorID=0&yearID=5 (accessed 2005).

Makotsi, Phil. "Blacks Play Key Role in Relief Aid." *The City Sun* (New York), March 27, 1985.

"Malawi: USAID gives US $14 million to fight hunger." IRIN. www.irinnews.org/Report.aspx?ReportId=32555 (accessed June 18, 2002).

Maxwell, Simon, and Margaret Smith-Buchanan. "Development Aid: Killing with Kindness." *The Guardian* (London), November 23, 1994, Society, 4 sec.

McCann, James C. "Climate and Causation in African History." *The International Journal of African Historical Studies* XXXII, no. 2/3 (1999): 261-79.

McNeil, Donald G. "Bush's Global AIDS Effort Limited by Restrictions." *The New York Times*, March 31, 2007, A12 sec.

McQueen, Michel. "Feast and Famine, City of Stability Ignores Continent of Strife." *The Washington Post*, November 27, 1980, DC1 sec.

Meredith, Martin. *The fate of Africa: from the hopes of freedom to the heart of despair: a history of fifty years of independence.* New York: Public Affairs, 2005.

Meriwether, James Hunter. *Proudly we can be Africans: Black Americans and Africa, 1935-1961.* Chapel Hill: University of North Carolina Press, 2002.

"Midcity at the Crossroads." Shawmainstreets.com. www.shawmainstreets.com.

Milner, James. *Refugees, the state and the politics of asylum in Africa.* Basingstoke [England]: Palgrave Macmillan, 2009.

"Monetization and Barter Contribute to Food Security." Alliance for Food Aid.com. www.allianceforfoodaid.com/Default.aspx?tabid=58&metaid=H9NK0915-7af (accessed August 21, 2007).

Montesquiou, Alfred de. "Chad-Darfur fight reflects resource needs." *Laredo Morning News*, February 18, 2007, 18A sec.

Morano, Marc. "Africare Dinner Sponsors Try to Mute Belafonte Controversy." http:///www.cnsnews.com (accessed October 25, 2002).

Moyo, Dambisa. *Dead aid: why aid is not working and how there is a better way for Africa.* New York: Farrar, Straus and Giroux, 2009.

"Namibia; Lack of Data and Resources Affects OVC Interventions." AllAfrica.com. http://allafrica.com/stories/200503071585.html (accessed March 7, 2005).

"Namibia; Osire Refugees in Furore Over Paraffin." AllAfrica.com. http://allafrica.com/stories/200406070685.html (accessed June 7, 2004).

"Namibia; Refugees Voice Their Unhappiness." AllAfrica.com. http://allafrica.com/stories/200505160741.html (accessed March 13, 2005).

The Namibian (Windhoek). "Namibia; Chaos Erupts at Osire Refugee Camp." October 20, 2003. http://www.queensu.ca/samp/migrationnews/2003/oct.htm#Namibia.

Nhema, Alfred G., and Tiyambe Zeleza. *The roots of African conflicts the causes & costs.* Pretoria: UNISA Press, 2008.

Nicholson, Sharon E. "The Methodology of Historical Climate Reconstruction and Its Application to Africa." *The Journal of African History* XX, no. 1 (1979): 31-49.

"Niger; Africare Team Reflects on 35 Years of Work." AllAfrica.com. http://allafrica.com/stories/200510140269.html (accessed October 14, 2005).

"NIGER: NGOs in north calling for peace." IRIN. www.irinnews. org/Report.aspx?ReportId=74009 (accessed August 29, 2007).

'*No Place for us Here,' Violence Against Refugee Women in Eastern Chad.* London: Amnesty International, 2009.

Oilseed Processing, Technologies Adoption Survey. Case of Yenga Oil Press Technology in Southern Province. Report. Farming Systems Association of Zambia, 2002.

"Oprah, Bono team up to fight AIDS in Africa." MSNBC. www. msnbc.msn.com/id/15242216ns/entertainment-celebrities/ (accessed October 13, 2006).

"Oprah Winfrey." Hollywoodreporter.com. www.TheHollywood-Reporter: SHOWBIZ411.com (accessed June 22, 2009).

Oxfam International. "Liberia Government Encourages Resouce Mobilisation for WASH (Water, Sanitation and Hygiene)." Oxfam International. Web log entry posted n.d. [2008]. www. oxfamblogs. org/westafrica/wpcontent/uploads/2008/10/children-washing-their-hands.jpg.

"PanAfrica; Why Famine Stalks Africa." AllAfrica.com. http://all-africa.com/stories/200212230529.html (accessed December 23, 2002).

Payne, Ethel. "Africare aids Ethiopia, The progressive approach." *The Washington Afro-American*, March 8, 1985.

Pierce, Ponchitta. "African American Philanthropy." *Carnegie Reporter*, Spring 2008.

Pletcher, James R. "Agriculture and the Dual Transition in Zambia." *The Journal of Developing Areas* XXXIII, no. 2 (Winter 1999): 199-222.

Plummer, Janelle, and Piers Cross. "Tackling Corruption in the Water and Sanitation Sector in Africa. Starting the Dialogue." *Water Integrity Network* (2006). www.Waterintegritynetwork. net.

Polgreen, Lydia. "Attacks Pushing Darfur Refugees Into Chad." *The New York Times*, February 11, 2008, A3 sec.

Polgreen, Lydia. "Refugee Crisis Grows as Darfur War Crosses a Border." *The New York Times*, February 28, 2006, A1 sec.

Powell, Aimee. "Zimbabwe: African Well Fund repairs broken wells and sanitation systems serving 2,000." WaterWebster. www.WaterWebster.org (accessed 2006).

"Prevention of Blindness and Visual Impairment." World Health Organization. www.who/int/blindness/causes/priority/en/index3/html.

Prunier, Gèrard. *Africa's world war: Congo, the Rwandan genocide, and the making of a continental catastrophe*. Oxford: Oxford University Press, 2009.

Raspberry, William. "Blacks Helping Blacks." *The Washington Post*, May 15, 1972, A23 sec.

Raspberry, William. "Famine Relief: The Africare Effort." *The Washington Post*, September 28, 1973, A29 sec.

Raykov, Annie. "CAR parliament approves refugee law." Humanitarian and Development Partnership Team—CAR. http://ochagwapps1.unog.ch/rw/rwb/nsf/db900sid/MUMA-79S42V?OpenDocument (accessed December 10, 2007).

"Rebel Leader Stages Coup; Refugees Flee." Www.unwire.org. www.unwire.org/unwire/20030317/32620_story.asp (accessed March 17, 2003).

Resnikoff et al., Serge. "Policy and Practice, Visual Impairment in 2002." *Bulletin of the World Health Organization* LXXXII, No. 11 (November 2004): 847-848.

Revkin, Andrew C. "Study Finds a Pattern of Severe Drought in Africa." *The New York Times*, April 17, 2009, A17 sec.

Rieff, David. "Charity on the Rampage: The Business of Foreign Aid." Review of *Michael Maren, The Road to Hell: The Ravaging Effect of Foreign Aid and International Charity. Foreign Affairs*, January/February 1997. http://www.jstor.org/stable/20047914 (accessed June 09, 2009).

"River Blindness Program." Cartercenter.org. www.cartercenter.org.

"Rough Cut, South Africa: The Play Pump." In *FRONTLINE/WORLD*. PBS. October 24, 2005.

Sachs, Jeffrey D. *The end of poverty: economic possibilities for our time*. New York: Penguin Press, 2005.

Samra, Cal. "Young Ypsilanti Doctor Follows in Tom Dooley's Footsteps." *The Ann Arbor News*, September 26, 1971.

Schelle, P., and J. Pittock. "Restoring the Kafue Flats." Panda.org. http://assets.panda.org/.../restoringkafueflatsschellepittockriversymposium3sept05.pdf (accessed September 3, 2005).

Scruggs, Danielle. "AKAs Raise $21,000 for Africare." *The Hilltop*, January 23, 2004. www.thehilltoponline.com.

Scully, Mary-Louise. "Southern Chad—The Forgotten Crisis." *Travel Medicine Advisor*, December 2008.

"Small-scale Rural Oilseed Processing in Africa." International Development Research Center. www/idrc/ca/en/ev-26984-201-1-DO_TOPIC.html.

Smith, Gayle. *Ethiopia and the Politics of Famine Relief.* Report no. 145. Washington, D.C.: Middle East Research and Information Project, 1987.

"SoyaCow & SoyaGoat. VitaGoat Fact Sheet." Malnutrition Matters. www.malnutrition.org (accessed 2009).

Spagnolo, Maureen. "Self-help for Africa gets boost." *The Washington Times*, May 2, 1984, 2B sec.

"Sub-Saharan African HIV & AIDS Statistics Summary." Avert.org. www.avert.org/subaadults.htm (accessed March 15, 2007).

"Sudan: New Janjawid Attacks Force More People Into Camps." IRIN. www.irinnews.org/Report.aspx?ReportId=58030 (accessed February 3, 2006).

"SUDAN-CHAD: Twelfth camp opened for Darfur refugees." IRIN. www.irinnews.org/Report.aspx?ReportId=54241 (accessed May 4, 2005).

Tanaka, Kenneth. "Humanitarianism-Dedicated Doctor in Africa." *The Hawaii Herald* (Honoluu), October 8, 1970, II, No. 7 sec.

Tenywa, Gerald. "First Lady to promote hygiene." The New Vision. www.newvision.co.ug/D/8/13/671027 (accessed February 10, 2009).

Terrell, Angela. "Africare in Action." *The Washington Post*, July 17, 1973, B3 sec.

Thomas, David S.G. "Sandstorm in a Teacup? Understanding Desertification." *The Geographical Journal* CLIX, no. 3 (November 1993): 318-31.

Tisdall, Simon. "No way out for nearly 3 million trapped in cycle of despair in Darfur's camps." *Guardian* (Manchester), February 3, 2009. www.guardian.co.uk/world/2009/feb/04/darfur-refugee-camps.

Tschirely, David L., and Michael T. Weber. *Mozambique Food Security Success Story.* Publication no. 19. East Lansing, MI: Michigan

State University, Department of Agricultural Economics, N.d. [1998].

"U2 fans from around the world donated over $26,000 ..." Water-Webster.org. www.WaterWebster.org (accessed June 23, 2008).

"U2 Fans Raise over $34,000 in Honor of Bono's Birthday." PR Web. www.prweb.com/pingpr.php/UHJvZilFbXBOLVNxdWEtUGInZy1U-aLVplcm8= (accessed July 5, 2007).

UN Volunteers. "Now we're in business: longer-term solutions in Chad." UN Volunteers. www.unv.org/nc/en/current-highlight/world-refugee-day-2008/doc/now-were-in-business.html (accessed June 20, 2008).

Under the Baobab Tree (Washington, D.C.). "High School Essay Contest Winner Travels to Africa." November/December 1984, I, No. 1 ed.

United States. The Library of Congress. Congressional Research Service. *Primer on P.L. 480—Program History, Description, and Operations: A Brief Compilation of Explanatory Documents.* By Susan B. Epstein. Washington, D.C.: Library of Congress, 1984.

"U.S. Still Fuels War in Angola." *Washington Notes on Africa,* Spring 1990.

USAID. "Assuring Food Security Means Better Health for Village Families." USAID.com. http://africastories.usaid.gov/print_story.cfm?storyID=324 (accessed 2005).

Varnis, Steven. *Reluctant aid or aiding the reluctant?: U.S. food aid policy and Ethiopian famine relief.* New Brunswick: Transaction Publishers, 1990.

Verney, Kevern. *Black civil rights in America.* London: Routledge, 2000.

Vestal, Theodore M. "Risk Factors and Predictability of Famine in Ethiopia." *Association for Politics and the Life Sciences* IX, no. 2 (February 1991): 187-203.

The Wall Street Journal (New York). "The Trouble with Harry." October 21, 2002.

Washington Informer. "Africare Takes Lead for African Refugee Relief Efforts." September 2, 1992.

Winter, Roger P. "Refugees, War and Famine in the Sudan." *Issue: A Journal of Opinion* XIX, no. 2 (1991): 56-61.

Wintz, Cary D. *Black culture and the Harlem Renaissance.* Houston, Tex.: Rice University Press, 1988.

Zambia. Fisheries and Aquaculture Department. *Status of fish stocks and fisheries of thirteen medium-sized African reservoirs. Kafue Flats.* Lusaka: Government of Zambia, N.d. www.fao.org/docrep/005/V4110E08.htm.

Zeng, Ning. "Drought in the Sahel." *Science* CCCII, no. 5647, N.s. (November 7, 2003): 999-1000.

"ZIMBABWE: Soya beans, the 'wonder crop' transforming lives." IRIN. www.irinnews.org/Report.aspx?ReportId=53215 (accessed March 1, 2005).

Personal Interviews

Alemian, Alan. September 20, 2006.

Banner, Laurin. September 19, 2006.

Benn, R. J. June 22, 2006.

Bond, Larry. April 13, 2006.

Carlbom, Cosco. October 14, 2005.

Chikowero, Sekai M. October 27, 2006.

Chipere, Cassie. August 17, 2006.

Coles, Julius E. May 16, 2009, and other dates.

DeBose, Charles. October 4, 2006.

Derryck, Vivian. August 15, 2006.

Dickson-Horton, Valerie. September 19, 2006.

Effiong, Chinwe. September 18, 2006.

Eitches, Eddie. April 17, 2007.

Enger, Warren J. February 6, 2007.

Epstein, Eve. June 29, 2006.

Foote, Melvin. April 12, 2006.

Hall, Clarence. October 6, 2006, and November 4, 2009.

Hamil, Rebecca. August 14, 2006.

Harper, Alameda. March 17, 2006.

Harrigan, Brian. August 6, 2006.

Height, Dorothy I. April 6, 2006.

Henderson, Will. July 24, 2006.

Hicks, John F. May 10, 2006.

Idriss-Outman, Al-Hassana. October 14, 2005.

Johnson, Jacki. July 26, 2006.

Kennedy, Joseph C. April 5, 2006, and other dates.

King, Elton. October 4, 2006.

Kirker, William O. December 9, 2005, and March 9, 2006.

Lagoon, Michael. June 20, 2006.

Lowther, Kevin. August 16, 2006, and other dates.

Lucas, C. Payne. April 11, 2006, and other dates.

Mans, Darius. April 12, 2010.

Maslowsky, Stacey. July 26, 2006.

McEvoy, Nan Tucker. September 13, 2006.

Mhango, Anatasia. July 28, 2006.

Miles, Mary G. June 26, 2006.

Miller, Michael. July 26, 2006.

Mufute, Ruth.

Mwale, Siteke. November 1, 2006.

Ngosi, Anthony. October 11, 2006.

Noble, William P. June 21, 2006.

North, W. Haven. March 1, 2006.

O'Neill, Michael. May 18, 2009.

Peasley, Carol. July 27, 2006.

Persell, Peter M. August 16, 2006, and other dates.

Richardson, Clyde B. June 27, 2006.

Rosenthal, Irving. June 27, 2006.

Saccardi, Vicky. October 14, 2005.

Scott, Jeannine B. August 16, 2006.

Sempebwa, Ernest K.K. October 16, 2006.

Seon, Yvonne Chappelle. July 25, 2006.

Short, Michael. November 4, 2009.

Smith, Stager Clay. May 3, 2006.

Stacy, Roy A. June 29, 2006.

Staff, Tanzania Africare Office, Dar es Salaam. October 2006.

Staff, Uganda Africare Office, Kampala. October 2006.

Staff, Zimbabwe Africare Office, Harare. October 2006.

Tackie, Gladys. 2001–2009.

Takasaki, Myra. September 6, 2006.

Tarver, Harold V. March 12, 2008.

Thompson, Lee. June 16, 2009.

Torrence, Everett. April 12, 2006.

Watriss, Wendy. August 26, 2006.

Watriss, Whitney. August 17, 2006.

Winsor, Curtin. June 29, 2006.

Index